W9-BVL-033

PREVIOUS BOOKS BY NICHOLAS LUARD

THE WARM AND GOLDEN WAR (1967)
THE ROBESPIERRE SERIAL (1974)
TRAVELLING HORSEMAN (1975)
THE ORION LINE (1977)
THE SHADOW SPY (1979)

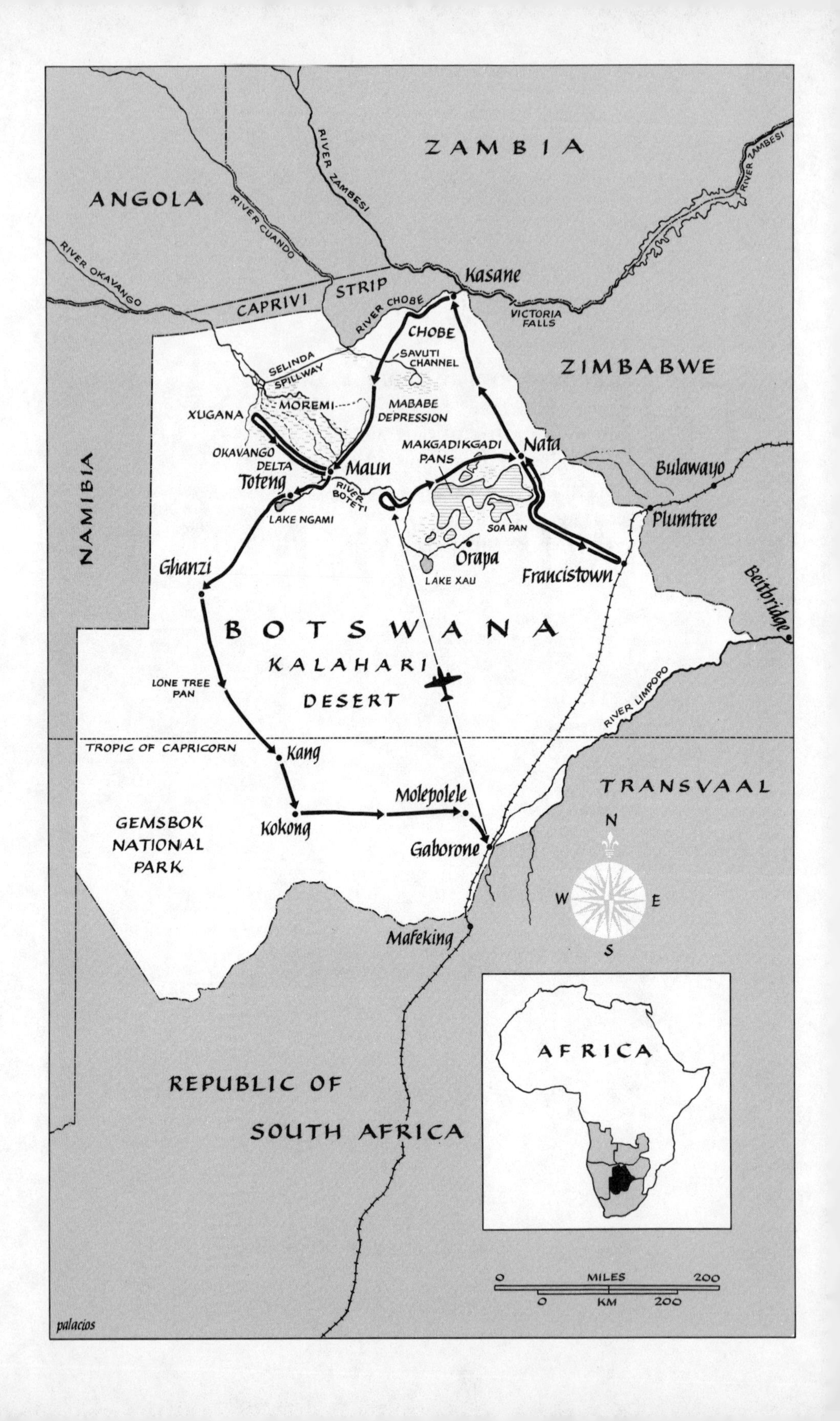
ZAMBIA
ANGOLA
RIVER ZAMBESI
RIVER CUANDO
RIVER OKAVANGO
CAPRIVI
STRIP
Kasane
RIVER CHOBE
VICTORIA FALLS
CHOBE
SAVUTI CHANNEL
SELINDA SPILLWAY
ZIMBABWE
MOREMI
MABABE DEPRESSION
XUGANA
OKAVANGO DELTA
MAKGADIKGADI PANS
Nata
Maun
Toteng
RIVER BOTETI
Bulawayo
Plumtree
LAKE NGAMI
SOA PAN
Orapa
LAKE XAU
Francistown
NAMIBIA
Ghanzi
Beitbridge
BOTSWANA
KALAHARI DESERT
LONE TREE PAN
RIVER LIMPOPO
TROPIC OF CAPRICORN
Kang
TRANSVAAL
Molepolele
GEMSBOK NATIONAL PARK
Kokong
Gaborone
N
W
E
S
Mafeking
AFRICA
REPUBLIC OF SOUTH AFRICA
0
MILES
200
0
KM
200
palacios

# THE LAST WILDERNESS

## A JOURNEY ACROSS THE GREAT KALAHARI DESERT

Nicholas Luard

SIMON AND SCHUSTER • NEW YORK

PUBLISHED BY SIMON AND SCHUSTER
A DIVISION OF GULF & WESTERN CORPORATION
SIMON & SCHUSTER BUILDING
ROCKEFELLER CENTER
1230 AVENUE OF THE AMERICAS
NEW YORK, NEW YORK 10020


DESIGNED BY EVE METZ
MANUFACTURED IN THE UNITED STATES OF AMERICA

10 9 8 7 6 5 4 3 2 1

Library of Congress Cataloging in Publication Data
LUARD, NICHOLAS.
THE LAST WILDERNESS.
1. ZOOLOGY—KALAHARI DESERT. 2. KALAHARI
DESERT. 3. LUARD, NICHOLAS. 4. AFRICA, SOUTHERN—
DESCRIPTION AND TRAVEL. I. TITLE.
QL337.K3L8 1981 916.81′1043 81-1584
AACR2

ISBN 0-671-41264-7

Like all who travel in remote places, in crossing the Kalahari and later in writing this account of a desert expedition I incurred debts of gratitude to many people. First to the people of Botswana for their unfailing courtesy and hospitality in the wild. Next to the many individuals who before, during and after the expedition helped me with advice, assistance and support. Then to my friend and guide, Syd Youthed, and his wife, Sheila. Last, and most of all, to my companions on the journey—Elisabeth Luard, David Towill, Robert Fermor-Hesketh and David Grenfell.

To each and every one, my thanks.

Cameras for the expedition were provided by Olympus Optical Co. (UK) Ltd. Principal photography by Robert Fermor-Hesketh. Additional photographs by the author and other members of the expedition.

FOR ALL POETS AND ALL POLITICIANS

# 1

THE VENERABLE Athenaeum chess club meets on Monday evenings. Normally after my own game had finished I lingered in the lofty clubroom to watch the distinguished international masters among the members at play. To watch and study and afterward discuss the intricate patterns they had wrought.

That Monday was an exception. I had an engagement to keep. At nine o'clock I left. Outside in the darkness the late-November air was chill and damp. A cold wind swept down Whitehall. There was mist on the Thames, and distant barges were hooting from the docks downriver. Beneath the lamps flaring on the Houses of Parliament I could see the patrolling policemen rubbing their hands together for warmth.

I crossed St. James's Park, hurried through the streets of Belgravia, climbed a flight of steps and rang the bell. For a moment I stood there shivering. Then the door opened and I stepped inside.

Instantly there was warmth, and a long table heavy with old silver, and candlelight playing over the faces of the gathered guests. Behind their heads, vases of late-autumn flowers scenting the air. Beyond, a log fire through the drawing-room arch, flames gleaming on decanters of port and brandy, books piled everywhere. Rare books, expensive books, the important new books, books of analysis, comment and ideas. And scattered among them newspapers and journals from across the world, from San Francisco, Paris, New York and Bonn.

The house and the evening belonged to a London that has almost vanished. An imperial London, capital of one-quarter of the globe, where in the private salons of the great hostesses weighty issues were debated, gossip and scandal exchanged, political alliances forged, cabinets made and broken.

The substance has gone. Here the style remains. A hostess still holds court. There is still a trade in intrigue, government policies are argued by those who fashion them, a new writer, painter or Pope is discussed and judged. Here Members of Parliament still come and go answering the call of the division bell.

I arrived that night as dinner was ending. There was a poet at the table. Inevitably, a politician too. The poet was a man of honesty and intellectual vigor, a powerful, combative man with a voice like a cathedral organ, deep and clear and resonant. The politician a lesser creature, furtive and whey-faced. He too wrote. His forum was a weekly column in the country's most staunchly conservative newspaper. Every Sunday honest burghers across the land turned eagerly to read his views: the death penalty for all murderers; birching for child delinquents; incentives for the entrepreneur; swingeing fines for scroungers, Communists and shop stewards. To retired colonels, golfing stockbrokers, fringe bankers, justices of the peace, lords mayor with building interests, his was the voice of reason and moral rectitude. He reaffirmed their granite beliefs, extolled their virtues, echoed and molded their opinions. And because he was eloquent, shrewd and plausible, his following was vast.

The poet, in contrast, was a spokesman for the radical left and had been so all his life. For more than a generation his verses had declared his passionately held, passionately opposed views. Predictably, they were ill at ease in each other's company. On every issue —freedom, justice, capital, labor—they bellowed in antagonism like two mastodons disputing a primeval swamp. On every issue except one. Late in the evening the debate turned to the future of Western society, to the forces that would change and direct it, and the shape our civilization would assume.

What role, I asked, would the birds and animals of the wild play in the world that they were constructing from the opposite ends of the political spectrum? I spoke of the falcons falling in rains of death from the air, poisoned by the chlorinated hydrocarbon pesticides of the fifties. Of the elephant herds slaughtered to the verge of extinction for their ivory. Of the gassed timber wolves and the vanishing whales. What provision, what safeguards, would be made for the creatures that remained?

For a moment I caught the attention of both. They heard me out in puzzled silence. Then the poet interrupted.

"Listen, my friend," he said. "You talk about birds and animals. Personally I have little interest in either. Birds disturb my morning sleep. Animals bite. I even have wounds from plants. Yet I accept that for some such as you, the wild has a certain attraction. A vague romantic appeal—the appeal of lost causes. Well, let me remind you of this. Lost causes are lost because there is no cause."

The politician nodded in confident agreement. All evening he had confronted an implacable foe. Now at the end the enemies were united. Left and right had found common ground.

"You speak of provisions and safeguards," the poet finished. "We create those for what concerns our own survival. In doing so we are neither philistines nor sadists. We are merely pragmatic—as pragmatic as any of your tigers or eagles. Does the wild concern *us?* Answer me that. If you cannot answer, the matter is ended."

I was silent.

At midnight I left. The mist was much thicker now, a Dickensian winter fog. I searched unsuccessfully for a cab. The drivers had prudently retired to their beds. I walked back through the deserted streets with my hands clenched tight in my pockets and plumes of steam lifting from my mouth.

Does the wild concern us?

Pacing the icy sidewalks, I felt a gathering anger. Anger first against the poet and the smugly acquiescent politician, and then against myself. I had been asked the most basic of all questions about the wild. And I, who for years had traveled and lived in and loved wilderness places, had not been able to provide an answer.

There were, of course, replies I might have given. They ranged from the esthetic value of a stooping eagle or a hunting tiger to human responsibility for sharing the planet with its other inhabitants. They were worthy and well-worn replies—the justification of a thousand conservation groups and a million concerned individuals.

They were not enough. Under the poet's interrogation, his questions would have followed remorselessly had I offered them, they would have proved worthless. Beauty and responsibility are products of the human consciousness. Neither has any meaning to the eagle or the tiger in the wild. And if the concepts are meaningless there, why should they reckon in our own relationship with the wilderness?

Does the wild concern us?

Stubbornly, I still believed it did. In anger that November night, I determined to find out why, to find an answer that would silence both poet and politician.

I knew, too, where the search would take place. If the wild did have relevance to our lives—not a cosmetic, self-indulgent relevance but a deep and permanent relationship with what we do and are—then it would be found in a place where wilderness was at its most harsh and remote and alien.

I knew with utter certainty where that was. As with all certainties, its foundations had been laid long years before.

# 2

WHEN THE *Generalissimo* died, the Most General, the coarse and brutal little man who for forty years held a noble country paralyzed in a grip of bigotry and corruption, the exiled writer Salvador de Madariaga was asked if he could not find one thing to say in the Spanish dictator's favor.

"For twenty-four hours I have searched my heart and mind," Madariaga answered. "In truth, I can find nothing."

My childhood had much in common with Franco's Spain.

Not the childhood rhymed out in song by Dylan Thomas where the hayfields ran high as houses between sun-bright streams, and the evening air was soft with moths and bells and owl calls. But a prison. Sentence was handed down on a charge never specified. There was no appeal. No option of a fine to be paid in lieu. The term was served inside chill flint walls where the permanent season was winter and the patches of sky above a sour unvarying gray.

I did sixteen years' hard. When the gates finally opened and I walked out to freedom, I could only pass Madariaga's judgment on what lay behind. There was one difference. In Franco's jails books were banned. Where I served my time, even the lifer had access to the prison library.

Access was one matter. To read in peace and privacy, away from the warders' eyes, another. That required stealth and cunning. Others among my fellow inmates furtively collected stamps or sportsmen's autographs to fill the sterile hours. I became a specialist in architectural flaws.

There was a house in Tehran, a hotel in Cairo, a mansion in the Hebrides, an apartment in London. To this day I could burgle them all. I know every window with a faulty latch, every hidden landing, every unused staircase, every forgotten garden door.

It was in one of those secret, undiscovered places where I did my reading that I first came across the name Kalahari.

> The Road of Death. August 1911. 9.30 of the morning.
>
> Dear A—. Last night the cattle ran away. I have no more water. I despair. I left the waggon on foot in the hope of reaching Kokong, but my strength fails. My private papers and my stamps send to my children and inform them that I have died of fever in the desert. As well inform B to this effect. Charlie and the new Kalahari boys are mainly responsible for this. The thirst kills me. These are the last words of a dying man.
>
> Your true friend—M.
>
> P.S. A little water would have saved me.

I sat very still with the book on my knee in an icy corner between the cook's and the housemaid's bedrooms. I was eleven. The floorboards were painted blue, and there was frost on the windowpanes, and a portrait of Lord Kitchener hung from the wall.

Who were the dying M and his friends A and B? Why those bare initials in place of their names? What were the stamps willed to M's children? Why on his deathbed was there no mention of his wife? What role had the villainous Charlie played? Where was the Road of Death?

Questions and images (hyena and jackal had got to M's body before the colonial policeman found it) tumbled fearsomely and insistently through my mind. But as I pondered them I realized there was a larger issue to be dealt with first.

What and where was the Kalahari itself?

My grandfather had assembled his library in the days when the globe was largely colored red and God was still an Englishman. His sternly bearded cartographers wore frock coats with gold chains across their stomachs. They spoke the language of Shakespeare and

Milton, and used sturdy no-nonsense names like Araby, Cathay and the Land of the Tartars.

The atlas I consulted was a massive leatherbound volume which smelled of cigar smoke. Not an atlas for the armchair traveler, but a practical work of reference for men. Men of empire, soldiers, explorers, colonial governors and sportsmen. The index referred me to the African continent. I turned the pages. There, toward the southern tip of a map of Africa, I found what I was looking for.

A scarlet oval plateau labeled simply with the legend "The Great Kalahari Desert."

It was Christmas. At Christmas, childhood's equivalent of the convicts' concert was a party. Both events were equally joyless. That year the festivity was hosted by a neighbor. When the chilling ritual of party games was announced, I slipped away. There was, I'd learned, one invariable sanctuary in the houses of the county bourgeoisie. The nursery. A warm, well-lit place guarded by the sleeping dragon of the family, the Nanny.

I opened the door quietly. The dragon was, as usual, slumbering. I hid myself in the shadow of the nursery bookcase. By chance I found I was kneeling against a row of encyclopedias almost as old as my grandfather's atlas. I pulled out the volume H–K and looked up Kalahari.

"Grey, grim and featureless," I read. "A barren wasteland, it can be likened to a vast landlocked island of sandstone scorched by the pitiless African sun. The forsaken desert, as the countless piles of bones discovered by intrepid explorers testify, is incapable of harboring life."

M's letter was brutal evidence in support of that. I read on. There followed an arcane description of the Kalahari's geology. Then at the end of the article I noticed a cross reference to another entry:

"For further observations on this inhospitable region the reader is referred to Dr. David Livingstone *(q.v.)*."

I put the book away and took out the volume that followed it. I had just found the entry when I heard footsteps in the corridor outside. Not the quick gallop of a child but the unsteady lurching of an adult. Any moment a large stockbroker who drove a maroon Jaguar and reeked of gin and tonic would blunder through the door rounding up the stragglers.

I searched frantically through the dense columns of print.

"That there were terrible wastes ahead of me I had no doubt." I was reading Livingstone's own words now. "But beyond the Great Thirst, as the natives called it, I was told stories of a land of water, of meadows and trees and flowing rivers. I immediately resolved I would cross the Kalahari and determine what truth there lay in these tales."

The footsteps were very close. A hand fumbled on the doorknob. I thrust the second volume back into the shelf, hurdled the still-sleeping dragon and departed through the window into the night.

At school across those years I acquired two acquaintances—friendship was much too warm a term for our relationship. The most we achieved was a wary tolerance of each other. It was enough.

The first was small, squat, bespectacled and taciturn. His home was in the shires, and he bore a name like Warrington-Bates. From the gamekeepers on his father's estate he'd learned old poachers' tricks. Together we'd climb the school walls at dusk and roam the surrounding hills—setting snares for hares and rabbits, dunking grain in alcohol to stupefy pheasants, laying gin traps for foxes whose pelts we'd sell in the local market.

The second was a boy named Speedwell. He was tall, beak-nosed and courteous. No one in authority suspected Speedwell of anything. He was clean but not overclean, studious but not remarkably so, a trifle vague perhaps but always conscientious and willing. An unexceptionable boy, authority assumed, a useful member of society. Good mortar between the bricks.

Authority's assumptions about Speedwell were catastrophically wrong. In reality he was a natural anarchist, a high-explosive bomb detonated by remote control, the worm relentlessly gnawing at the heart of things. Where Speedwell went, sedition and disaster followed. Always at a distance, always long after he'd passed by.

In the laconic company of Warrington-Bates I first discovered how to live with and off the wild. From Speedwell I learned other techniques of prison survival.

"What are *your* plans?"

Speedwell passed me the bottle of sloe gin Warrington-Bates had looted from his father's cellar.

"Plans?" I frowned.

Sunday. A shining May morning on the Hampshire downs. In the distance the cathedral bells were chiming. We had skipped Matins.

The hawthorn hedge was bright with flowers, and round us pairs of lovers were coupling under tartan blankets on the warm spring grass.

The three of us had been discussing the future, what we'd each do when the cells were finally unlocked. The other two had given their views. Now it was my turn.

I thought, and suddenly there on the green hillside images of the great desert came back to me. The parched, despairing M, the Road of Death, the Great Thirst, Dr. Livingstone and the tales of a land of trees and meadows and flowing rivers. There was a mystery and only one way to solve it.

I realized at that moment that I had always known what I was going to do.

"Oh," I said casually, "I've decided to cross the Kalahari."

Three companions. Warrington-Bates now farms his dead father's estate and rents the shooting to oil-rich Venezuelans. He is reputed to drink two bottles of vintage port each evening after dinner. I see him occasionally on the steps of his St. James's Street club. Doughy and rotund, with a bowler hat on his head and an expression of glowering malevolence on his face. The other members, I am told, have a deep and cordial loathing for him.

Speedwell made a killing on the commodities market and retired at the age of twenty-seven. He lives as a tax exile in a Monte Carlo apartment. During the off season he plays backgammon against the Swiss-based professionals across the border. Speedwell wins.

I went to the Kalahari.

When my grandfather's atlas was first published, the Kalahari desert was unencumbered by national boundaries. An unexplored plateau three thousand feet above sea level, it lay like some vast and unclaimed island of stone at the center of the southern tip of Africa.

Today the map of the desert is dissected by lines. In common with all the continent's great natural formations, the Kalahari has been arbitrarily divided up and its territory allocated to a number of countries. Part lies within the Republic of South Africa and part within Namibia. But the largest part of the Kalahari, half its entire area and including the desert's heart, belongs to Botswana—formerly the British Bechuanaland Protectorate.

Botswana, which became independent in 1966, is a landlocked

state rather larger than France with a population of some eight hundred thousand people. Most of the inhabitants are concentrated in a narrow belt along the eastern border. The rest of Botswana's huge expanse is the desert—the wild. In a sense the country and the desert are synonymous.

A journey across the Kalahari is a journey across Botswana.

Politically, from independence until his death in 1980, Botswana was ruled by Sir Seretse Khama, its elected president. A wise, courageous and scrupulously fair man, and one of Africa's outstanding leaders, Khama created and maintained a genuine multiparty democracy in spite of the country's appalling poverty. The poverty, in large measure, remains, but while Khama's writ ran, Botswana was tolerant, stable and peaceful.

Soon after that November London night I sent a cable to the small town of Gaborone, the country's capital. Two weeks later I received a telegraphed reply. It read simply: YES. The signature was SYD YOUTHED.

I had had to wait twenty-five years since the May morning on the Hampshire downs before I finally went to the Kalahari. It had happened three years earlier, and my companion into the desert then had been Syd Youthed. Syd was a veteran white hunter who specialized as a Kalahari guide. I'd asked him if he would assemble a safari and accompany me again the following spring.

Once I had his answer, I set about preparing for the journey in earnest. I had already planned the route. Starting at Gaborone, on the southern edge of the desert, we would travel north across the Kalahari, swing west at the northern limits and then make a great sweep south to Gaborone again. In all it was a distance of some two thousand miles and with luck would take us two months to cover.

The next crucial decision was whom I should take with me. Syd would bring two Tswana camp hands and a cook. The safari's logistics left me with space for four more. About the first there was no problem. As a wildlife painter, my wife, Elisabeth, was used to expedition life. EBL, as she was known from the initials with which she signed her paintings, was coming to record the birds and animals of the Kalahari.

For the final three places I began by making lists. Broadly based lists to start with. Afterward, shorter and shorter ones. Finally I set about interviewing people. Formally in certain cases, dropping the idea like a fly on the stream in others. Some candidates were unavailable because of prior commitments. Others for one reason or another quickly disqualified themselves.

But the great majority turned away out of a sense of apprehension that was difficult to define. Somehow the size, the remoteness, the fabled savagery of the great stone plateau menaced and troubled them. They listened. They considered. Then they made their excuses and left.

By early spring I had torn up every list. A month before we were due to start I had no one. In my mind's eye I still had a clear picture of the people I would have liked. Lean, long-striding men with their gaze on distant horizons. Men of quiet laughter and few words round the campfire at night. True pioneers capable of reading stars and wind. Men who loved space and open sky, to whom the smoke, clamor and greed of the urban sprawl were anathema.

That was the breed I was after. What I got was Big David, Little David and Bobby. Big David was the first to sign up.

Years before, I had lived in a house at the head of an Andalusian valley. A large, dreaming house where I would wake early and lie in sunlight reflected from the sea listening to the Mediterranean wind. One morning I woke to a sound I'd never heard before. A cross between an old-fashioned dental drill and a concrete pile driver.

The bed throbbed. The pictures on the walls were quivering. Even the deep-set floor tiles vibrated. I followed the noise to the kitchen. A figure was standing in the middle of the room gripping an instrument that looked like a sawed-off Uzi machine gun.

"Morning, old bean," he said. "I thought it was prudent to bring my own cocktail shaker. For breakfast I had in mind a banana daiquiri. How about you?"

He handed me a tumbler full of golden liquid. I looked at my watch. It was 7 A.M. I had never seen him before.

"I don't think we've met," I said.

"We have now. A refill?"

So David came into my life. It was the Kalahari hunters who christened him Big David later. Not so much for his height as for his awesome capacity for alcohol and the sheer majestic bulk of his physical presence—250 pounds of bone and muscle preceded by a belly like a butt of Shakespearean Malmsey. Walking very slowly, flat-footed, his arms curving outward and then in again, bow-shaped at the wrists, David in movement from the rear can easily be mistaken for a silver-backed gorilla.

David is in business. The business is principally conducted in late-night taverns to the artillery of champagne corks. I have never asked its nature. But business brought him to the Kalahari. He had viewed the preparations for months with interested skepticism. Then one chill March evening the bell rang and he appeared through the door.

"This desert wheeze," he said. "I think it might be advisable if I came along."

I gazed at him astounded. Here was this quintessential creature of saloon, gambling club, racecourse and raunchy discotheque proposing he should cross the Kalahari.

"Are you serious?" I asked.

"Absolutely, old bean."

"Why?"

"There are negotiations afoot," he answered. "It would be diplomatic if I absented myself from the smoke for a while."

"But what are you going to do in the desert?"

"I shall as usual be responsible for vulgar and loutish behavior. Also, I am a dab hand with differential problems in heavy sand."

He reached for the morning newspaper and disappeared down the passage.

Bobby came next. Bobby matched David in thirst and size. He too had unspecified business interests. But where David was direct and uncompromising, a blunt instrument with the honed blade of his tongue at the tip, Bobby was quieter, more devious and oblique, a private man and a dreamer. His world embraced paintings and rare books, Palladian country houses and the Scottish deer forests where he was counted an outstanding rifle shot.

Lastly, a week before we left, Little David joined up—"Little" only to distinguish him from his namesake. Although he lacked Big David's monumental frame and build, he was in fact the taller of the two, a piratical, debonair figure with an acid tongue, sharp blue eyes and the features of a dissolute Rupert Brooke.

"So why do you want to come?" I asked him.

Little David stared thoughtfully over my shoulder. Ostensibly his reason was to combine the expedition with a visit to a family ranch in Zimbabwe on the Kalahari's eastern border. The reason was plausible. It wasn't wholly convincing.

He lit a cigarette, flared out his cuffs and laughed.

"It sounds like an adventure, Colonel," he said. "I rather fancy adventures."

For better or worse I had my third foot soldier.

My choice of the three was greeted in several quarters with astonishment that approached disbelief. I knew rather more about them than the popular view. Big David had traveled several of the world's wilder quarters and roamed alone on foot high into the Himalayas. Bobby had spent six months cut off in the Amazon jungles, emerging with half his normal body weight, festering inch-deep sores and his usual lazy smile. Little David had been tempered by a childhood in the African bush.

All three had elected to make their way in London smoke. They were raffish, hard-drinking, and their language would flush the cheeks of a Marseilles docker. They hadn't been chosen for parlor conversation. We had two thousand miles of Kalahari sand, scrub and thorn ahead. The guerrilla bush wars that were flaring round the plateau's borders in Zimbabwe and Namibia. The malarial and tsetse belts of the Okavango delta, the Great Thirst to the south, the Road of Death at the end.

Little David had called the expedition an adventure. In the old-fashioned sense, he and the other two were all adventurers. They had volunteered themselves, and I'd accepted them, on no more than the simple and unspoken premise that they'd stand firm if occasion demanded. I had no doubt about that. It was, after all, what adventurers are traditionally expected to do.

At the last minute, for obscure reasons connected with his negotiations, Big David had to postpone his departure. He was due to fly out and join us in Gaborone forty-eight hours later. Equally abruptly and obscurely, Little David found himself delayed even longer. He planned to cross the Kalahari by air and join the expedition midway along the route at a trading post in the northern desert.

EBL, Bobby and I left London on a damp and gray mid-April afternoon. Spring rain glistened on the sidewalks, and the trees were quickening with green. As our cab crossed a quiet square, Bobby suddenly leaned forward and tapped the driver on the shoulder. The cab stopped. Bobby jumped out and sprinted away. A moment later I saw him locked in an embrace with a passing blonde.

"Stroke of luck, that," he said when he returned. "Last chance of a nipple-feel for an eternity. Right, Colonel, we're on our way."

The cab turned into the Cromwell Road and headed toward Heathrow and Africa.

# 3

WHEN BRITAIN TRIMMED the imperial sails before the African winds of change, a manual was prepared for the navigators in Whitehall.

It listed the urgent requirements of the former colonies for independence. The most pressing was a national flag, and the College of Heralds was retained to advise about design. Next came a patriotic anthem. Afterward, brass-buttoned uniforms for the local militia, flowers and fireworks to celebrate the great day, a small royal personage to grace the occasion, and a team of gray shire horses—on loan—to add an authentic touch of pageantry.

Checking the list, as independence neared for the country about to be born as Botswana, a colonial mandarin made an unnerving discovery. Flag, flowers, fireworks, a diminutive but perfectly formed royal, even the shire horses had all been ordered. Everything was apple-pie ready. Everything but one.

The new nation lacked a capital city.

Or rather, and even more embarrassingly, it had a capital—but the capital was in another country. For almost a century the Protectorate had held the distinction of being the only country in the world whose seat of government was outside its borders. It was administered from Mafeking, twenty miles away in the Republic of South Africa.

Flowers and fireworks, the mandarin uneasily realized, not to mention the coiffeured royal, would look a little gauche if the day of destiny dawned and there was nowhere to bloom, detonate or parade in white gloves except a space of desert sand.

On the spur of the moment the decision was taken to create a capital for Botswana. The chosen site was Gaborone's, a little village on the Ngatwane River in the south of the country named after a minor Tswana chief. The circle of huts was cleared, and almost overnight Botswana had its London, Paris, Washington or Rome. Officially its name is now Gaborone, but fourteen years later few people refer to it other than as "Gab's."

If you want an instant toy capital on the cheap and your definition of long-range planning is to guess what might happen next Tuesday by consulting a chicken's entrails, then Gab's is what you get. A miniature version of the parliament houses at Westminster. A shopping precinct called the Mall. A ring of barrackslike administrative buildings. And a scatter of suburban villas for anyone quixotic enough to live there.

The town was "planned" for a population of a few thousand. Today it has fifty thousand inhabitants spilling out in chaotic ripples from the center. The number rises each year. Yet in spite of its explosive growth, Gaborone retains something of the intimacy of the old chief's village. Unlike almost every other African capital, it is relaxed, friendly, unpretentious and welcoming.

Our flight from Johannesburg landed at sunset on a humid and cloudy April evening. Two days earlier Syd Youthed had left for the central desert to set up our first camp. In his place to greet us was his wife, Sheila. From the airfield she drove us to the Holiday Inn —one of Gaborone's two hotels and the favorite meeting place for the prospectors, ranchers, hunters, pilots and traders who worked the desert to the north.

The following morning we met the flight from Johannesburg that Big David had promised to catch. He wasn't on it. We returned to the hotel to check if he'd left a message. There was nothing. Then we settled down to wait out the day. By evening there was still no word from him. Finally at 8 P.M. I was called to the telephone.

"Can you hear me?"

I could, but only just. David's voice rose and fell through waves of static. I hunched myself deeper under the transparent plastic canopy and cupped my ear with my hand, trying to shut out the clamor from the bar.

"Where are you?" I bellowed back.

"Spot of bother, old bean. Thick fog over Nairobi."

The static increased and I lost him. There were several hazards attached to landing at Nairobi. In April, fog wasn't one of them.

I waited. A young lady tapped on the canopy. She was slim and black and bright-eyed, wearing a skin-tight white satin pants suit and with a bronze coin in her hand. Black and white and bronze. Desert colors at dawn. I smiled at her and waved, silently imploring her to be patient.

"Listen, David"—the line had cleared, and I was shouting again —"will you just tell me where the hell you are?"

He might have been calling from almost anywhere in the world. To judge from the level of interference, Tokyo seemed a reasonable guess.

"Not to worry." His voice traveled in curves through the electronic crackling. "I'm virtually next door. Quaint old Jo'burg, to be exact. What happened was this—"

I cut him off. "I'm not interested in what happened. We leave at eight A.M. tomorrow. All I want to know now is whether you'll be there."

"No problem, Colonel. There's a connection at five. I'll see you in the morning."

The line went dead. I surrendered the telephone to the young lady and walked upstairs.

Normally I sleep deeply and well. That night it was different. I woke at one, at two and again at three. Each time, I got out of bed and paced restlessly for a few minutes. EBL never stirred. As if instinctively storing up reserves of energy for the days ahead, she lay motionless and untroubled.

Finally, waking once more, I dressed and went to the window. I slid back the glass panel and stepped out onto the balcony. I was looking north. I could feel the wind set at an angle to my face. By now it should have been blowing from behind me, from off the Transvaal mountains to the south. In late April the Kalahari summer, the season of the desert's most searing heat and occasional deluging rains, should be over. I had planned for clear, dry days and cold, starlit nights. If the wind remained in the north, we could expect sandstorms, stifling humidity, perhaps even a late downpour that might briefly make the desert impassable.

I stood for a moment frowning in the darkness. Then I realized it wasn't the unseasonal northern wind that had made me sleepless and uneasy. The wind would create hazards and problems—but something else was grating at the back of my mind, something I couldn't immediately pin down. I went over everything again trying to find it.

Syd Youthed would be waiting for me four hundred miles away in camp at the Boteti River. Since my first cable to him I had made some changes in the expedition's route. The basic plan, a circular crossing of the Kalahari, remained. But I'd trekked the first stage overland from Gaborone on my last visit and I knew the terrain. This time I'd decided we would fly straight to the central desert and start from there.

Much depended on our expedition guide, Syd. Much, in the Kalahari, can mean nothing less than life itself. Was there, I wondered, something wrong there? I knew Syd could be difficult, stubborn and cussed. He was also vastly experienced, loyal, conscientious and hickory-tough—a true old-fashioned professional hunter who'd give the devil his soul in barter sooner than short-change his companions in the bush.

No, I decided—whatever else happened, Syd wouldn't be found wanting.

My three foot soldiers, then? I doubted their loyalty and competence as little as I doubted Syd's. Perhaps the problem lay in the route after all? In planning to cover two thousand miles, I had set the expedition a daunting task. Even Syd, in his few and cryptic communications, had expressed reservations about what we were taking on. Yet I knew it was possible.

With the right companions, the right supplies, the right will and determination, the journey could be completed. I was sure I had them all. So what was vexing and nagging me as I stood there gazing north toward the desert under the wheeling Kalahari stars?

An animal.

The realization came suddenly and late. It wasn't so much a realization as the resurfacing of an image that had haunted me ever since

I'd been there before. I'd returned to search for an answer to the poet's question. I had also come back on a quest of my own. The animal I was looking for, and the image of it which had risen out of the darkness, belonged to the night.

I had returned to the Kalahari to search for the black leopard.

"No." The man by the fire shook his head emphatically. "I've read those findings and I don't give a goddamn what they say. They're wrong."

Still shaking his head, he gazed at the flames.

It was a night on my first visit to the desert, and the speaker was a hunter who'd joined me at the fire after supper. We'd been discussing the rarest and most elusive of the Kalahari's predators—the leopard. Known to science as *Panthera pardus*, the common leopard is, of course, a large spotted feline, a ferocious and normally solitary nocturnal hunter. But there is another and much less common creature which appears identical to the spotted leopard in every characteristic but one: its coat is black.

It was called a black panther, and for decades there was speculation whether the two animals belonged to the same or different species. Then in 1966 the results of a lengthy series of experiments were correlated and published. The experiments had taken place in zoos. They involved mating captive specimens of the spotted and the black.

The ability to breed is the classic, although not infallible, test for determining specificity. In the zoo tests, spotted and black bred successfully without distinction. Analyzing the coloration of the cubs in the litters, the monitoring zoologists found a consistent pattern. The pattern conformed exactly to the Mendelian theory of genetics.

Spotted and black were the same creature. The appearance of a black cub in a litter from "mixed" parents could be ascribed to a recessive gene. The same recessive gene that at predictable intervals in humans could produce a blue-eyed child from two brown-eyed parents, just as with equal predictability it had caused color variations in Gregor Mendel's monastery flowers.

For the zoologists, the old Austrian monk had been proved right again. The speculation was ended. The case was solved and the file closed. Not in the intractable Kalahari it wasn't.

"You still believe the two are different?" I said.

"I don't believe," he answered. "I know."

"How?"

"Where the hell did those black panthers come from?"

It was a rhetorical question. We'd discussed and agreed on the answer before. The zoo specimens had all been caught in the mountainous rain forests of Asia. Not even the zoologists disputed that. The arid stone plateau of the Kalahari might be many things. A permanently damp and hilly rain forest it was incontrovertibly not.

"So the environment, the habitat's totally different," he went on. "Yet we've got the black here. And that's not all. You know what the panther's skin looks like?"

I nodded. The skin of the black panther, the animal bred with the spotted in the conclusive experiments, had been a pure, unvarying jet. No marks, no trace of pattern—nothing except a total silken blackness.

"I've seen the hides of the Kalahari black," he said. "Two of them. I was a kid, maybe fourteen. I was out in camp with my old man. A group of Bushman came by. They had these skins they wanted to trade. Showed them to us. . . ."

He frowned. He was over sixty, and his face had the fierce concentration of someone trying to communicate a scrupulously accurate picture of something seen almost fifty years before but which was still as vivid now as it was then.

"It was early—six thirty, seven. Good clear light. My old man, he held the skins up against the sky. Then he knuckled them round his fist. The hides were stiff. Stank of dry blood and piss and salt. He said, 'Look at them.' I looked. They were black—Jesus, they were black. . . ."

He hunched himself forward and stirred the fire.

"But there was something else. Every single hair had a pale rib. Spread the skins flat and they made roses. Black roses on black fur. No way you could miss them. . . ."

He paused.

The black panther came from high rain forests and showed not a trace of the roseate pattern of the spotted. The Kalahari black came from the desert and was printed with flowers.

"I tell you"—he jabbed out his arm—"out there you've got another animal. It's different."

He was pointing at the immensity of the plateau beyond the flames in the darkness.

I heard other stories of the Kalahari black that trip. Other recollections, other rumors, other tales told round a campfire at night.

There was never anything concrete in the stories, and many people flatly rejected them. Instead, they spoke of the dark-skinned leopards of the desert. There were, beyond doubt, in the Kalahari leopards with fur so dark that in the half-light of dusk or dawn they could appear black. On the rare occasions when one of those was shot it invariably turned out to be an ordinary spotted.

A dark coat, uncertain light and gullibility. To the disbelievers—the majority—that was the explanation of the so-called Kalahari black. In their view the truly black leopard was a desert fable, a companion to the phoenix and the unicorn. Those, on the other hand, who believed in the animal were equally adamant about its existence. Hides were still reputed to appear occasionally in remote trading posts. Others as well as the hunter with whom I'd first discussed the leopard claimed to have examined them—although not for years now.

They remained just as certain as he that what they'd seen wasn't the skin of a spotted—it had belonged to the black.

I spent a month in the desert. I left skeptical but puzzled. The evidence against the creature was overwhelming. In a court of law there would have been no case to argue on its behalf. Yet it was all negative evidence, and I remembered that improbable sea animal, the coelacanth. Marine biologists had proved conclusively that the last coelacanth had perished millions of years ago. As a species it was extinct—at rest with the dinosaur in the distant past.

And then one day a fisherman in the Indian Ocean pulled in his net and a living, gulping organism armored with spikes and bony plates tumbled onto the boards of his boat. The marine biologists were astounded. The fisherman was not. He'd been saying quietly for a long time that coelacanths still survived—he knew because periodically one of them patterned his net with scales.

Whatever the truth, an image of the Kalahari black took shape in my mind. It stayed with me long after I left the desert. Months later a feral black silhouette would come padding into my dreams. Waiting for a telephone call, I'd find myself sketching a feline head against a barrier of thorn. Once, sitting late at a dinner table, I glanced down and discovered I'd drawn a rose above a line of pug-marks in the spilled wine.

Trying to rid myself of the shadowy presence, I combed through the journals of the nineteenth-century hunters who'd ventured into the Kalahari before the plateau was pillaged. If the leopard existed, or even had existed once, it would surely be there in the meticulous and detailed records of men like Andersson, Gordon Cumming and Selous. If they failed to mention it, then the animal could be dismissed.

I did not find a single entry in any of the journals that might even be construed as referring to the Kalahari black. Yet stubbornly the leopard still refused to depart. Reluctantly, then, I reconciled myself to living with it. Over the months that followed, the animal began to acquire another dimension. It was still an emblem of itself, of a rare nocturnal species that might or might not inhabit the desert. But it also began to represent the entire Kalahari and all the issues raised by any consideration of a great wilderness.

They were, of course, the issues implicit in the poet's question. When I returned to the desert in search of the answer I had not been able to give then, I was also returning to search for the black leopard. The animal and the wild were indivisible. The two quests had become one.

I understood at last what was troubling me that night in Gaborone as I stood gazing north into the wind. My chances of finding the leopard were infinitesimal.

I went back to bed. I still could not sleep. I lay on my back watching the stars until the sky grayed with dawn.

# 4

"MORNING, old bean."

Big David surged through the throng of arriving passengers like a liner encircled by tugboats. He was wearing dark glasses, a quilted down jacket, bottle-green cord breeches and an immense pair of metal-studded mountaineering boots laced with scarlet ties.

"French," he explained as I gazed at the boots. "Fell off the back of a truck outside Toulouse."

"We're not planning an assault on the Eiger," I said.

"True, Colonel," he agreed. "But at fifty francs they were irresistible. Furthermore, I have judiciously brought the serum."

He dumped a chinking bag at my feet. I looked inside. I could see bottles of malt whisky, some flagons of St. James's rum and several magnums of champagne.

"Stirred, shaken and imbibed in sufficient quantities," he added, "they are widely regarded as antihemo and nervotoxic both."

David beamed. In the pale dawn light he looked like a Mafia hit man disguised as the Red Baron. At least he was there.

The passengers drifted away, the little terminal emptied and we walked out onto the runway. The air was thin and clear. Above the control tower the flag of the sovereign republic of Botswana strained out before the morning wind. A broad black line ran horizontally across it. The black was for the country's majority population, the eight Tswana tribes. Above and below were slender bands of white to mark the legacy of European settlement and empire. The background was blue.

The blue stood for *pula*. In the Kalahari, *pula* signifies greeting, prayer, sacrament and celebration. *Pula* is the Tswana word for rain. When Botswana created its own currency to replace the South African rand, it was almost inevitable that the principal unit should be named a *pula* too.

"Ho-ho!" David said. "What have we here?"

The plane due to fly us north to the landing strip in the central desert was an Aero Commander. From a distance it had the silhouette of an aging prizefighter. Rugged, heavy-shouldered, its wings gnarled with scar tissue. Closer, we could see that the fuselage was listing lopsidedly, as if it had just taken some heavy punches to the body.

David glanced underneath, spotted a flattened tire and gave it a speculative kick.

"Technical hitch number one," he chuckled happily. "Time out, I think, for a first beaker. Follow me, my fat friend."

He and Bobby strode to the runway's edge, where they settled themselves comfortably in the dry winter grass. A moment later I heard the pop of a cork. Then Brian Whitley appeared.

There are three main categories of pilot who fly the desert routes. The young cowboys who mainly work the hunting camps and take any other job that's offered without asking questions about the cargo. The professional free-lances filling in time between other African assignments. And the Kalahari veterans. All three groups are good. The veterans are the best. Whitley was a veteran.

"Good to see you again," he said.

Whitley smiled and held out his hand. I remembered him from before, a spare, quiet-voiced man with steady eyes in a tanned and wrinkled face.

"We seem to have a small problem," I remarked.

Whitley glanced at the tire.

"At least we can fix it here," he answered. "Last year I did an overnight run to a camp at Tsane. Midnight I heard a bang like a cannon going off. I belted over to the plane with a flashlamp. When you leave a kite out in the bush, you often get buck licking the paint for minerals. This time it was a hyena. It had been chewing at the tire when the tube exploded. Blew its goddamn head right off."

He chuckled. "I was stuck all day waiting for someone to fly me out a replacement."

Whitley disappeared beneath the undercarriage.

An hour later we were airborne. Apart from the pilot and copilot, the Aero Commander had seats for four passengers. I sat beside Whitley in the copilot's seat. Behind us were EBL, David and Bobby. There was room for one more.

"This is Ted Armitage," Sheila Youthed had said, introducing a young man, when we arrived at the airfield. "He's never flown the desert. Can you take him with you for the ride?"

Armitage was pleasant and open-faced. He worked as an assistant manager at the Holiday Inn. He had the neat appearance and easy conversation of the professional hotelier, but I sensed a certain tension in him. After we'd talked for a while I discovered why.

Armitage had a snake problem.

"Vipers, spitting cobras, puff adders," he said wearily. "You name it, we've got it. Jesus, yesterday we even found a black mamba by the bloody swimming pool. Can you imagine how a guest's going to feel about sharing his lunchtime Bacardi and Coke with that?"

I sympathized with him as he shuddered. A black mamba's venom can kill within fifteen minutes.

The plague of snakes troubling Armitage was partly due to two successive drought years, and partly the result of Gaborone's growth. The staple diet of many poisonous snakes is small rodents. With the failure of the rains, the desert's rodent population had dropped sharply. Searching for food, the snakes had moved toward the Kalahari's townships and villages.

There, as in any place of human settlement, they found an abundant supply of man's inevitable parasites—rats and mice. Gaborone had become a particularly rich larder. The snakes thrived and bred. For them the town was a cornucopia. To men like Armitage, responsible for running hotels, it had become a nightmare.

Armitage sat silently in the back throughout the flight, gazing through the window. He was meant to be looking at the desert. I doubt he even noticed it. I think he was offering up dark curses against the fate that had made him responsible for plump white tourists and thin black mambas.

Our destination was a landing strip four hundred miles northwest of Gaborone. Although there was nothing there—no nearby village, no hut, not even a wind sock—to identify it, the strip was known as Tsoe.

Tsoe, as Whitley said, was a very small needle in a very large haystack. Instead of heading for the strip directly on a diagonal line across the desert, we first flew due north. Our immediate object was to find a village named Nata. With few radio beacons and virtually no ground features, air navigation in the Kalahari is carried out by compass, experience, observation and guesswork. Nata was one of the rare fixed reference points. At Nata we could orient ourselves for the approach to Tsoe. At Nata, too, we could check if there was water in the Sua Pan. Pans, shallow depressions in the desert's surface, are a recurring feature of the Kalahari landscape which we would encounter at intervals throughout the journey.

We gained height and Gaborone disappeared behind us. As Whitley leveled the plane, I sat forward and stared down. Most landscapes are open and revealing from the air. Not the Kalahari. Spreading out from horizon to horizon in a vast and desolate expanse of wilderness, the desert gives nothing away. It radiates defiance and hostility. That morning a grainy screen of heat and dust hung unmoving above the summer-baked earth like smoke from smoldering battle fires. Occasionally a vulture spiraled on a thermal above the haze. Beneath the circling birds the only colors were the colors of war.

The thorn was dried to the dark leathery brown of a hide shield. In the empty watercourse the pale rocks shone with the goose-feather gray of an arrow's quill. The pans glittered sword-metal bright. The bush hurled back the light in ripples of chain mail. The dead trees were angled like resting lances in the bitter earth.

The stone citadel was mantled in silver, black and tawny armor. It was ancient, cunning and pitiless. I remembered the dying M. The Kalahari took no prisoners.

"Nata," Whitley said, pointing, two hours later.

I peered forward. Below, in rows of tiny studs like snail shells, was a cluster of huts. We overflew the village, banked and turned west. Then we angled down. The Sua Pan complex lay just to the south of Nata. If there was any water left in the pans we'd make our second camp there.

As we descended, the haze dissolved. The ground came into focus in planes of gleaming steel linked by whorls and crescents of bone-colored sand. Suddenly the surface was stippled by lines of tracer fire. The bullets ricocheted upward and detonated in flares of rose and white.

"It's drying fast," Whitley said. "But I guess there's still a foot left. You've got maybe ten days."

The exploding flashes were flocks of flamingos and pelicans. They were feeding in water that had fallen the year before in Zimbabwe, hundreds of miles to the northeast. After months of forcing its way south through the sand, the water had finally reached the pans. Now it was evaporating, but we'd be back before it dried out completely and the birds left.

"Right," Whitley added. "Let's go hunting for needles."

Still keeping low, we flew on. The pans ended and we were over the bush again—tracts of dry grass and scrub stretching out between scattered trees. For the first hour the plateau had looked incapable of supporting any but the most primitive forms of life. It was the Kalahari of legend, of long-received wisdom, implacably bleak and sterile. The Great Thirst traversed only by the Road of Death. The few vultures, the birds of death, seemed merely to confirm that view.

In reality, of course, their presence meant the opposite. Vultures are indicators not of death but of life. Where vultures fly there must be carrion below. Carrion in sufficient quantities to sustain them all year round. Carrion in turn means animals—and animals all year round. However improbable it appeared from the air, the Kalahari was inhabited throughout the seasons by creatures large enough to support the wheeling vultures. The incontrovertible proof was written clear in the silhouettes against the sky.

"Prettiest goddamn birds you'll ever see."

Three years earlier. I was standing with an old hunter in the shadow of a kopje in the western desert. Overhead, a group of griffon vultures was beating lazily upward.

"Vultures follow game," he went on. "Game follows water. So long as you've got those birds above you, you're safe. Somewhere close there's both food and drink. It's only when you can't see them you're in trouble, real trouble. Shit, man, a sky without vultures, that's serious—that's death."

He shook his head, chuckling quietly. "I tell you, those birds, they're beautiful."

So much for the received "wisdom." As the old hunter knew—not from witchcraft or the whispering perversions of rumor but from the strong direct experience of living—where the cleansing vultures go, there goes life itself.

We had seen vultures. Now we saw what nourished them. Not directly, but in the calligraphy scrawled on the sand beneath. Everywhere the bush was serrated with tracks. Some were narrow spidery corridors wandering at random through the thorn. Others pressed die-straight ahead in broad furrowed lanes. They converged, crossed each other, parted and then met again. All of them were patterned with the stamp of countless hooves.

Over the next two hours we glimpsed no more than a dozen solitary buck. But multitudes of animals had traveled below—and traveled so recently that the desert wind hadn't had time to erase the imprint of their passage.

Until Nata, Whitley had been relaxed and communicative. From the moment we angled west he became increasingly taut. He sat upright over the controls. His eyes narrowed in concentration. At shorter and shorter intervals he glanced at his watch, the compass, the frayed and grimy map spread out on his knees. Then, ninety minutes after we left the pans, he stiffened and stared intently ahead.

I followed his gaze. For several moments I could see nothing except the limitless expanse of the bush. It was as flat, monotonous and unvarying as it had been from the start. Then at the extreme limit of my vision I registered what he'd spotted. On the rim of the horizon, almost indistinguishable from the encircling grass and thorn, there was a tiny thread of brushed earth. The Tsoe landing strip.

"I reckon we've found our needle," Whitley said.

He glanced round and gave me a quick smile. There was no pride or elation in his face, only a small private satisfaction. He'd flown four hundred miles across the featureless wilderness without hesitation or correction, and he'd arrived unerringly at our destination. It was what he was paid to do, and he did it well.

The strip came closer. We dipped and swept over it. Briefly I saw a truck and a silhouetted figure, arms lifted in salute. We banked steeply, circled and came in to land. The fuselage juddered as the wheels bounced over the pitted sand. Then Whitley cut the engines and I climbed out.

"Welcome back, *amigo*."

Syd ambled forward to meet me. I gripped his hand and clapped him on the shoulder.

It was exactly three years since I'd seen him last. With something of a shock I noticed how much he'd aged. His tall, spare frame was leaner and more angular, his hair sparser, his face hollowed and deeply lined. Even for a young man the Kalahari is a brutal and demanding place to work. Syd was approaching sixty. He worked the desert for eight months each year. The strain was beginning to show. But his handshake was as vigorous as before, and he heaved our heavy bags up into the truck effortlessly. Even at sixty he'd still be more than a match for any of us in the bush.

I introduced Syd to the others and greeted George, who'd been with me on the last expedition. George, a stocky, smiling Tswana in his forties, was Syd's longtime lieutenant on safari. He'd started as cook; graduated to driver; now, under Syd's direction, he ran everything in camp. He was reliable, tireless, consistently good-humored and a fine tracker.

We talked for a few minutes. Then I returned to where the rest of them were standing in the shadow of the plane's wing.

"How's everything at Boteti?" I asked.

The camp was an hour's drive from the strip, on the edge of the Boteti River.

Syd rubbed his jaw and frowned. "I'm afraid we've got a spot of trouble."

Big David had been examining him warily. For the next month, like the rest of us, he was going to have to live at close quarters with Syd on a journey across some of the most difficult terrain in Africa. At the mention of the word "trouble" a flicker of interest came into David's eyes.

"What sort of trouble?"

"The supply truck," Syd answered. "We made it to camp. Then I discovered a break in the chassis."

Any Kalahari expedition that departs from the few recognized tracks, as we'd be doing, needs at least two vehicles. Even on a track it can be days before someone else passes the same way. A breakdown with a single vehicle off the tracks can mean disaster.

We were taking a Toyota Land Cruiser as lead truck and a lumbering six-ton Ford, which Syd had acquired from a South African Army war-surplus depot, for backup and supplies. The Ford must have hit an aardvark burrow near the camp and fractured its chassis by the back axle.

Whitley, Syd and I walked away from the plane to discuss the problem. We decided that instead of returning to Gaborone, Whitley would fly Syd up to Maun, a little trading post two hundred miles to the northwest which was used as a base by several of the Kalahari hunting companies. There, in one of the fixed hunting camps, Syd might be able to find a mechanic and a welding unit. If he succeeded, he'd fly back that afternoon, buzzing the camp as he passed to signal us to pick him up from the strip. Meanwhile the rest of us would head for the Boteti in the Toyota with George. If we hadn't seen the plane by four o'clock, we would know Syd had failed. In which case Syd would return to Gaborone with Whitley, obtain another truck and rejoin us as soon as he could.

The accident and the arrangements made to deal with it were typical of the hazards of Kalahari travel, but I knew Syd was bitterly disappointed. A desert expedition involves balancing complex and expensive equations made up of carefully calculated factors such as scheduling, distance, fuel, supplies and water. Now, right at the start, the whole elaborate structure had been thrown off balance. At best we'd lose one day, at worst three or more. Whatever happened, the financial cost would be fearsome. But much more than money was at stake. There was Syd's pride. He was a perfectionist who had been preparing for this journey for months. All he'd been able to greet me with when I finally arrived was the news that we were stranded.

"I'm truly sorry, *amigo.*" He shrugged ruefully. "It's just one of those goddamn things that happen."

"Don't worry," I said. "There's serum, stores and guns at the camp?"

Syd nodded. "George knows where everything is."

"We'll be fine."

Five minutes later the plane took off again. We watched it disappear over the horizon. Then David marched purposefully toward the Toyota.

"Right," he said. "Let's inspect technical hitch number two."

We climbed into the truck and with George at the wheel set off through the bush for camp. The track was a faint double line of tire marks in the bumpy sand, rimmed with wiry desert grass. On either side, walls of thorn and scrub pressed in shoulder high against us. Occasionally the scrub parted. There were open glades beyond, and scattered clumps of low-tree shade, and once a desert bustard broke from the ground and drummed noisily upward.

Twenty minutes after we left the strip, George braked. As the Toyota bumped to a halt, a group of vultures heaved themselves into the air.

"Lion," George said.

He pointed down. Crisscrossing the track by the wheels were lines of pugmarks. Each print had the round, full-blown shape of a Tudor rose. A few hours earlier they'd been crisp and fresh. Now, as the sun sucked out the dew that had bonded the night sand together, they were fading like flowers in an old tapestry.

I swung myself out and followed the pugmarks through the low bushes. Ten yards from the truck I found the remains of the kill, a zebra foal. All that was left was a few bones and some tattered strips of hide. The scraps of gristle on the bones were still moist. The lions had killed late, toward dawn. They'd be lying up somewhere close in pools of shadow beneath the thorn.

I glanced slowly around. It was midday. The sun high. The bush gray and gold and shimmering. The air clear, arid and hot, so hot that even as I stood still sweat was pouring down my body. The lions were invisible, but just as unmistakably present as the unseen thousands of animals whose tracks we had seen below us on the flight from Nata.

I walked back. In the Kalahari to know the meaning of indicators, to read the calligraphy of bone, blood and print, the spoor left by wind, plant, smoke and cloud, is everything. Not merely the difference between survival and crass, ungainly death—but the very stuff of living. Instinctively, with a painful stiffness from using long-unexercised muscles, I'd started to interpret the writing again.

Forty minutes later we reached the Boteti River and our first camp.

By desert tradition a camp is not a camp until it's been named. The name can be as prosaic or fanciful as the traveler chooses. Most sites are named after a physical feature, such as a tree or a pan; others, after an incident in a hunt or trek. Some names, whimsically, have no more connection with the place they represent than a story once told there over the fire at night. In Ngamiland there is a camp named The Major and the Maiden. No one, not even the oldest Kalahari hand, remembers who the Major was or what he got up to with the Maiden, but both of them are immortalized in a few square yards of sand beneath a lonely camel thorn tree.

The tradition is no desert idiosyncrasy. On the stone plateau good campsites are shelter, haven and sanctuary. Safehouses in the guerrilla warfare between the Kalahari and man. They are also a coinage to be bartered. To describe their location accurately and in detail is, of course, essential. But to give them identity, to fix them permanently in the human mind, requires naming. As the Zulu warriors know, there is magic in names.

The camp on the Boteti River was called the camp on the Boteti River.

The ideal site requires water, shade and firewood. Water is always diamond-rare. Shade is treasure of lesser value, but treasure nonetheless. Firewood, apparently the easiest criterion to satisfy for a good camp, is by no means always available even when timber is abundant. A fire is the strong, bright heart of any camp. Yet the logs from many species of African tree are virtually useless for burning. They stink, they smolder coldly, they refuse to yield the smallest flame. At the Boteti River there were diamond, treasure and by night the sturdy blaze of honest branches.

The camp was set in a grove of acacia trees on the river's eastern bank, a steep escarpment rising twenty feet above the water. The river below was wide, slow-running, dappled with sunlight and shadow. On the far side, lush grass meadows reached down to the water's edge. At a bend upstream, a pair of fish eagles mewed and called. Pied kingfishers hunted the shallows, and lily-trotters scurried among the broad leaves between cream and buttercup-yellow flowers.

"For the center of the Kalahari desert," David commented, "I find this rather jolly. Are you sure you've read your maps right, Colonel?"

I had read the maps correctly. Our journey was starting here, close to the desert's heart. And here, in the afternoon heat, the loudest sound was the rippling of deep water against reeds. The brightest colors the blossoms of the floating lilies.

We were back once more in the territory of received wisdom, where vultures are the emblems of death and deserts consist solely of sand. Nothing can live on sand without water. There is by definition no water in deserts. Therefore, so the wisdom runs, the Kalahari is an arid, sandy and lifeless waste. Every educated person knows that—and none better than the professional naturalist whose job it is to know the wild throughout the world. In a recent issue of the magnificent periodical published by America's leading ornithological society, an eminent writer delivered an eloquent warning about the dust-bowl consequences of new practices in intensive agriculture.

"The land," he concluded grimly, "will rapidly come to resemble the Kalahari desert, barren and sterile without even a blade of grass."

I tossed a twig into one of the shadowed pools. A sleek silver-scaled bream swam up to inspect it. For a moment the fish nuzzled the bobbing stem. Then it switched its tail and drifted back into the depths. The water was dark and flecked with bronze. I turned. Suddenly the air was clamorous with song. Multitudes of doves thronged the trees. A chanting goshawk belled from the high branches. Lilac-breasted rollers dived, climbed and swooped again.

I walked through the copse. Beyond, where the trees ended, was the grass-covered plain. As far as the eye could see, there was nothing but the rich, gently coiling stalks of grass. We had flown over them for mile after mile. Now they lapped in waves round my ankles, my knees, my waist. I walked on. Finally I stopped and stood chest-high in a billowing golden sea, dizzy with the smell of the spilled grains.

"Without even a blade of grass."

What had led a responsible and distinguished naturalist, writing in the last quarter of the twentieth century, to project such a grotesquely inaccurate picture of the Kalahari?

The Kalahari has been bedeviled by the label "desert" from the time of its discovery by Europeans. It was so called originally for convenience, as a form of shorthand. The stone plateau was evidently harsh and dangerous. The Tswana who were already there referred to it as the Great Thirst. The later naming of the Road of

Death confirmed their view. To call the plateau a desert seemed the most effective way of adequately conveying its ferocity. For once, the incomparable richness of the English language was found wanting. In reality, all the Kalahari shares with a conventional desert is the lack of permanent water. Aside from that, the term is meaningless. The plateau stands like a vast table tilted gently toward the south. Covering the flat limestone surface is a shallow layer of sand. Each year the sand is fed by the summer rains and by water draining into it from a river system that originates far to the north; the Boteti was one of the system's southernmost channels.

Nourished by the rains and the slow-seeping river water, the sand mantle rears a community of plants—grasses, trees, flowers, bushes, tubers and vines. Lacking soil, the searing Kalahari sun burns up dead vegetation and prevents the formation of humus. The plants have had to adapt to the plateau's demanding living conditions. They have adapted so successfully that they in turn support great communities of birds and animals. The birds and animals have also been forced to adapt.

The water from the river system irrigates only part of the plateau. Even in the areas it reaches, its flow fluctuates from year to year. The rains are more unpredictable still. They vary in both strength and location. Often they fail altogether. The wildlife either migrates, following the water's random patterns, or learns to survive off the moisture that remains even in drought. Feeding in the night dew, a buck can extract almost one hundred times as much water from a leaf as the same leaf will yield by day.

The rains had failed for the past two years. Still, we had seen the spoor of countless animals from the air. I still had to wade through the waving grass. There were still lilies on the Boteti, bream in the dark waters below, congregations of birds circling the banks.

I turned back toward the camp. I decided then to compile another list of people. Not people I'd discarded and left behind when the expedition set out, but those whose names had never occurred to me —the ones I should have taken into the wilderness.

"Welcome back, Colonel," Big David said when I reached the Boteti. "You're just in time to advise on technical hitch number three."

"What's the problem?"

"Your foot soldiers are involved in a delicate grass-round-the-balls-and-up-the-bum situation."

I gazed at them. He and Bobby were standing shoulder to shoulder. They too must have walked out onto the plain. They were both wearing long khaki pants. Hundreds of barbed heads of the grass had hooked into the loose fibers and broken off. In the tree shadow they looked like two enormous yellow porcupines.

"You're under a misapprehension, fellows," I said. "There isn't a blade of grass in the Kalahari. To prove it, ask EBL to cut those pants down to shorts."

EBL did some swift tailoring for all three of us. Afterward there were fewer problems with the desert grass.

I had the first name for my list. It was the name of an educated, well-meaning and very dangerous man—the naturalist who believed the Kalahari was a dust bowl.

The afternoon passed. From three thirty onward I checked my watch every few minutes. The hour hand moved toward four, touched it and traveled on. Then, just as I'd concluded that Syd must have failed, George stood up and cocked his head to one side. I listened. Very faintly I could hear the hum of an engine.

Moments later the plane circled the camp. George climbed into the Toyota and left for the strip. He reappeared at dusk with a mechanic, a welding unit and a triumphant Syd. Syd linked the welder to the supply truck's engine and rigged up a lamp. Before darkness closed in, showers of sparks were spraying up from the chassis. By morning the expedition would be mobile again.

However many times one has been out on safari in the Kalahari bush, the first evening meal is unlike any other. Flying up from Gaborone, we'd been able to bring fresh meat with us. From then on until we shot sand grouse, guinea fowl or perhaps a small buck, we'd be eating out of cans. That night it was big, tender steaks. George grilled the steaks over the embers. He served them with potatoes cooked in the hot ash and bread he'd baked that day over flat stones in a hollowed-out sand oven.

David rummaged in his cavernous serum bag and produced two bottles of wine to accompany the meal. The wine was dark and red and strong. The meat tasted of charcoal and woodsmoke. The potatoes were sweet and the loaves light and fresh. We ate swiftly and hungrily, leaning toward the flames as the wind lifted from the river and the stars glittered through the leaves overhead. Afterward

Bobby, not to be outdone by David, casually handed round a box of fine Havana cigars.

I took one, lit it and leaned back on my stool. I could hear the water and bell frogs in the reeds and somewhere a zebra mare scolding her foal. After the near catastrophe with the supply truck, the meal had been a fine and reassuring start to an expedition across the stone plateau.

Later we left the mechanic at work and drove for two hours along the bank. We traveled slowly, stopping often to scan the ground and the surrounding bush by flashlight. The night was quiet. Away from the river the air was soft and warm. Through the rolling waves of dust that billowed up from the wheels the eyes of startled springhares gazed back at us, scarlet and green and unblinking in the glare.

For Syd and me it was a matter of orientation, of determining what creatures shared the Boteti with us at the start of the Kalahari winter. The springhares were the only animals we saw, but there were fresh tracks everywhere. Buffalo, reedbuck, wildebeest, zebra, hyena, jackal, lion, caracal and mongoose. Syd read out the list from the prints on the sand as quickly and surely as if he'd been reading newspaper headlines. Then we drove back.

"What a pair!" Syd chuckled. He nodded toward Big David and Bobby. The mechanic had finished and the others had retired to their sleeping bags. Now Syd and I were sitting together by the flames.

Normally Syd, by his own admission, is tense at the start of a desert safari. Tonight for once he was relaxed and cheerful. In part it was due to his relief at having fixed the supply truck. But the other three had contributed too. The foot soldiers' conversation at supper had baffled, intrigued and finally delighted him.

Predictably, he'd taken to EBL at once. Syd didn't need to watch Westerns to learn how an old pioneer behaves toward a young woman in the wilds. He has a naturally rugged and sentimental protectiveness that John Wayne would have envied. If the Cheyenne war parties came down from the hills, he'd be there between her and the whistling arrows.

"So what brings you back?" he asked.

"You got my letters."

Syd nodded. "We cross the desert. The lady paints. The lads are here in support. Well, that makes sense. We've got rough country ahead—you've picked one hell of a route."

"I know."

"Sure, it gives you most of the Kalahari in a single expedition, but the journey's a real bastard." He shook his head doubtfully. "Why are you doing it?"

I stared into the fire.

Since that now remote London night, I'd formulated many strategies for my return to the plateau. In the end I'd discarded them all. I'd been thinking conventionally, but the very nature of the wilderness and the leopard ruled out a conventional approach. The Kalahari is vast. Even with a starting point, a systematic search for an animal as elusive as a nocturnal hunter would have required an army and limitless time. I had neither time, starting point nor army.

My only chance, I had finally seen, was to abandon every preconceived idea, every orthodox attitude, and instead come back in stealth. I would treat the wilderness like the underworld and the leopard like a stolen diamond. Somewhere, someone in the community of thieves knew its whereabouts. Walk into the taverns where the criminal fraternity congregates in search of a missing jewel and shout—and you will learn nothing. But if you slip in quietly, settle down in some unobtrusive corner and wait with patience, you may eventually learn what you want to know. A whisper caught in passing, a gesture across the room, a fragment of conversation overheard late at night, the distant clink of coins in some furtive transaction.

I had returned without trumpet or drum to take my small patrol quietly across the plateau. So quietly I would not even explain why I was there. I was going to listen to the underworld of the wild.

"Leopard?" Syd ventured as I remained silent. "I reckon there's leopard in it somewhere."

I looked up startled, and Syd chuckled.

"This route you've figured out," he went on. "It's leopard country almost all the way. Also, I remember before."

I should have known better. The last time we were together in the desert, we'd looked for leopards unsuccessfully. Now Syd had analyzed the terrain, put animal and habitat together, and drawn his own conclusions.

"Bait," Syd said. "That's the only way you'll ever get leopard. Without bait you don't stand a prayer."

Syd was talking as a hunter. In big-game hunting the leopard is the hardest trophy of all to obtain. The standard method of trying to kill one is to shoot a buck, rope the carcass to the branches of a tree and wait in a nearby blind at dawn and dusk. If you're lucky, on perhaps the third day you'll get a shot when the animal climbs up to feed on the decomposing meat.

I'd brought the bait with me. It was roped to a branch in my mind. If the black leopard came, it would come to me.

We slept on the banks of the Boteti under the desert stars. All night lions roared around the camp. I was listening for another sound. A deep, rasping bark. I did not hear it.

Out of long habit I woke early—thirty minutes before Kalahari daylight. I climbed out of my sleeping bag and stood shivering in the dew-laden grass. There was mist on the river. The fire was low but still bright with flame. George had risen to fuel it at intervals throughout the hours of darkness.

I walked forward and studied the campsite in the glow from the embers.

In addition to George, Syd had hired two other Tswana camp hands for the expedition. Elvis and Mtimba. Elvis was small, wiry and sullen. Mtimba amiable and vacuous. The three blacks were lying in line to my right. Next, at an angle to them, the two foot soldiers. Equally bulky and inert, but distinguishable by the volcanic snores that rumbled up from Big David. Then the still, slender silhouette of EBL. Afterward my own empty bag. Finally, at an angle again, Syd with a loaded 12-gauge shotgun beside him on the ground.

The sleeping figures made a rough U-shape coiled round the fire. Behind them the two trucks had been drawn up, fender to fender, in a protective wall. Farther back, encircling the camp, scraps of cloth hung from stakes driven into the sand. The cloths—oil-stained rags, dirty towels, sweat-and-dust-encrusted shirts—had been placed there by George.

Desert lore says lions find human and mechanical smells offensive. George has a healthy respect for desert lore. He has a much healthier and more pragmatic respect for lions. Lions select their own paths to water and follow them undeviatingly night after night, ignoring any obstacles in their way. George's cloths were our outer ring of defense in case we'd unwittingly chosen a site on a lion path.

The sky paled. A gust of wind plucked the mist from the river and sent long gray streamers whirling through the trees. In the gray half-light the trucks looked like covered wagons. For an instant the encampment might have belonged to some early pioneering column trekking north from the Cape into the interior. Then Syd sat up yawning. George padded over to the fire and rested a kettle on the coals. A few minutes later everyone was awake.

We left camp in the lead truck after breakfast, heading out onto the plain where I'd walked the day before. Syd was at the wheel. EBL beside him in the passenger seat. I and the two foot soldiers cramped knee-to-knee on the narrow metal benches at the back. Above our heads an observation hatch had been cut in the Toyota's roof. Standing with feet straddled on the benches we could look out through the hatch over the surrounding landscape.

From the start I took the front viewing position. If all three of us were standing wedged in line together and the truck hit a burrow, the ripple effect in the hatch was like a multiple subway-car pileup. Well over two hundred pounds of Bobby cannoned into Big David. David, weighing considerably more, slammed against me. With close to five hundred pounds crashing against my back, I pitched forward and collided with the roof bar of the cab.

"Gentleman's relish," David muttered. "Otherwise known as the Colonel providing the sandwich filling. How are the ribs, old bean?"

I massaged my trunk. There were deep weals on my skin from my chest downward. We rearranged ourselves and continued. It was to happen again and again over the days to come.

Plotting out the route I'd chosen on the desert charts and using his experience of the ground, Syd had chosen twelve campsites along the way. Each, on the average, was a day's Kalahari travel from the last. The plan was to alternate three days' exploration from the successive fixed bases with one day's movement between them. The days of exploration would start as early as possible every morning and end with our return to camp at dusk. When we'd finished with one sector we'd move on to the next.

As a plan it was of necessity rough and ready. On some of the travel days, where the route followed a track that had been cleared and leveled, we should be able to cover almost three hundred miles in eighteen hours' driving. On others, where our path lay through bush, sand and rock, we'd be lucky to put eighty miles behind us in the same time. Eighty miles in eighteen hours—which meant a start and finish in darkness—was less than five miles in each unbroken hour. Sometimes we would not average even that. A hundred years ago, by oxcart, our daily target would have been a mere twenty miles.

By the end we would have traveled through most of the plateau's distinctive habitats. From the air the Kalahari had been the desert of legend—arid, grim and pitiless. The grass and waters of the Boteti had already proved how deceptive that first view was. We had, as Syd said, rough country ahead, but I knew the stone citadel held other surprises.

Throughout, EBL would paint, sketch, record and note, filling her books with a visual chronicle of the journey. The foot soldiers, riding shotgun to the caravan, would watch, guard and supplement her chronicle with the expedition's cameras. I would be watching too, and listening. Watching above all for a fugitive black silhouette pacing the corridors of thorn.

I heaved myself up and stood gazing out. Beneath me the chassis heaved and rocked. The air was filled with the song of desert larks, and the morning sun was warm on my face.

From the Boteti River the plain spreads eastward to the rim of the Makgadikgadi Pans—the great shallow bowls of white and silver we'd flown over on the way to Nata. The area surrounding the river, including a section to the west, is officially designated the Makgadikgadi Pans Game Reserve. The reserve covers some three thousand square miles. That day and for the two days following we set out to explore it.

Game and the need for reserves are not normally associated with the Kalahari any more than dark water or floating lilies. In fact, almost one-fifth of all Botswana has been declared a reserve or national park. More areas still are under consideration as wildlife reservoirs. On a map, the neat lines ruled around vast sections of the plateau look most impressive. They were certainly put there by thoughtful and well-meaning men. Viewed from the ground, the situation appears rather different.

There are, first of all, virtually no wardens. The country's resources do not permit the training and paying of more than a token force to police the unproductive wild. As there are almost no visitors either, this matters less than it would elsewhere in Africa. There are, however, poachers. The Kalahari's game reserves have their own defenses—remoteness, isolation, the lack of communications. But if those defenses are breached, the wild can count only on itself. Against trucks and automatic weapons it is helpless—and both are increasingly available to those who wish to raid it.

Poaching is only the most obvious threat to the bravely created network of sanctuaries. There is another, subtler and much more dangerous menace to the creatures the reserves have been designed to protect. By declaring an area a reserve, man automatically declares open season for himself in the territory surrounding it. The two are indivisible. If what is inside is reserved for the wild, what is outside must, logically, belong to man.

On the lonely stone plateau the incisions have still largely to be made. For the moment, the neat lines on the maps are like markings for surgery. They show where the knife will go, not where it has already cut. Yet even in the Kalahari there are places where the attempted partition between man and the wild of an ecologically self-contained unit has begun. We would see the consequences later on the journey. Meanwhile, we had the Makgadikgadi reserve in front of us.

North from the river lay savanna—grass plain patterned with thorn and, incongruously, groves of palm trees. The palms have spiny trunks, clusters of vegetable ivory fruit and drooping fronds. Once, walking back across the plain in the dusk, I sat down and gazed at a grove with the setting sun behind it. The early-winter evenings were heralded by wracks of cloud gathering on the horizon. Against the sunset the clouds were stained opal and turquoise and emerald. There was not a trace of crimson or red—only the water-pale glow of sea and desert stones.

In front of the cold radiance of the coming night the trees stood in dark and wistful silhouette. The desert wind lifted, the fronds moved slowly; then they were still again. I could hear cicadas and the rustle of windblown sand. A cloud shadow crossed the air like the filling sail of a Nile dhow, and the trunks creaked. For an instant I might have been in some little harbor on the Arabian coast as the ancient shallow boats put out for the night's fishing.

Then a lion roared. The roar started with a deep-voiced challenge to anyone who might have considered hunting the plain that night. The challenge rumbled down into a warning and then into a rebuke.

Afterward the call died away in a series of mildly irritable grunts. According to desert lore, each grunt was supposed to signify a year of the lion's age. I counted twelve.

To the east and south there are no palms. There the plain alternates between long, flat expanses of grass and scrub, and low, rolling dunes covered in grass alone and set with watchtower clumps of acacia trees. At the foot of the dunes there are broad winding lanes of bare crusted sand. Sometimes, cresting a ridge in the truck, we'd surprise animals below—a herd of springbok, some ostriches, a solitary hyena. For an instant they'd gaze at us startled. Then they'd race away.

The first animals we'd seen had been individual zebras and wildebeests coming to drink from the Boteti at dawn near the camp. On the plain we saw them again in small herds, seldom consisting of more than two dozen individuals. At the start of winter the game of the Makgadikgadi is widely scattered. The summer rains had failed, but there was still just enough water in the outlying pans to support the animals across the whole range of the reserve. When the water dried up they'd begin to drift toward the river, congregating more and more closely as they converged on it.

Unlike the game in most African reserves, conditioned by years of observers, the animals of the Kalahari are wary and elusive. Man and his trucks are still almost unknown, an alien, threatening presence. The herds studied us suspiciously from a distance, analyzing the strange smells, the unfamiliar noises and silhouettes. In the bush every animal takes on the color, almost the texture, of its surroundings. The hides of the watching zebras weren't the crisp black and white of captive specimens but a grainy thorn-umber and sand-red. The jackal fur had the translucent sheen of the dry leaves. The mongooses and ground squirrels, the paleness of desert stone.

On the third morning we came on a herd of over a hundred springbok—by far the largest group we'd seen. They spread out in a nervous crescent around us, leaping from time to time in the characteristic springbok pronk in which the pouch of hair on the back is erected in a stiff warning fan.

"For Christ's sake!" Syd said suddenly. "Look at that animal at two o'clock."

I swung my binoculars in the direction Syd had indicated.

In the middle of the herd and half-hidden by a screen of grass was a patch of white. For a moment I thought it was the glaze of sunlight reflected off a length of dry bark. Then the herd moved. The patch of white moved too, and the grass parted. Through the glasses I saw a single springbok appear. It wasn't a pale tawny chestnut like the others: from head to hooves its coat was a pure, dazzling white.

"Jesus," Syd added, "in fifty years I've never seen anything like that. Hold tight!"

He dropped back behind the wheel. A moment later the truck was bucketing forward over the plain.

The herd whirled away and broke into a gallop. We roared after it, juddering and lurching and rocking. Behind us, sand rose in towering plumes from the wheels. Ahead, the racing animals pressed in on one another, jumping and plunging and then soaring again. Sometimes the herd fused into a single densely packed wedge. At other times it split into arcs and sprays like the final flower-burst of a Halloween rocket, before merging again in its silent, wind-swift flight.

Soon the herd began to outdistance us. But right to the end of the chase, long after we had lost contact with it, I could see the white springbok. The animal seemed to soar higher, run faster, trace wilder and more delicate arabesques over the plain than its companions. The whiteness was absolute, unclouded by any smear of chestnut or gold. Even through the dust and sun-dazzle and the combing rain of dead grass flung back against our faces, the color was flawless. It was the color of arctic snow, the color of a unicorn's flank, the austere heraldic color of faith.

"Jesus!" Syd repeated as he finally braked. "Now I've seen that, I'll believe anything."

The truck came to a halt. We climbed out panting and sweating. I rinsed my mouth with water from one of the leather gourds that hung from the mirror supports on the Toyota's fenders—suspended there to cool in the passage of air as we traveled.

I had come to the Kalahari in search of a night-black leopard. I had found in the first week an antelope the color of ivory. It was probably an albino. Probably, but not necessarily. An albino is a genetic freak —a poor, inadequate and doomed member of its species. There was little of doom or inadequacy stamped on that powerful soaring creature at the vanguard of the herd.

Perhaps its determining genes had been handed down from another time, another climate and another place—a place where at that blending of weather and moment it had been supremely well equipped to survive. Perhaps it was equipped to survive still at the heart of the stone citadel. Like Syd at that instant I was prepared to believe in anything—I was prepared to believe in the black leopard.

We had stopped beside an acacia copse. I glanced at the truck's odometer, left the others to rest in the ragged tent of shade and walked away. It was midafternoon and our last day in the Makgadikgadi reserve. Distance on the days of exploration was unimportant, but for me the run since breakfast had a particular significance. In the six hours we'd been on the plain, we had traveled eighteen miles from the river.

Behind me the copse vanished in a fold in the ground. I unlaced my boots, hung them round my neck and continued barefoot. I walked very slowly, feeling for the earth with each step before I put my weight down. On the surface, the sand was hot and barley-colored. Beneath, cool and gray, the luminous gray of a goshawk's wing in flight. In front the sun-glazed plain ran in wavering panels of white and beaten gold to the horizon. I paused and inhaled the air. There was nothing, not the faintest trace of scent or spore. Only the utter arid purity of the winter. I broke off a grass husk and shredded the pods between my teeth. They tasted as harsh and clean as the desert wind.

I moved forward again. A puff adder uncoiled and slid lazily away between the stems. From a distance a herd of wildebeests inspected me warily. Their dust-layered hides shone a glossy gunmetal blue. A black-backed jackal trotted delicately along the crest of a ridge and vanished. A hunting kestrel hung against the sky.

Finally I stopped once more and stood quite still. I inhaled the air again. I gazed steadily across the burnished plain to the hazed meeting point of land and sky. I was alone, and I had rid myself of everything—deliberately stripping and scouring my body and mind. All that was left was my senses. The sand was pliant between my toes. The lingering grass taste bilberry-sharp in my mouth. I saw the movements of the birds and animals, felt the sun and the wind on my skin, heard the echo of the trotting jackal's paws and the rustle of the parting stems in the adder's wake.

If the paleontologists are right, man originated near where I was standing on the desert grass plain, eighteen miles to the east of the Boteti River. There in the afternoon light I was seeing the world exactly as the first child saw it at the moment our nature was formed.

I was standing at our beginnings.

By now the paleontologists' answer to the obsessive questions about man's origins, questions that have haunted the human consciousness since the start of recorded history, has been well documented. The paleontologists believe in an African genesis. Five million years ago, they assert, a belt of land running diagonally across Africa heaved and crumbled. The belt, now known as the Great Rift Valley, started at Mombasa. It ends in the Kalahari.

When the upheaval rumbled into stillness, the surface landscape had been changed and enriched dramatically. In place of an uninterrupted expanse of forest, the ground was laced with rivers and gorges; studded by mountains, hills and lakes; patterned with savanna, marsh and plain. For the animals of the old forest the changes had only one meaning. There were new sources of food in the newly created habitats—if they could adapt and learn to use them.

The forest apes adapted. They came down from the trees and learned to exploit the plain. For a while they became amphibians of forest and grass. Then as global climatic disturbances swept Africa, the forest began to retreat. The more it retreated, the more the apes were pushed off the branches of their treebound sanctuary, down into the open. Soon the plain was the only territory available to them. Once more they were forced to adapt. Dispossessed of the sentinel trees, they learned to stand upright and scour the grass for predators. New hunting techniques were needed. In the forest hunting had been a solitary activity. On the plain a group effort was required to kill the swift game—and a group activity demanded communication. Just as important for their survival as hunting was gathering. The herds of antelope which were their prey might disappear for months on migration, but the fruits of the grass plain—the seeds, berries, tubers and grubs—were always available.

The apes learned to harvest them—individually at first and then for sharing among the group. Sharing was more economical of the group's energy. It meant that not all members were committed to the same activity and so risked the consequences of failure. Instead some could hunt and some could gather, and the whole community benefited from whichever party was successful. Finally there were tools. Like other animals, the apes had used tools for millennia. On the plain these tools became more and more elaborate.

To the crude club, seized from the ground and wielded in self-defense as a threatened baboon still wields it, was slowly added a whole range of implements with different functions—rough killing axeheads, chipped-stone hide cutters, hammers and gouges to extract marrow from bone. Walking upright, communicating, living in family groups, using tools and harvesting fruit, the hunter-gatherer apes were pressed more and more closely into the mold of man.

Where and when the final changes took place not even the boldest primatologist will hazard. Quite possibly they happened in several different places at about the same time. But perhaps half a million years ago, on a stretch of plain like the one by the Boteti River—eighteen miles was a reasonable hunting journey from water—the sun rose on a group of figures.

One evening they encircled and killed a half-lame springbok in a copse on a small mound to the west—the mound where I had left the others resting in the tree shadow. For a while a lion disputed the kill. They drove the lion off with volleys of stones, dismembered the buck and carried it back to their camp, a few small hollows scooped in the sand. There they gorged themselves on the raw meat before sleeping through the night.

At dawn they cracked the remaining bones, sucked out the marrow, ate a handful of mongongo kernels stored in a jackal-hide pouch and drank water from ostrich-shell containers. Afterward they headed back for the river.

They were the Kalahari hunter-gatherers. But they were no longer apes. Hundreds of thousands years older than Cro-Magnon man, by convention the earliest human, they were nonetheless the same as he. They had become *Homo sapiens.*

I knelt and replaced my boots. The black-backed jackal reappeared and examined me curiously, a front paw motionless above the sand and its lungs pumping rhythmically. Each time the lungs expanded, a little flare of goose-feather light bounced off its flanks and seemed to ripple away across the grass. I turned and headed back for the copse.

The paleontologists' account of creation has been under strident and sustained attack of late. It is not difficult to understand why. As people they are in the main an unlovely group—dogmatic, arrogant and avaricious. What they advance about evolutionary forces and man presses even harder on the raw nerve of religious faith and rational philosophy than Darwin's claims. And all they have for evidence is a handful of old bones gleaned from the fossil leavings in Africa's lakeshores and gorges—bones which they cast like runes across time's immensity. Yet what if they are right and the answers to the haunting questions are indeed to be found here at the desert's heart? What if the hunter-gatherers still inhabited the stone plateau?

In that case the Kalahari would assume an incalculable importance. If Africa were confirmed as the birthplace of life, it would mean almost certainly that the Kalahari was the cradle where the child was rocked. I kept an open mind about the paleontologists, but I knew about the hunter-gatherers. They are called the Bushman, or San, they still roam the desert, and I had seen them before. With luck I would meet them again before the journey ended.

The next day we were leaving the Boteti. We had started the journey as I wanted—close to water on the grass plain at the center of the Kalahari. Now we would head east for the pans.

After supper I left the others preparing for tomorrow's move and walked alone southward along the bank. The moon was high and full and the light flared off the Boteti below, but I moved with care, pausing often to check the spaces between the trees for eyes. Throughout the night animals would be coming to the river to drink. Bucks would choose the shallows, but the bank's steepness here would prove no barrier to leopard or lion. Half a mile from the camp I saw the glow of another fire. I walked quietly toward it and stopped thirty yards away in a cone of tree shadow. I could see the silhouette of a man sitting by the flames. He was wearing a hat and gnawing at something.

"How you doing?" a voice called.

I stiffened. With the distance and the shadow I was certain he couldn't see me. I glanced around. There was no one else. Then I came forward.

"Fine," I said.

He picked up a bone-handled knife stuck in the earth beside him and sliced a strip from the length of biltong he'd been chewing. I took the strip and sat down on a log.

"Where are you bound?" he asked.

"Nata. Down to the pans. Then north. What about you?"

He grunted. "Moving."

There was silence for several moments. I tasted the biltong. It was black, leathery and tough and then, as the fibers broke down and the locked-in juices came out, strangely sweet. Biltong, the dried meat of game animals, was the staple diet of the Boers on trek. Its preparation after the first hunt at the start of each season is still an important yearly ritual for the Kalahari old-timers.

This one was very old. Seventy or more, I guessed. His hat was of faded and tattered leather. Under it his flat, expressionless face was hatched with scars and wrinkles like the bark on an ancient thorn trunk. His eyes were amber-colored in the firelight, and his neck tendons stood out wire-tight from scoops of wasted flesh.

Suddenly he chuckled ferociously. "Jock," he said. "That's how."

I looked at him startled. Still chuckling, he leaned down and patted something under his chair. I hadn't noticed it before, but there was a dog lying behind his heels. A scrawny bundle of matted black-and-white fur that looked as old as he was.

"Knows them all," the old man said. "Wildebeest, zebra, waterbuck, lion. Just one whiff on the air and he tells me. People? The same. White or kaffir, man or woman, he knows."

I understood then. The dog was the old man's private radar, signaling anything that approached his camp. It was the dog that had heard or scented me.

"How can you tell what's coming?" I asked.

"Didn't I teach him? In the growls, set of his fur, way he holds his head. And you never heard nothing, did you?"

"No," I admitted. "Much too smart for me."

He laughed happily again. Then he held out his hand.

"Maritz," he said, "Piet Maritz."

His hand was hard, clawlike and crushingly strong in spite of the arthritic pads over his knuckles. Briefly, as he patted the dog chuckling, his face had blazed with an almost crazed delight. Now it was blank and shuttered again. Yet I sensed that some bond had unaccountably been forged between us.

It had happened to me before in chance encounters with those who spend months on end alone in the wild. For the first few minutes nothing is given away except the traditional courtesies of the fire. But then if the traveler passes some mysterious unspecified test, everything is thrown open to him—not just the fire but the man who has built and guards it.

It happened then. Maritz began to talk about his life.

He was seventy-six. His father had been a South African hunter and trader. In 1895 he'd headed into the interior. Eight years later he had returned to the Cape with a cargo of ivory. He wanted a wife and children. The only source of women he knew was the seafront red-light quarter.

There in a dockside whorehouse he made a deal with the madam for an Irish girl. She was named Teresa. Maritz' father paid for her in gold from the ivory he'd sold. He mounted her on their wedding night in the "Captain's Cabin"—so called because it was the room where the ships' captains were serviced. The following week he left for the desert again.

"You don't believe me?" Maritz said. "I'll show you."

He went over to an old truck parked beyond the fire and returned with a book. It was a Bible printed in Afrikaans. On the flyleaf there was a handwritten Afrikaans inscription followed by two names and a date. Maritz translated for me. The inscription recorded the marriage of Johannes Maritz and Teresa Patel. The date was March 11, 1903.

"Patel?" I frowned. "That's a strange name for an Irish girl."

"Hell, man," Maritz said. "She was Roman. My father was Dutch Reformed. She wasn't going to marry a heretic. She used the name of the woman who ran the house."

I tried to work it out and gave up. Many arrangements made in turn-of-the-century Africa had their own logic which defied analysis three generations later. If Johannes and Teresa were satisfied at the time, that was enough. I believed Piet.

Two years later his father came back. Teresa had gone. She'd honored her part of the contract. Nine months to the day after the marriage she'd given birth to a son. She gave part of her golden dowry to the madam for the child's support and set sail for Dublin. Piet stayed in the cathouse under the madam's care for a further five years.

"Son of a whore, raised in a cathouse, paid for with ivory." Maritz gave his ferocious chuckle again. "Not many came up that way."

When he was seven, Maritz' father returned again. He settled his final account with the madam, collected his son and trained north on the new railroad to Jo'burg. At Jo'burg they transferred to an oxcart. Then they set off for the Kalahari. The year was 1911.

"Lion," Maritz said. "That's what I remember best. Folk think of the Kalahari, they think of water, the thirst. But that trek it was lion. . . ."

Some years earlier white settlers had reached Ghanzi. They had sunk boreholes and started cattle ranching. Maritz' father had been engaged to escort the herds south to the slaughtering yards. His job was to protect the cattle against the huge concentrations of lions which by then had established themselves along the route. The route was four hundred miles across the southwestern desert. He traveled it three times yearly on horseback with his son. It was known as the Road of Death.

Maritz shook his head. "Didn't kill one the first trek. Had to wait another two years. Then at ten I got my first. Spring following, I dropped fourteen."

Maritz was eleven. At the same age, I was a small gray-faced boy in the gray-walled prison of a Sussex boarding school. Maritz was in the Kalahari killing black-maned lions under the desert sun. His wages were a daily biltong ration, a rand a week and the lion hides, which went to his father. Like his father he'd become a gun for hire —a hunter. He'd been a hunter ever since.

"What about leopards?" I asked.

"Then? Hell, yes," he answered. "But not so much on trek. Trek belonged to lion. Leopard stayed round the ranches. We'd get them there with traps and poison—hundreds of the buggers."

"And now?"

"You come across them time to time. Nothing like before. But they're strange, those cats. Know what they say about them?" Maritz wrinkled his face. "Game smells rain—leopard smells trouble. It's true. You corner a leopard and that bugger, he'll fight harder than everything else in the bush together. But when there's trouble on the way they know it, they're the first to go. You find veld where the leopards have gone and you know something bad's coming."

"Have you ever shot a black leopard?" I said.

Maritz thought for a while. Then he chuckled once more.

"There's funny creatures in the bush, I tell you that for sure, man," he replied enigmatically.

Afterward he changed the subject and spoke not about leopards but about the past. For sixty-five years he'd roamed most of Africa, traveling wherever there was work to be found. He'd escorted big-game clients as support gun to the guiding professional in Kenya and Uganda between the wars. He'd been a scout for the expeditionary columns in the minor campaigns of World War II. He'd shot elephants under government contract in Tanzania's Luanga Valley.

Always he'd returned to the lonely fortress of the stone citadel. Why? I wondered.

"Providing he's got this . . ."

Maritz pointed at his rifle. It was leaning against his chair, an old .405 with a silk-smooth stock and a gleaming barrel.

". . . a man can live here any way he goddamn wants. They leave you alone—the desert's big enough. You reckon on heading out into the bush and keeping moving, you just go. Out there you got all the space and more than you'll ever need. . . ."

He paused. "Well, that's how it used to be. Maybe it'll see me out. I don't know for how much longer."

He stopped and shrugged. Then he added abruptly, "You making for Chobe after the pans?"

"Yes."

"Maybe I'll see you again."

I said good night and walked away. At the bank I glanced back. Maritz was wrapping himself in a kaross, a cloak of animal hides. As I watched he lay down on the sand. I could see the dog lying like a sack at his head.

Early in the morning I went back. Maritz had gone. There was no trace of his camp. The fire had been carefully covered with sand and the earth brushed clean with a leafy branch. All that was left was the faint spoor of his truck heading into the desert. From the tracks, the tires were totally bald.

# 5

PITCHING OR striking camp in the Kalahari is like working through an elaborate Japanese puzzle. There is only one way to solve it, and that requires following meticulously a complex sequence of movements. A single wrongly placed item and the entire process has to be started again.

Between them Syd and George have years of experience. They also have Elvis and Mtimba as assistants. It is still three hours after breakfast before we are ready to move. The supply truck leaves first, with George at the wheel. We follow an hour later in the Toyota. Two hours later still, we overtake George. We continue for a while and then stop to let him catch up again.

The leapfrogging from point to point continues all day, as it will during every day of travel. If either of the vehicles doesn't reach a rendezvous within a given time, the other will retrace its spoor in search of it. With the exception of major accidents like a broken chassis, the two vehicles together carry enough spares and equipment to tackle virtually any mechanical breakdown.

Nata is two hundred miles due east of the Boteti. By Kalahari standards the journey is not a difficult one. After an initial run across the plain there is road for the rest of the way. "Road" on the stone plateau needs definition. With the exception of a few tentative black settlements on the eastern border in the fifteenth century, the human history of the Kalahari until 1750 is the history of the San peoples.

The apparently innocuous word "Bushman" is a corruption of an abusive term coined by early Dutch farmers in the Cape of Good Hope. It had, and in several quarters still has, much the same derogatory racial overtones as "kike" or "nigger." The San bitterly resent the word and the humiliating stereotype it represents, and ask to be called by their own name.

The San, the little apricot-skinned hunter-gatherers, had no need of roads. They went their own ways across the desert, and the plateau remained unmarked. Then in 1750 small parties of two other black groups, the Yei and the Herero, moved into the Kalahari. Their arrival was the result of two events that had taken place almost simultaneously a hundred years earlier and convulsed all southern Africa—the twin invasions by white settlers landing at the Cape and migrant Bantu tribes pressing down from the north.

The two land-hungry waves advanced toward each other and collided. Caught between them, a number of smaller, weaker groups, mainly Tswana, fled sideways and began to colonize the outer ramparts of the Kalahari. By 1800 the plateau was surrounded. Every locality where there was permanent surface water had been settled by cattle owners.

Even then it was a considerable time before there was any real need for communications. As little as one hundred years ago there were no recognized routes across the desert. The rare traveler navigated by his compass or the stars, plotting his course according to the season and where he knew or guessed he might find water. Later, as the cattle settlements expanded on the outlying battlements and the first trading posts were established, thin, spidery tracks emerged to link them.

They were printed as much in memory as on the ground. A single summer rainstorm and every trace of where they ran would be erased. But the rains passed, the routes were used again and gradually the passage of hoof and wagon wheel and foot carved out identifiable corridors in the earth.

They are the Kalahari roads. A few, for brief stretches in the south and along the Zimbabwe border, are now surfaced. Others are periodically leveled and filled by grading machines. Most remain as they were—faint, wandering lanes on desert rock and sand, as vulnerable as ever to wind or weather.

The road on which Nata lies, the road from Maun to Francistown, alternates between graded track and fragile Kalahari lane. We reached it late in the afternoon. By then we had seven hours of plain behind us. On the firm open ground, we could have covered the distance in a quarter of the time.

We were not traveling quickly. We'd been searching, as we'd searched for the past three days, for the springbok and gemsbok herds of the central desert. The largest we'd seen was the herd with the white springbok. That afternoon we found what was left of them.

Witnessing the moving springbok congregations of the late nineteenth century the embattled Boer farmer used the same word for them as for his own God-willed and irresistible migrations—the trek. He trekked when the spirit moved him. So did the springbok. In 1896, the herds trekking south across the Kalahari covered an area of two thousand square miles. Like lemmings, they were experiencing one of their irregular irruptions. A good breeding year had dramatically increased the springbok population. As a consequence, the locally available food had been exhausted and they'd been driven to seek fresh pasture elsewhere.

They pressed on toward the Cape in an unbroken rippling chestnut tide. Other animals were caught up and swept helplessly along with them. Everything in their path was smashed and flattened. They came to rivers and drowned in columns fifteen miles wide, filling the banks from side to side. The survivors surged on. Finally they stopped. The uncontrollable force was spent and the migration was over. Those which had survived the trek split into smaller herds. If their journey had ended in suitable habitat, they established themselves there. If not, they died out. It did not matter either way. Behind them on the plateau more than enough were left to ensure that sooner or later the columns would be on the move again. The springbok would migrate at intervals forever.

Or so it seemed. Within fifty years the migrations on the scale that had been common in the nineteenth century and for thousands of years before were over. The great tides of animals belonged to the past. The herds had gone. Much of the explanation for their disappearance was undisputed. Wanton hunting and the loss of distant desert pastures to cattle were obvious causes. But they were not the only ones. Whatever carnage was inflicted on the springbok around the plateau's borders, whatever territory was lost there, the Kalahari and its resources should have been large enough to permit the animal to build back to some recognizable level of its former strength.

BOTETI SUNSET

ALBINO SPRINGBOK

PALM TREES ON THE MAKGADIKGADI
GRASS PLAIN

AFRICAN LILY-TROTTER ON THE BOTETI RIVER

YOUNG OSTRICHES AT DUSK

PALM TREES ON THE MAKGADIKGADI GRASS PLAIN

THE MAKGADIKGADI PANS FROM THE AIR

THE SUA PAN

LIGHTNING-FIRED GRASS

A FLAMINGO FEATHER

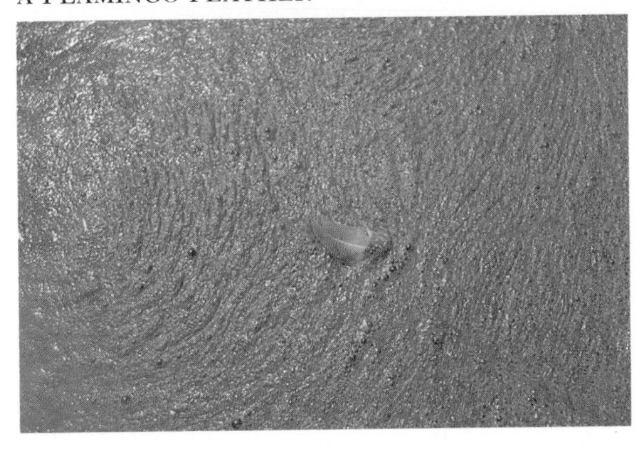

SUA FLAMINGOS

CHOBE ELEPHANTS

GREATER KUDU

CHOBE HIPPOS

WATERBUCK

PUKU

SPUR-WINGED GEESE

CHOBE RIVER AT MIDDAY

CHOBE RIVER SUNSET

KALAHARI TRACK

SAVUTI CHANNEL

WILDEBEESTS

LIONS

IMPALA RAM

SASSABY

BAOBAB

SACRED IBIS AND MARABOU STORKS

ZEBRAS

SAVUTI WATER HOLE

SAN ROCK PAINTINGS AT SAVUTI

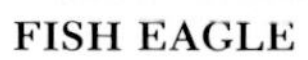

FISH EAGLE

WHITE EGRET

UMBRELLA ACACIA

WATERWAY AND PAPYRUS IN THE OKAVANGO DELTA

GROUND HIBISCUS

WATER LILY

HERERO

OKAVANGO DARTER

REEDS AT MORNING ON LAKE NGAMI

LAKESIDE CONVOLVULUS

GEMSBOK

CATTLE STOCKADE

SOUTHERN KALAHARI GRASS PLAIN

SAN

THE EXPEDITION

THE GABORONE DAM AT EVENING

It did not. The herds were crippled. They broke down, and they failed to recover. I watched the remnants in the afternoon light.

Mingled with them were gemsbok. The springbok were small, alert and graceful, glossy chestnut above with a dark bar along the ribs and a white belly below. The gemsbok—the African oryx—much larger, a heavy, powerfully built animal with a melancholy bovine face and a magnificent pair of horns. They were true desert weapons, the gemsbok's horns, long and straight and dagger-pointed. Occasionally lions are found impaled upon them, predator and prey lying locked together dead after the gemsbok had inflicted the fatal wound but could not drag itself free of its attacker.

In light or shadow, the springbok glitters. In the sun the gemsbok are dun-colored with black and white markings. But as soon as they move into shadow they become a deep dusky purple, and the drifting sand coils over their flanks like smoke. Then, standing shoulder to shoulder, heads uplifted and the lancelike silver horns bright in the darkness of some copse, they might be strange armored and caparisoned warhorses gathered to charge in battle.

Both species are superbly equipped for the Kalahari's living conditions. They will drink when water is available, but they can adapt their diet to survive long periods of drought. The springbok feeds at levels that vary with the season, tracing a curve downward from the shoulder-high vegetation that follows the summer rains, to the dry ground grasses that come next, to the subterranean roots and tubers of midwinter—digging deep to excavate them when there is no moisture anywhere else. The gemsbok follows the same pattern. So efficient is its use of moisture that the few drops of urine it occasionally and reluctantly releases have the consistency of tree gum.

Two species. One, the swift and bright chestnut-gold, scatters, shaken like kaleidoscope flakes over the desert grass. The other, stately and ponderous, canters through the winter stubble with its war-ready lances and the violet-mahogany damask of its haunches. They should both have been there in the thousands, the hundreds of thousands; in the case of the springbok, the millions. The gemsbok was always less numerous than the other, but it too had been present in hordes. But now, under the palms and through the haze-distorted thorn, we saw little, fragmented groups of both.

"You can take just one clump of grass," Syd said. "Uproot it and you start to unravel something. You don't know where the unraveling will end. It could be miles, hundreds of miles away. But wherever the zip runs, everything's going to be changed. It may be changed forever."

It was one of Syd's favorite themes. The intricate interwoven life-fibers of what he scornfully dismissed as ecology—dismissing not the reality but the vogue word that represented it and the arrogant young man with long hair and a Fifth Avenue T-shirt who lectured him from the World Wildlife Fund data books.

After long years of living with it and from it, true ecology was Syd's trade and passion. Ecology to him was a hunting lion and a distant antelope and the myriad linked factors in the complex chains of earth, water, air, plant, insect and bird that joined them.

Gazing across the plain as the light began to fade, I knew what Syd meant. Someone somewhere, perhaps unwittingly, had tampered with one of the links. It might have happened hundreds of miles away, but years later, there on the Boteti grass plains we were left with the consequences. The springbok and the gemsbok had gone. I wondered what had happened to the black leopard.

The northern reaches of the Kalahari are dominated by two main natural features—the inland basin of the Okavango delta and the complex of the Makgadikgadi pans. We would come to the great delta later in the journey. Meanwhile we were heading for the pans.

Ranging from the size of a football field to that of a small country, there are pans scattered throughout virtually all the Kalahari. On one level the homely kitchen term describes them well—shallow, rounded bowls with a marginally raised lip set in the desert sand. The bowl's surface consists often of a hard skin of mineral salts bonded by a combination of rain, evaporation and sun. Often too, on the low banked rim that encircles it grows a selection of plants and grasses unknown in the surrounding bush.

The exact relationship between the pans and the Kalahari's wildlife hasn't yet been fully determined. To the desert animals their function is clearly crucial—so crucial that if the pans disappeared it is possible the whole life structure of the plateau might break down. What is known is that the surface lick salts provide iron and vitamins unavailable elsewhere, the rare herbs and grasses perform a similar nutritional function, and the pans' ability to store water after rain is vital.

Once a vast lake which dried up thousands of years ago, the two principal pans of the Makgadikgadi basin—the Ntwetwe and the Sua—cover between them some six thousand square miles. Our destination was the Sua Pan in the west, at the point where the Nata River drains into it—the point where from the air we had seen the birds rising from the surface like tracer fire.

Fifty miles from Nata the temperature of the night air suddenly began to fluctuate wildly. One moment we were slumped warm and drowsy in the back of the truck. The next we were bolt upright and shivering, with a raw chill pricking our skins. Five minutes later the warmth returned. Then the cold swept back again. The abrupt changes continued until it seemed as if we were swimming through alternate layers of hot and icy water.

"If I want a sauna I normally go to Finland," Bobby said as another wave of chilling air enveloped us. "What the hell's going on?"

The explanation lay in the landscape, invisible in the darkness beyond the Toyota's open sides. Where the ground was covered with bush, as it had been until then, the vegetation absorbed and held the day's stored heat like a thermal blanket. But as soon as the bush gave way to barren earth, the surface cooled swiftly at nightfall and the temperature plunged.

We had reached the rim of the Makgadikgadi. Small satellite pans, incapable of supporting plant life on their crusted soil, lapped out from the main complex and bit into the plain along the course of the track. Each time we crossed one we felt a shock of cold. Then the pans retreated, the bush drifted back and we were cloaked by the warmth of the desert evening again.

The gyrations lasted for two hours. We rumbled through Nata, turned south beyond the village and wound across the plain. Thirty minutes afterward, we found our camp. A lonely fire beneath a lofty acacia, the worried but smiling face of George, the scent of roast guinea fowl on the night breeze. For an instant it was everything a camp should be at the end of a long day in the bush—a scene from the illustrated journal of some early hunter's wanderings in Africa.

We climbed gratefully out of the truck. Suddenly, without any warning, everything changed. We were enveloped in a blizzard of aphids. They blotted out the firelight. They drummed on the canvas sleeping-bag covers like sheets of torrential rain. They swarmed and drifted and billowed in thick gray-green clouds, choking nostrils and mouths, silting up on food plates and water bottles, layering everything with a dense patina of glutinous wriggling bodies.

A few minutes earlier the site had looked ideal. Now it was uninhabitable. Then, as we stood there blinded and dripping with insects, Syd discovered what had happened. Once again it was a matter of temperature. The fire had heated the surrounding soil and provoked an immense hatch of pupae lying dormant beneath the surface. The aphids were pouring up in columns from half a dozen tiny holes ringing the flames.

The remedy was gasoline. The ground was doused, the eruption stopped and twenty minutes afterward the air had cleared. We slept as before with the Kalahari stars brilliant above our heads.

Between the camp and the pans was a ten-mile strip of tree-covered grassland. When we left at eight the next morning the sky was clear and the day promised to be hot and still. But by the time we reached the end of the grassland a wind had blown up. It was coming from the south, and it rose steadily in strength until when we drove onto the pans the truck was rocking. The sun had vanished, and the horizon ahead was lost in dark, churning mist.

We stopped and got out. Instantly the full force of the gale struck us. What had appeared to be mist turned out to be a whirling screen of sand and salt lifted from the surface and hurled across the pans by a winter storm. The grains stung our skins, forced their way into our mouths, tasting raw and sharp on the tongue, and drew tears from our eyes.

"Good God!" David said, peering around. "Nanny's brought us to the seaside."

I walked away from the truck with Syd and gazed blinking toward the south. Syd shook his head and swore. Our target was the stretch of water we'd seen on the flight to Tsoe, but we both knew it was unattainable. We couldn't navigate in the storm, and there was every chance we'd bog the Toyota down in a patch of still wet sand below the saline crust.

There was no choice except to turn back. We climbed into the truck again and returned to camp.

It was still only 10 A.M. The day before, we'd had problems with the Toyota's wheel bolts. Syd suggested taking the truck into Francistown, a hundred miles to the east, where he knew a garage that might be able to fix it. With a good road from Nata onward, the journey should take under three hours and he'd be back sometime after dark.

Big David volunteered to accompany him as relief driver. I agreed. As the supply truck needed refueling, I decided we'd go in convoy to Nata. Syd and David would push on to Francistown, while the rest of us would drive back to camp after George had finished at the pump.

I'd seen the village twice before. First as a little heat-laden cluster of brown and ocher huts from the air. And then, the previous evening, driving through it in darkness when all that was visible was a ring of dung fires studding the night like desert glowworms. Now I could examine it in daylight.

There was very little to examine. Some meandering lanes of trodden sand, a few fly-haloed dogs, knots of torpid children playing silently in the earth, the dust-veiled rows of huts, the open space of the *kgotla*—the tribal assembly place and debating forum. Everything had a makeshift and impermanent air. The European builds his dwelling places from rock, and for eternity. Not so the Tswana. Like their remote Moorish neighbors to the north, they treat their villages as seasonal bivouacs, to be dismantled, moved and reerected as warfare, weather and the tides of fortune demand.

Nata's fragile huts had more in common with the towers, arches and minarets of the Alhambra than with the solid architecture of the Empire which had decreed that the village should become a trading post.

I found the store and went inside to escape the sun. A moment later I heard a voice behind me.

"May I have two glasses of water, please?"

It was a woman's voice with a quintessential South African accent. Hard and flat and toneless, with all the vowels compacted into a single "i."

I turned. There were two silhouettes in the doorway, dense black against the glaring light outside. One was small, compact and erect. The other, taller and slimmer, with a bulging stomach, a drooping head and a slumped shoulder—a slack, motionless bundle propped up on splayed legs.

"Here." The owner, an Indian trader, pushed two glasses across the counter.

The pair came forward. The taller was a pregnant black girl of about fifteen, listless and sleepy-eyed. The second, a white woman in her late forties. She picked up the glass and drank. Then she noticed me.

"Good morning."

I returned her greeting and we started to talk. She ran a school, she told me, for San children—she used the colloquial "Bushman" to describe them. I studied her as she spoke.

She was wearing a simple printed cotton dress, faded lilacs on a cream background, and worn leather shoes. Her hair was a wispy gray, her skin pale and barely touched by the desert sun, her face utterly unremarkable. It was a face I'd seen since childhood all over Western Europe—behind stalls at charity bazaars, waiting in line at the spring sales, poised over mops on the doorsteps of city streets. Colorless, homely and endlessly patient. Accustomed to the rawness of life—to its blood and semen—but always implacably prim and respectable.

"How do you find the Bushman children?" I asked.

She shrugged. "Children are children everywhere. Some bright, some slow, most between the two. They're no different."

In her terms, and although she was too polite to say so, it had been a foolish question. She lived with them. She taught them. She fed, scolded, nursed and looked after them. A San child was the same as any other child.

"Is communication a problem?"

"They learn Tswana. When they arrive, of course, it isn't easy. I'm fortunate in having Thlama"—she indicated the black girl. "She's part Bushman and she translates for me."

"Into Tswana?"

She nodded. "I've spoken that all my life. But there's something about the Bushman language . . ."

She broke off and shook her head, smiling a little sadly, a little wistfully.

She was a member of the Dutch Reformed Church and a missionary. Her church had sent her into the Kalahari to bring God to the San. She'd begun with a single wooden hut in the desert south of Lake Ngami. From there she'd sent out word to the San that she was offering board, lodging and education to their children, free.

At the start the San elders had been puzzled and wary. Board was already available in the Kalahari as desert fruit and running buck. Lodging too was there in a scoop of sand or a leafed shelter. Education was simply a matter of patterning their young to understand and use the plateau's resources. They saw no need of what she offered. But her arrival was followed by successive years of devastating drought. Water and pasture dried up. Game, cattle and people died by the thousand. The San, their territory long since eroded and wasted by the Tswana herders, were ravaged by disease and starvation. In desperation they began to send her their children.

"So God smiled on your mission?" I suggested.

She thought for a moment. Then she nodded in agreement.

"I was very fortunate," she said. "It was one of the worst droughts this century. It was a miracle."

The first pupils paid nothing. Afterward, when the school was established, their parents were encouraged to contribute one *pula* —about eighty cents—each semester. By then the drought was over, but the habit of dependence had been formed. The children were housed, fed and educated. They were also taught about God.

"Will they go to Heaven when they die?" I asked.

"No, of course not. They're blacks. . . ."

She hesitated. The answer had been immediate and spontaneous. Now she qualified it.

"Well, that's for the Lord to decide."

"Can you guess how He'll make up His mind?"

"I'm not here to guess," she said. "I'm here to obey and fulfill the teachings of the Church. The Church says they are black. I accept that."

As all men regardless of color or creed are considered equal under the Botswana constitution, I suggested that she might be breaking the country's laws in teaching the San that they weren't in line for paradise.

She considered again. Then she shook her head. "The government help support the school. They'd have to pass a special law to send the children to Heaven."

It was my turn to be silent. There seemed to be a gray area between the authority of Seretse Khama's government and that of the Almighty. As we were clearly entering deep theological waters, I changed the subject.

"What else do you teach them?"

"The normal curriculum we use for black children in the Republic."

Most blacks in South Africa live in densely populated urban townships. The illustrations in the mission-school textbooks I'd seen reflected their environment. I asked her if she used the same books.

She understood my point and frowned unhappily.

"Yes, at the moment we have no choice. It can be very difficult. Sometimes, frankly, I give up. Traffic signals, for example—they're impossible to explain. I say they're trees."

She looked relieved at my smile and added, "We're really trying to equip them to fit into today's society."

One of the principal requirements for entering contemporary African society is a job. The problem in the Kalahari, I suggested, was that there weren't any jobs available.

The expression of unease returned to her face. "We can only trust that in time that will change," she said.

"What happens meanwhile?" I asked. "Do you send them back to the bush?"

"No, not if we can help it. If they return to the bush they can lose everything they've been given. Besides, few of them want to go."

"So they stay at the mission."

"Mostly, yes."

"What do they do?"

"They chop wood." Her face brightened. "In winter we have wonderful fires. If you pass through Ngamiland you must stop and see our fires."

"I would like to very much," I said.

We talked for a while longer. She was on her way from the mission to Francistown, where she was going to take the pregnant Thlama to the hospital. Thlama wasn't the only passenger she had with her in the ancient mission truck I could see through the window. There were another girl, younger still, a youth with a withered arm and rolling eyes, and an old woman who muttered constantly to herself. For all I knew, there were more—an entire army of the desert's walking wounded traveling with her. To the good lady it made no difference. She navigated by the bright, unchanging star of faith and its satellite moon patience. All were welcome to join her on the road she trod.

"Thank you." She gave the glass back to the Indian and smiled.

The trader spread out his hands and bowed. Many conventions govern life in the Great Thirst. One is more than a convention. It is an iron rule. As by the medieval law of hospitality—if a man comes to your door seeking shelter, even your deadliest enemy, he is entitled to your roof and his life sacrosanct under it—so in the desert you share your water.

"I enjoyed your company." She turned to me and held out her hand. "Please don't forget our fires."

The smile she'd given the Indian was warm. The one she gave me was dazzling.

She went out. Through the window I saw her silhouette against the glare of the dusty track once more. Her head was covered by a sun hat, and her cotton dress flapped slowly in the heat above her scuffed shoes. She was holding Thlama by the hand. For no apparent reason, Thlama was weeping.

"That lady is the salt of the earth," I said to the Indian.

"Yes, sir," he answered.

He had hooded, calculating eyes, and he made no sound as he moved in the shadows behind the counter.

The mission truck disappeared. In a little school four hundred miles to the west, San children were diligently learning that traffic signals were trees, and Heaven was denied them because their apricot skins were black. Outside the school, their jobless and dispossessed companions were chopping wood—great mounds of wood, to build wonderful Kalahari fires.

"She can also arrange harvest-festival flowers," I added, turning from the window.

"Yes, sir," the Indian agreed again.

He'd been searching for something on the shelves. He found what he was looking for and handed me a packet to inspect.

"We have salt too, sir," he said. "Excellent salt. The Bushman collect it from the Makgadikgadi. Please taste."

I opened the packet, tipped some crystals into my palm and licked them up with my tongue. The salt was white and dry and tasted of the sea. The Indian was watching me apprehensively.

"If you come back in summer, sir," he said, "I can arrange flowers also. The salt we have all year. But for flowers, you understand, now is difficult."

"I'll take the salt," I said.

It seemed a discourtesy to refuse him a sale. He wrapped up the packet in brown paper and I took it outside. George had finished fueling the truck, and we set off for camp.

I held the parcel to my chest as we bucketed across the plain. She was such a kind and caring and honorable woman, I wanted to send her a gift for the mission. I racked my brain to decide what would be suitable. Suddenly I realized I already had it there in my arms. The salt gathered by the San from the Makgadikgadi pans.

I would go to the school and pour the salt on the winter fire and watch the faces as the crystals flared gold and green and turquoise. The children would laugh. The teachers would laugh. The lady would laugh. It was even possible the God of the Dutch Reformed Church might laugh too.

The Toyota reappeared through the darkness at 10 P.M. with David at the wheel. There was no sign of Syd as the truck stopped, and for a moment I thought he must have stayed behind in Francistown.

Then I heard a low groan from the back. I walked around and peered over the tailgate. Syd was lying flat on the floor inside with his hands clasped to his head. I carefully helped him out, guided him over to the fire and offered him a drink. Syd looked at the glass and shuddered.

"I think our Syd's caught a cold," David ventured.

"A cold?" I glanced at David suspiciously. "You were under strict orders not to lead him astray. What the hell have you been up to?"

"Ah . . ."

David's eyes glazed over, and he stared thoughtfully into the night beyond my head. I waited. Whenever David's gaze settled on the far distance, I knew from long experience he had something to hide.

"We encountered a little local difficulty," he said. "The tinted mechanic at the garage was somewhat coy about assisting us. 'You can go fuck yourself, white man,' as he put it. Syd tried to reason with him with the help of a monkey wrench, but to no avail. At which point I suggested a mild restorative might be in order."

I knew David's definition of a mild restorative. It would cause panic in an overstocked distillery.

"Do that again, foot soldier," I said, "and it'll be a drumhead court-martial at dawn."

By the fire Syd groaned again and asked weakly for aspirin.

By daybreak the storm had died away. We drove down to the edge of the pans, and the air was clear and still. Yesterday the southern horizon had been hidden by a stinging wall of sand and salt. Today it stretched out in front of us clean and bare and glittering in the early light. We turned and began to work our way slowly toward the east.

The crow's-flight distance to the water was only ten miles, but the journey took us three hours. Beneath the salty crust the ground was damp and spongy. It meant we had to follow the wandering spits of land that straggled in and out across the pans no more than eighteen inches above their surface. Sometimes one spit would be separated from the next by only fifty yards, but we'd have to make a detour of half an hour to reach it. The saline lane between was too fragile to support the truck's weight. At others we'd stop, climb out and test the salt in case the soil below had dried out enough for us to risk a quick scramble across.

Wherever we halted, the crust was printed with spoor: the great flat disks of elephant feet, the cleft incisions of deer, the round pads of lions. Some of the tracks were months old, and most of the animals had vanished, retreating north as winter pushed across the plateau. But occasionally a springbok or a jackal would appear in the wavering belts of mirage, gaze at us for a moment and then break away to dissolve in ripples of bending light.

"I think I'd better stay here," Syd said when we finally reached the water.

He glanced wildly around, searching for inspiration. Suddenly it came to him.

"Just in case we're robbed," he added.

I looked at the uninhabited immensity of the black-and-silver landscape reaching out on every side. Then I nodded.

"Sensible precaution," I agreed.

Syd sank gratefully to his knees in the truck's shadow. He rolled over and lay on his back nursing his forehead in his hands. As we walked away, I heard intermittent moans of anguish behind us. His cold certainly hadn't improved.

The water was ankle-deep. We stepped into it and moved forward.

---

Lapping over our boots it was no longer silver but dark bronze and flecked with particles of gold. I cupped my hands and drank. The taste was rank and lemon-sour and the smell in my nostrils acid. I spat. A dark trickle ran down my shirt. The moisture evaporated within seconds and left a fur of white crystals on the cotton.

We splashed on. The surface was ridged with bands of scum. They lapped over one another, fused, divided and drifted away. Beneath our feet puffs of creamy mud opened like sunken azalea blossoms. Above our heads the sky was a pitiless glaring white. The sun seared and blistered our skin, the light throbbed against our eyes, the heat saturated and dazed our bodies.

A mile from the shore I called a halt. The charred spit of land, the truck, the inert figure of Syd in the pool of shadow had all vanished. We were entirely alone in a shimmering, dazzling world of water and salt and sun.

Alone, apart from two million birds thronging the horizon in unbroken crescents and clouds of rose on every side. We were encircled by one-third of the world's population of lesser flamingos.

Dreaming Alice watched them being used as mallets in games of croquet. Before her, Pliny insisted their pickled tongues, thick and oily, were an essential delicacy at any serious banquet. Before Pliny, the ancient Phoenicians bartered their feathered skins with the Cornish for tin and the Netherlanders for amber—explaining to both that the bird was the legendary phoenix.

Now we were enveloped by them. They marched, wheeled and displayed in endless regimented columns, each a thousand strong. They retreated unhurriedly as we advanced, folding round us in delicately pacing thickets a steady forty paces away. They lifted in sudden tumultuous flocks, beat through the bending haze and planed down again.

Everywhere the water was stippled with tiny crimson breast feathers and the air filled by murmuring calls and the clamor of wings. Everywhere both water and air were colored and charged with the presence of the elegant, wistful and improbable birds.

I sat down and drenched myself against the heat. Beneath me the salt splintered like ice. On the Boteti I'd been surrounded by golden grass. Here, still at the desert's heart, it was water and rose as far as the eye could reach. I thought again of that distinguished American naturalist who believed in a Kalahari without grass, water or birds.

How indeed had it come about that such a vast congregation was assembled on the pan at the start of the Kalahari winter? The reason lay in the birds' diet. Like all flamingos—four species survive, with Africa the principal home for two of them—the lesser flamingo is a highly specialized feeder. It lives exclusively off the algae which thrive in the sour water of soda lakes and lagoons. Using its inverted head as a combined trawl, filter and pump, it extracts the minute organisms from below the surface and expels the waste.

The water's composition is critical. So too is the depth. If the level rises or falls outside certain narrow tolerances, the feeding ground becomes useless. Either the algae fail to reproduce or the flamingo's delicate gathering mechanism is unable to crop them. At that moment the bronze film of water on the Sua Pan was ideal in every way.

The birds had flown perhaps a thousand miles to get there. They traveled at night, navigating by the stars and the earth's magnetic field. They would stay for as long as conditions on the pan remained stable. When the water level dropped through evaporation and the algae died, they would move on. One evening the pan would be carpeted with the huge roseate flocks. At dawn next day it would be deserted.

Since the flamingos' survival was a matter of random migration dictated by the changing availability of their food, the pattern of their movements could never be constant. One year a lake might meet all their demanding requirements. The next, through flood or drought, it would be barren. So the birds roamed the continent like trusting pilgrims. If a certain staging post was closed, another farther along the road would be open. The God of the *Phoeniconaias*, the crimson water nymphs in their Linnaean name, would provide.

The Sua Pan was a flamingo staging post, one of a network scattered across Africa. It was neither more nor less reliable than any other. From time to time the distant Zimbabwe rains would be thin, the southward press of water would spend its energy in the sand, and the pan would be bare. That was a hazard of the seasons. When it happened, the ripple effect could be followed thousands of miles to the north in a legacy of abandoned nests, dying birds and decimated flocks.

---

In the Sua water failure was rare. Much more often the pan filled at summer's end, the algae flowered and the flamingos drifted down in skeins through the darkness to harvest them. They reaped the saline layer of protein and drank at intervals from the clear, sweet streams that fed the shallow basin. There they might be taken as prey by jackal, hyena, lion and other waiting predators. Such were their multitudes that the loss of a few incautious individuals was irrelevant to the survival of the flocks.

The flamingos trusted Sua with the skeptical and pragmatic wisdom of the wild. It functioned or failed to function as a feeding ground according to the remote and uncontrollable vagaries of climate. At least it was always there. It had been there, tilted on different gradients and sown with different vegetation, for hundreds of thousands, even millions, of years.

It was like Lake Xau, to the west. The huge expanse of Lake Xau, with its population of hippos and crocodiles and water-treading bucks, had also been there from the beginning. It was marked on the earliest desert charts. It appears as an area of blue on the map of the Kalahari made from U.S. Air Force satellite photographs. Lake Xau is one of the citadel's few permanent and unchanging features.

Fortunately for the flamingos, they depend on neither charts nor photographs for navigation. Despite what the satellite's cameras recorded, Lake Xau is not there. It has vanished.

Fifty miles west of where the maps locate the lake is a place called Orapa. Approaching Orapa on the ground is an eerie, almost surreal experience. For mile after mile there is nothing but Kalahari bush and wilderness. Suddenly the bush is sheared off in a die-straight line as if it has been trimmed by a gigantic knife. Beyond, the ground has been cleared in a broad corridor a mile long. At the center of the corridor stands a towering chain-link fence.

That is all. There's no sound, no trace of human habitation, no sign of anyone. Only the grim and forbidding fence barring the way in silence. It continues at right angles at both corners, and then again at the ends of the arms. Inexplicably and at vast expense, a square mile of bush has been cordoned off like some escapeproof desert prison camp.

Twenty minutes later the fence has disappeared as abruptly as it came into sight. So abruptly that it lingers in the memory as a desert mirage. It is no mirage. Every link in the metal wall is of tempered steel. In the middle of the enclosure lies the second-largest known diamond pipe in the world.

The discovery was made in 1967. A few years later the pipe was being worked. The machinery used for diamond extraction requires large quantities of water. There was no water at Orapa, but Lake Xau was only fifty miles away. In diamond-mining terms, fifty miles is a stroll to the corner store. Lake Xau ceased to exist.

In fairness to the interests that removed the lake from the ground, if not yet from the maps, the hippos and crocodiles had gone from Xau over a hundred years before. The lake was shrinking and changing long before even Livingstone crossed the plateau. The point is important not just in relation to Xau but more widely in the Kalahari and elsewhere. Far too often, change is blindly attributed to the tampering hand of man. In reality there never was a moment of stasis, a time when the balance of green and perfect Eden was struck forever.

The natural state of the wild is constant and often violent flux. The impact of the ice ages on life forms, for instance, was arguably as profound and in the common sense as destructive as anything man has done. The two processes operate side by side. Man's rearrangements of the environment are swifter and more arbitrary. But regardless of anything he does, the wild is always rearranging itself.

At Lake Xau the effect of man's intervention was immediate and dramatic. The lake was moved like the venue of a football game. Its water was taken and poured into small holes in the earth. Out of the holes tiny pebbles were washed. The pebbles were cut, polished and bartered. Some ended up on the heads of drills probing for further pebbles. A few were draped around or over the necks, breasts and wrists of old—or more rarely, young—women. Most were returned to the earth in vaults.

The story is the same as the story of gold. At Xau, by a remarkable alchemy, the water was converted into stone. The stone was put back where it had come from and stored there rather less safely than before. The lake had been truly buried.

At what price? No point in asking the roughneck drillers spinning the cutting head onto the thread of the bore pipe. Their concerns are with lubricant mud, the set of the platform and the blood seeping through the seams of their gloves. No point in asking the men who sent them into the desert. They are preoccupied with balance sheets and the return on capital. No point in asking the craftsmen who cut the stones, the women who wear them, the attendants who lock them away in subterranean safes. They all have different interests—and not one is the lake.

There is no one to ask. Perhaps in the case of Lake Xau it does not matter, for the lake may have been shrinking and vanishing of its own accord.

But what if a diamond pipe were found fifty miles west of where the Nata River joined the pan? What if pipes were discovered all over Africa wherever rivers fed into pans and soda lakes?

Part of the price then can be swiftly reckoned. It would include the extinction of the flamingo. Denied one source of food, many birds can adapt and survive successfully off another. Some, like the peregrine falcon, are so flexible in their feeding and living requirements that they can flourish in almost any environment. The specialist feeders like the flamingo cannot adapt. When the algae vanish, so, instantly, will the birds. Throughout Africa that year men were prospecting for new diamond pipes.

Much later, I stood up and walked slowly back to the shore. Just before I reached it I paused and turned around. The sun was lowering, and a glow was spreading across the western sky. The glow was the same pale pink as the flamingo feathers. It spilled onto the surface of the water and raced across, staining the pan, for mile after endless mile, rose. At the same instant all the birds lifted, and there were not two million of them but four—two million in clamorous flight and two million in beating reflection below.

For a few moments the entire universe was an incandescent rose —sky and sun and water, clouds and air and the great traveling skeins; even the early Kalahari stars glittered pink between the churning wings. And suddenly, as I watched, a new name came to me for my list. Not one of the drillers, a board director, a craftsman cutter or a keeper of the vaults. They are all tied to the diamonds for their keep. But the one person who could accept or refuse the stones of choice—the woman who wears them.

I wanted to take her with me into the same rose flamingo sunset. There we would discuss the price of diamonds. When she asked me how much her next would cost, I would be able to point at the birds and say in complete truth: "Those."

I climbed into the truck and we drove back. Homing flamingos flew above us all the way.

We are a week and five hundred miles out. Tomorrow we strike camp again and head north for the Chobe River. So far everyone is in good heart. But after the Chobe there are Savuti, the delta and tsetse fly, the walls of mosquitoes at Lake Ngami and then the long, bruising trek south.

I study the faces round the fire wondering how each will stand up to what lies ahead. Of the three black Tswana, two, Elvis and Mtimba, are enigmas. I guess they will remain so to the end. Elvis (did the King ever imagine that among all his many legacies he would bequeath his name to a gun bearer in the wilds of the Kalahari?) is small and wiry and sullen. He would have made a fine barrack-room lawyer. He does his job, but he bears an air of truculent resentment toward life in general and us in particular. By contrast, Mtimba is amiable, vacuous and undemanding. In signing up to cross the desert, Mtimba may or may not have got lucky. Privately he is trying to work out which.

George is very different. Twice the age of the other two, not tall but immensely strong, with powerful sloping shoulders, a slow majestic gait, ebony features rounded by years of Kalahari wind and sand, a deep chuckling voice and laughter deeper and richer still, George in his world is a true king.

At night after supper George holds court on the far side of the fire. He is a romancer, a teller of prodigious tales, of adventures he has shared across so many years with his *morena* ("father," as Syd is known by Tswana custom), outrageous stories of desperate encounters and hairbreadth escapes from lion, buffalo and elephant. The others listen in silence. They doubt him, they express disbelief and envy, they mock and sneer at him, yet always they are captivated, held spellbound as by some ancient mariner.

Occasionally Syd will overhear their conversation and interrupt the quiet Tswana voices. "Remember that time near Kokong, George," he will ask, "the time I left you alone in camp? There was just one little mopane tree and a pride of lion walked in, ten of them and big buggers all. You climbed that tree like a squirrel and you stayed there all day with the lion beneath you. You tell the Colonel what happened."

Syd points at me and George will laugh, an immense, delighted earthquake of a laugh that starts at his ankles and rumbles upward until his whole body is shaking. And then George will tell the story.

From time to time, Syd, who despite a lifetime in Africa remains a product of another civilization, an expert in disciplines and technologies as alien to the Tswana as space travel, loses his temper with George. He rails and curses, calls George a black bastard, every name in a catalog of abuse garnered from the Cape to Cairo. George listens patiently. Then when the uproar subsides, George chuckles. After a moment, Syd chuckles too. He punches George on the shoulder, and peace is made again.

Technically, since independence the two are fellow citizens, with equal rights under the law. In practice, their relationship remains one of master and servant, paternal hunter and trusted gun bearer. Yet they are united by something stronger and more durable than citizenship or law, a bond of friendship forged by their shared experiences in the wild.

I have no doubts about George. He is a professional, an old hand in the bush. To him the safari, however long and arduous, is no more than another exercise of his craft. George will hold firm to the end.

Nor, on almost every level, do I have any doubts about Syd. Like George he is a professional, another old African hand who as a conscientious colonial officer spent thirty years trekking the length and breadth of the southern half of the continent. When the winds of change began to blow, Syd was forced to make a choice. Suddenly and inexplicably, the Empire was in retreat. He could retreat with it, casting himself on the global ebb tide of the white *bwanas, sahibs* and *morenas;* or he could stay, nail his feet to the only ground he knew, and attempt to hew something else from the new and bewilderingly volatile Africa.

Syd stayed. He resigned from the Colonial Service. Deeply and lastingly loyal to the Crown, troubled but sure of his course, he abandoned the safety and certainties of a British passport. He sank his roots in Kalahari rock and became a professional hunter. The change in occupation posed few problems. Syd had hunted all his life. The only difference now was that he was being paid for a craft he'd practiced out of instinct and delight since childhood.

He was a superb shot. He knew the Tswana people, he spoke their language, he understood their customs. He combined an expert's knowledge of the natural sciences with a passionate love of the wild and a deep understanding of the creatures that inhabited it. As a guide to the stone citadel he was peerless. And yet, hunched over the fire with my hands cupped above the flames, I feel again the two grating reservations I have felt from the start.

Syd is close to sixty. He has been tempered and hardened by the bush, he has adapted himself to its rhythms and patterns, he has learned to ride its assaults, to weave and roll and sidestep. Not even the old mongoose Archie Moore was more skillful with his counter-punches. But still the years accumulate remorselessly. In the end, as the mongoose found on that chalk-white square, their weight is unendurable.

Like Moore, Syd is cunning, obdurate and dauntless, but he cannot conceal the pressures bearing down on him. They manifest themselves in a haggard set to his face at dusk, in irrational outbursts of anger at some trivial problem such as a mechanical failure, in brooding silences over the midday meal when his head will droop and his eyelids close until, in rage against his body, he shakes himself awake bellowing furiously like a wounded buffalo.

For a hunter to retire from the bush is as strange and anguishing as for a deepwater sailor to retire from a lifetime at sea. In Syd's case, loath as he is to acknowledge it, the time will not be long in coming.

My second concern is less easy to define. It stems from Syd's nature. As expedition guide he has a specific job to do, responsibilities to fulfill, tasks to carry out. He deals with them all meticulously. By day, the bouts of weariness aside, he never rests. At night he sleeps with a shotgun cradled in his arms, waking instantly at the slightest sound—a crackling ember, the bark of a distant jackal, even the passage of a windblown leaf across the sand.

Syd is also a yearner, a dreamer, a man of fierce and impetuous pride. He does not only know the Kalahari—he *owns* the desert. It is his private fief, his personal territory. Somewhere deep inside him, the two forces—responsibility for the expedition and the iron conviction the citadel is his own possession—collide. He wants the desert to be seen in his way, through his eyes, as he knows and understands it.

Before we leave tomorrow, Syd and I will pace a slow wide circle round the copse, making the ritual morning check of the spoor of the animals that have visited the camp during the night. As we do so I will know there are tensions still to be resolved. Syd and I have matters to settle before the journey is done.

# 6

AT 5 A.M. the darkness is intense. I open my eyes and lie gazing upward. Overhead, I know, is a canopy of leaves, with the desert sky beyond. All I can see is impenetrable blackness. Perhaps he is there—my black-skinned leopard—merging so perfectly with the utter darkness that he will always remain a part of the environment that nurtured him.

Last night flames from the fire lit the ring of sleeping bags, and the Southern Cross flashed in sickle blades of brilliance between the moving branches. Now there is nothing. The fire dead, the wind gone, the stars eclipsed by a film of cloud that will dissolve with the coming dawn. It is the brief moment of stasis, of utter stillness and silence, between the night and the day.

Then immediately above me a pearl-spotted owl calls, and a flicker of silver patterns the dark. It has patrolled the camp since our arrival. A stocky, immobile silhouette in the hours of light. A predatory and roaming sentinel after sunset. To the owl our evening fire has turned the copse into a richly provisioned larder of insects, moths and aphids drawn to the flames from the surrounding plain. For three nights it has fed effortlessly and well, stooping at ease to select from the laden shelves of the thermals above the coals. Now, as the first shell of daylight rims the horizon, it is proclaiming the trees its exclusive territory.

---

The calls continue, raucous, challenging and insistent. Fifteen minutes later, the camp is alive. The morning air is chill and edged with frost. It rises in plumes into the grayness, leaving a metallic taste on the tongue. The night's wind blew from the snow-covered flanks of the distant mountains to the south, rolling the advance of the Kalahari winter with it across the plateau. In a few hours we will be mantled by the blazing heat again, but from now on every night will become inexorably colder.

George rebuilds the fire. Normally he would have been up at intervals to see that it flamed all night through. But here, with neither lion nor hyena on the pans, he has been able to sleep uninterrupted.

I stand shivering by the flames with a mug of scalding tea. I can see everyone except Big David. I search the camp and finally I spot him, ambling back through the trees with his arms curved out at his sides and a roll of toilet paper in his hand.

"Morning, old bean," he greets me. "Now, that was a deeply moving experience. 'Dear Diary: Today I went.' "

He beams and tosses the roll in Bobby's direction.

In David's vocabulary a deeply moving experience is the ultimate accolade. Not a term to be used lightly but one reserved for very special occasions. Over the years I have heard him apply it to a dish of *pâté de foie gras aux morilles* in a French provincial restaurant, a tumbler of St. James's rum after a long climb in the Spanish sierras, and to disaster—above all to disaster.

David is a connoisseur of disasters. He collects them with the passion and dedication with which other people collect Meissen porcelain or Rembrandt etchings. The worse, the more dangerous, painful and catastrophic, the greater their value. Disasters are events to be hoarded in mind, to be savored and recounted—growing always more epic in the retelling.

Three nights earlier, on the trek to the pans from the Boteti, we had broken down. It was early evening. The day had been long and bruising. As the bush cover gave way to the open crusted flats, the temperature dropped suddenly and the air was bitterly cold. I and the two foot soldiers were huddled in the back of the truck, an exhausted Syd and EBL sitting in front.

We hit an ardvaark burrow, there was a shuddering, plunging crash and the truck stopped dead. David had been trying to doze. The shock woke him instantly. But it was something else that an instant later sent him hurdling over the tailgate like a gazelle. Syd was already kneeling by the chassis cursing furiously. David looked down. His nostrils were twitching, and I knew immediately what he was thinking.

The supply truck had leapfrogged us for the last time an hour before. Camp was another forty miles ahead. It was almost dark. We were all drained. There was no food. The abrupt silence after the crash had, even to my mechanically untutored ear, a savage finality to it.

For David the situation had all the ingredients of what he loved best in the world. It was a potential disaster.

"Ho, ho, ho!" He chuckled. "Check the axle bearings, Sir Sydney, but I don't hold out much hope. No go, I'd say, old bean."

The chuckles went on. His delight was so pure and infectious that after a while even Syd started to laugh. Then as Syd slid under the truck, David turned to the rest of us.

"I remember a marvelous occasion south of Baghdad," he said wistfully. "We were out in the Wahdi depression and the differential got shafted on a rock. Took us two days to fix it. Then we discovered the tank had been ruptured too. Over a week before we finally got out. Even the party Bedouin almost died of thirst. Deeply moving it all was. . . ."

I could almost see nostalgia filming David's eyes as he told the story.

To his regret, the damage this time proved less serious than he and Syd had suspected. Within an hour we were on our way again, and we reached camp at nine. The Sua breakdown would go into David's collection, but it would be hung with the minor works in the hall, not among the masterpieces in the drawing room.

Looking at him now, as Bobby hauls himself to his feet and trudges away on the same errand, I have no qualms about David. While the desert continues to provide him with disasters and deeply moving experiences David will be happy.

Kazengula is two hundred and fifty miles due north of Nata. A few years earlier the journey would have taken several days.

Now, as a result of the Zimbabwe war, the two are linked by a die-straight, graded and rubble-surfaced road. We covered the distance in six hours. Once we made a brief stop to eat. We sat in tree shadow looking out over a shallow calcrete bowl. The calcrete, exposed and weathered limestone, was as white as sun-dried bone. In the midday light the glare was brutal and eye-aching.

There were scarlet butterflies and white convolvulus blossoms spilling out of the rock fissures and a dark chanting goshawk turning overhead. Sweat poured off us. The heat was too fierce for talk. We finished our meal in silence and went on.

The roar of the engine and the hammering of the wheels made talk inside the truck impossible too. But at least at speed it was cooler. As the curving fans of dust streamed away in our wake, I sat with my back to the cab, watching the landscape. It changed every hour.

The first change had been dramatic and obvious. The vast shimmering emptiness of the pans suddenly gave way to a salty grass plain. By Nata the plain had become tree-studded bush. From then on, the successive variations as one belt of vegetation shaded into another were perceptible only to the expert eye. It was a matter of leaf shapes, subtle gradations in color, the texture of a plant stem, the curvature of the barbed armor on a thorn tree. There was mopane-dominated scrub and woodland interlaced with acacia. Next, in an overspill from Zambia and Zimbabwe, Rhodesian teak forest. Afterward, as we neared the Zambesi, thickets of Natal mahogany mixed with acacia once more.

Rhodesian teak and Natal mahogany. African hardwoods and the myriad species of acacia. Grasses, ferns, lichens, flowers and mosses. A long botanical catalog, dry as the dust that trailed the truck, best consigned to the study of balding scholars poring myopically over leatherbound Victorian volumes in somber libraries.

"Smell this, colonel."

We had stopped briefly again to check the water level in the radiator. Syd plucked a swollen grasshead and crushed it between his fingers. I leaned forward and sniffed the broken grains in his palm. The smell was oily and sweet. Syd gave the plant's scientific name.

"It's an indicator of different soil composition," he went on. "Means there'll be *Acacia tortilis* bush too. And that should give us impala."

As he spoke, a troop of young impala rams bounded across the track ahead. They were the first we'd seen. Their flanks gleamed chestnut in the sun, and their slender horns were ebony-black.

Syd smiled. I had the expert eye. It came on loan from him. To the Kalahari hunter the study of botany doesn't belong in some cloistered library. Its place is out in the living desert. There it could mean the difference between a full stomach and death from starvation.

We drove on. I remembered talking to a geologist in the bar of the Holiday Inn. Three weeks ago he'd made the same journey. An hour from Kazengula, five men had suddenly run out of the bush and lined the road in front of him. They were all armed with Kashalnikov repeaters. He braked and glanced in the rearview mirror. Three more, also armed, were covering him from behind.

"Rhodesian guerrillas from across the border," he said. "Shit, was I scared! I didn't know what to do. I had maybe three seconds to make up my mind. I decided to shut my eyes and put my foot down. I was lucky. They let me through. But next time . . . ?"

He shook his head. "I'm not traveling that way again."

I looked at my watch. We were also an hour from Kazengula. I checked the guns in the rack above my head and leaned forward, gazing at the walls of bush on either side.

The guerrillas were elsewhere that day.

Fifty minutes later, David stood up to look for a first glimpse of the Zambesi. As he raised his head through the open hatch, the wind curled under his sunglasses and whirled them off his face. He'd already lost his other pairs. These were his last, his pride and joy, an elegant marvel of optical engineering. He hammered furiously on the roof, and Syd stopped.

We all got out. David to walk back and collect the glasses, glittering in the dust two hundred yards behind. The rest of us to stretch after the battering six-hour run. David ambled away. Then, in the distance, we saw the supply truck grinding toward us. It was the only other vehicle we'd seen all day, and its course would take it straight over the glasses.

David's face stiffened in horror. He started to run. We all started to run—shouting, waving our arms, bellowing for George to stop. At the truck's wheel, George peered forward. He realized something had happened and grimly slammed his foot down on the accelerator.

We converged—the bucketing truck and the panting, shouting group of figures. George, driving like a Grand Prix *maître* on the last lap of a race that would clinch him the world championship, got to the line a few yards ahead of us. There was a scream of brakes, and the truck shuddered to a halt. Its front wheel was resting neatly on top of the glasses.

David peered down at the sparkling fragments and the mangled frame.

" 'Dear Diary,' " he said: " 'Today glasses also went.' "

Ten minutes later we reached Kazengula. There were a gasoline pump, a little customs building and a few huts. Two members of the Botswana National Guard lounged in the shadow of a baobab. Some naked children played silently in the dirt. Beyond them, the waters of the Zambesi glistened a dull gray-brown in the afternoon sun.

It was a quiet, drowsy outpost, too small even to be called a village, which existed only as a landing stage for the ferry to Zimbabwe-Rhodesia. Yet there was a jarring sense of tension in the air. The two guards reached nervously for their guns as we drew up. The pump attendant examined Syd for several minutes through narrowed eyes before he came out to refuel the trucks. The children never smiled.

For twelve years Kazengula had lived with the guerrilla war a mile away across the river. A week before our arrival the conflict had come the closest yet. Rhodesian Army gunships had dropped out of the morning sky and sunk the ferry with rocket fire. In a few minutes the tiny community's function and entire economy had been destroyed. Now there was nothing to do except wait for the war's end under the constant threat of a raid by the feared Selous Scouts.

As soon as the trucks' tanks were full, we headed west. For a while we drove parallel to the Zambesi. Then the Zambesi curved away out of sight to the north. Half an hour later it was replaced by the Chobe River. The Chobe was in flood, the water level higher than Syd had ever seen it. We followed the bank for a further ten miles and stopped to camp on a little promontory above the water.

I walked down to the river's edge and stood looking north. We had crossed Livingstone's tracks before, first at the Boteti and then on the pans. But it was here, on the banks of the Chobe, that I felt his presence most vividly.

Livingstone was the first European to break through the stone citadel. As far as I could judge, I was standing exactly where he had stood when the epic journey ended—a journey from whose consequences the Kalahari had never recovered.

The safehouses we use are only as secure as time, shifting circumstance and the flux of war permit. Even to the *maquis* fighter, the agent in the field, the mercenary in a foreign land, the term is relative.

Yet each of us carries in mind a private image of the ultimate safehouse. A final haven. A place of incandescent beauty. A fortress invulnerable to treachery or assault. I found mine as a child. A small whale-backed island in the Hebrides. Green-wooded and sunlit. Patrolled by soaring eagles, with sleek seals in the rocky bays below. A castle looking out toward Staffa, Fingal's cave and the white sands of Iona, with the ramparts of the outer isles and the gray Atlantic beyond.

The island is named Ulva. From my first childhood view across the sound, Ulva has traveled with me. I consider myself an islander.

To the end David Livingstone referred to himself as an "islander" too. It was many years before I learned we both laid claim to the same last safehouse, the same island. His family were Ulva folk.

After his death it was estimated Livingstone had explored, mapped and opened more than one million square miles of southern Africa. His starting point was the Kalahari. Unwittingly, he proved the most dangerous and effective of all the spies sent to survey the citadel. Livingstone, strangely, never even saw Ulva. So where did he come from, this island-haunted, tormented and ultimately obsessed man?

He was born in Blantyre, south of Glasgow, where his father had settled after leaving the Hebrides. By trade an itinerant tea vendor, the elder Livingstone was also a minister, an evangelist and a man of learning. He was determined his son at least should be lettered. At ten, young David was sent out to work in a cotton-spinning factory. There, amid the smoke and clamor of the looms, he began his education, propping Greek or Latin grammars against the loom's frame and committing a rule, a sentence, a phrase to memory each time he passed with the flying shuttle.

Twelve hours a day. Six days a week. On the seventh he wandered the countryside round the bleak town, collecting and identifying the plants he found from an ancient copy of *Culpepper's Herbal*.

At twenty he made the decision to enter the service of his God.

Unlike others of his countrymen who made the same choice, Livingstone experienced no fire-flash conversion. For him it was the logical culmination of his austere childhood. To be a missionary, to go forth and spread the word, to take enlightenment to the most distant corners of the earth. Without debate or inner conflict he'd found his life's work.

That, certainly, was for long the popular assumption. More recently, attempts have been made to explain the extraordinary saga that followed in medical terms. Livingstone, it's been convincingly argued, was a victim of acute clinical melancholia. Looking down at the swollen river, listening to the screams of the baboon pack, I wondered if there wasn't another explanation still.

Livingstone invaded Africa. Africa, I believe, more fully and deeply invaded him. In fact it wasn't Africa he was drawn to first, but China. He studied. He equipped himself. He trained to become a doctor. He applied for admission to the London Missionary Society. With considerable doubts the Society accepted him. He was serious, that was beyond doubt. Yet he was also stubborn, contentious and deeply reserved. Something jarred in his physical presence too. Light and supple from the waist down, he widened noticeably above, with a broad chest, heavy shoulders and thick, muscular arms.

Livingstone had an athlete's build but lacked team spirit. The Society picked teams. The Governors were understandably wary of lonely long-distance runners. Good relay members were what they were after, not marathon men out on their own. Yet they took him on. Livingstone qualified as a doctor in Glasgow and moved to London. There in a boardinghouse he met by chance someone who was to change the direction of his own life and, in turn, the history of modern Africa.

Twenty years older than Livingstone, Robert Moffat was a fellow Scot from the same humble background—he'd been an apprentice gardener when he saw the blazing light. He too had joined the Society, trained, and then, with his "beloved partner," the dauntless Mary, he'd voyaged to southern Africa. From the Cape he traveled by oxcart toward the interior. Finally, at Kuruman, on the southern rim of the Kalahari, he unyoked his team, glanced around and made his decision.

Moffat was brave and determined and fired by missionary zeal. That was in his mind. But his eye and heart were the eye and heart of a gardener. Kuruman was on a river. There were year-round water, fertile soil and of course sun. At Kuruman, Moffat nailed his feet down. He would build a mission post in the wilderness, he would spread the word of the Lord, he would baptize, marry and bury in the ceremonies of the Christian faith. He would also make the desert flower. Moffat had found a garden to tend.

Seventeen years later, when he encountered Livingstone on a rare visit to Britain, Moffat had made few converts among the gay and dreaming Tswana—but he'd hewed a lovely garden from the wild. A neat, trim garden of rose and mayflower and hollyhock, good vegetables, fruit and corn, herb and lavender. Constant as he remained to the end, the Lord's lantern bearer in the darkness, the sturdy Moffat, I suspect, found his greatest satisfaction not in the pulpit but among the dung heaps, seedlings and blossoms of his Kuruman acres.

Livingstone, suddenly abandoning the idea of China, ventured to ask the veteran missionary if he could join him in Africa. The dour Moffat sized up his young countryman and grudgingly gave his approval. Two years later, in 1842, Livingstone, by now ordained and qualified, made the same trek to Kuruman.

*Culpepper's Herbal* had given Livingstone much. Over the years to come, the legacy of its order and disciplined observation was to be as important as the spoor he read from the land. What it hadn't given him was the patience of the true gardener. Moffat could pace sedately between the rows of his spring vegetables waiting without hurry for a harvest of souls in the fall. Livingstone could not. He was eager, impulsive and restless.

He tried to harness himself to the routine of the missionary station. He failed. His eyes wandered constantly toward the north—toward the heart of the stone citadel. Within a year he was on the move. Befriended by Sechele, chief of the Bakwena tribe whose son he'd cured, he trekked east and west—tentative treks, preliminary ventures toward an interior that increasingly occupied his thoughts. And then, as the footloose young man explored the desert's perimeter, the Kalahari struck back.

In August 1843, Livingstone found himself face to face with a huge desert lion. He had always detested killing what he considered were "God's creatures." At that moment he felt he had no choice. He fired both barrels of his gun at point-blank range. Apparently unharmed, the lion leaped on him. It gripped him by the shoulder and shook him like a rag, spewing his blood between its fangs.

Livingstone went briefly into what was probably a coma of fear and pain. The pain was so intense that afterward he could recall the experience only as a dream. Then one of his bearers hurled a spear at the lion's flank. The lion dropped Livingstone and attacked his new aggressor. A second bearer intervened and received the same treatment. Moments later Livingstone's bullets took effect and the lion dropped dead.

In the era before antibiotics, a wound from a carnivore almost invariably became infected—leading often to gangrene, amputation and frequently death. On this occasion, all three men had received numerous lacerations. None was infected. Never satisfied until he had an explanation, Livingstone concluded that the tartan jacket he was wearing contained special properties which had wiped the virus from the lion's fangs.

"What the hell's this?"

Big David was examining the list of required equipment I'd prepared for expedition members before we left.

" 'An adequate supply of tartan clothing is essential,' " he read, puzzled. "If you're planning Highland reels by the fire, Colonel, kindly remember I don't perform without the support of a full pipe band."

"Just do as you're told, foot soldier," I said.

David settled for a pair of tartan socks. In his case it was almost certainly enough. The most belligerent lion was unlikely to do more than snap at his heels.

Livingstone's recovery was slow, and he could never again lift his left arm above his shoulder. He convalesced at Kuruman, where he was nursed by the Moffats' eldest daughter, Mary. The result, in that lonely outpost, was predictable. In 1845, David Livingstone and Mary Moffat were married.

"She is not romantic," he wrote, "but a matter-of-fact lady, a little blackhaired girl, sturdy and all that I want."

Poor Mary. She has left no record of what she expected from life as she stood with her newlywed husband in prayer before the little Kuruman altar that January day. No doubt a quiet and stable family existence such as her parents enjoyed, isolated but rewarding under the benevolent eyes of God. What she got instead was a living nightmare. Appalling physical hardship. The heartbreaking death of a child. Summary exile to England. Icy alienation from Livingstone's family. Long years of separation when she had no idea whether her husband was alive or dead. Poverty. The collapse of her faith, which turned belief into despair. And finally a pain-racked death from fever at the age of forty-one.

They were all to be the consequences of something Mary did not know on her marriage day. Livingstone had already fallen under the spell of the Kalahari. From the north across the desert he'd heard stories of a land of water, trees and rivers—the stories I'd read in that long-ago encyclopedia. The land was ruled by a Makololo chieftain named Sebetuane. Livingstone was determined to reach it, but the problems appeared insurmountable.

There was the barrier of the desert. According to local wisdom it could be crossed only in years when, after exceptionally heavy summer rains, the succulent tsama melon blossomed. Even then the expense of fitting out an expedition on a missionary's salary, increased now with marriage to £100 a year, was prohibitive. Frustrated and impatient, Livingstone could only stand gazing north and listening to the Kalahari wind.

Then an answer suddenly appeared in the shape of a young English aristocrat. William Cotton Oswell, an officer in the Coldstream Guards, was rich, handsome and witty. The contrast between the two—the worldly gentleman and the ascetic missionary from a Glasgow slum—could hardly have been greater. Yet they became and remained firm friends. Oswell had come to Africa to hunt. Excited by Livingstone's stories, he volunteered to finance an expedition and invited Livingstone to go with him.

Livingstone naturally accepted without hesitation. On June 1, 1849, they set out. With them they took a friend of Oswell's, Mungo Murray, a trader named Wilson, eight Hottentots, thirty Bakwena, wagons, oxen, horses and supplies for a year. Even so, disaster almost overtook them early in the journey. They lost their way, exhausted the water they had with them and were on the point of dying of thirst. Then Oswell spotted a San woman. Galloping furiously, he headed her off on his horse and cajoled her into leading them to a spring.

Halfway across, they came on the Boteti River. They followed it northwest and reached Lake Ngami. Livingstone's goal, Sebetuane's country, was still two hundred miles ahead. But the lakeside tribes proved recalcitrant and unhelpful. Unable to obtain further provisions, they were forced to turn back.

The next year Livingstone tried again. This time he was without Oswell. Instead he took Mary and their three young children. From the start the journey was bedeviled by dangers and difficulties. In spite of his previous year's experience, Livingstone badly underestimated the water requirements of the wagon team. Often they had to travel continuously by day and night in search of a spring.

Finally, when they reached Ngami again four months later, Mary, the children and most of the men went down with malaria. The shore was infested with mosquitoes, and not one square inch of the children's bodies remained unbitten. Thwarted for the second time, Livingstone turned and headed back.

And then the following year, financed, equipped and accompanied by Oswell again, he made a third attempt. This time he traveled due north across the Makgadikgadi pans, leaving the Boteti River and Lake Ngami to the west. Once more their water failed. Now there were no wandering San to rescue them, no lucky discoveries of a remote spring. Nothing except the unending whiteness of the saline flats.

Livingstone had been close to death before. He would be close to it many times again. But never did he feel its presence so vividly and nearly as he did then. There was no choice except to press on. Gaunt, haggard and emaciated, he drove the wagons forward. In late July 1851 he reached the banks of the Chobe. Two weeks later he struck north with Oswell and found the Zambesi. The stone plateau had been crossed. The citadel of the Kalahari had been breached. Africa had been opened.

Our first evening on the pans, it had rained aphids. Here on the Chobe, it was baboons.

Ignoring the fire, they came closer with darkness, thronging the trees round the camp until every branch seemed to be laden with brawling silhouettes. The uproar as we ate was deafening—a screaming, grunting, growling, barking chorus that was silenced only by the intermittent roar of a lion.

At midnight David climbed out of his sleeping bag to relieve himself. Unknown to him, a large dog baboon had perched above his head and evacuated neatly beside his pillow. Fumbling sleepily through the darkness, David put both feet in the deposit. Then he clambered back inside.

He emerged next morning with his pajamas stained in harlequin streaks of dark yellow-brown and smelling like a sty. He examined himself carefully, wrinkled his face at the stench and glanced malevolently up at the tree.

" 'Dear Diary,' " he said: " 'Baboon went.' "

There was always half an hour between wakening and breakfast. I walked down to the river's edge and stood looking out across the water.

Livingstone came back here several times after that first breakthrough with Oswell, but from now on his journeys would mainly be to the north. The north and in two great scything curves to the west and east. He sent Mary and the children back to England. He rejoined them years later as a national hero. To his amazement, he found himself rich through his writings and lectures. He was even received in audience by the mighty Queen Empress.

And then he returned to Africa. The travels not merely continued. The urgency, the momentum behind them, seemed to increase. There was the epic encounter with Stanley, the shrewd, tough opportunist who obtained the greatest scoop in the history of journalism. There were failures, grotesque, laughable failures such as the government-backed attempt to chart an inland waterway. Mary, joining him for the expedition, was an almost casual victim of that one.

Still Livingstone went on. His children were strangers. His wife crazed, then dead. His fortune largely squandered. His health in ruins. And yet he pressed on.

What are we to make of this driven Scottish "islander"—islander of an isle he'd never seen, let alone set foot on? This man who single-handed unlocked more territory than anyone before or since?

Although Livingstone resigned from the London Missionary Society in 1862, to the last his journals record—in his tireless, vivid, simple and muscular writing—a staunch, unquestioning belief in his God. On one level I do not doubt him. He had a faith and a mission. The knowledge sustained him through peril, disaster and pain, which Livingstone accepted without complaint or protest. On one journey alone he suffered seventeen crippling attacks of malaria in nine months.

I believe the desert drugged and enslaved him. He became possessed of a daemon. His faith was the intellectual justification, but under it, insidiously, uncontrollably, the daemon took over and urged him on. Africa was a cobnut. He was forced to crack it, taste its sweetness and then show all the world what he had done.

Poor Mary that she ever set eyes on the stone citadel. Poor children, too. And then poor Dr. David, hauling his enchanted body's wreck up mountains, across swollen rivers, through dark forests. Plagued, leeched and raddled, but constantly, consumingly obsessed by a dream he never understood. Poor riven and disjointed family. But most of all, poor citadel. The Livingstones, mother, father and children, died. There was no such quietus for the Kalahari. The upland plateau had had a lance plunged into its guts. Now it had to struggle for life against the constant draining of blood.

Twenty miles west of the Kazengula landing stage is a low ocher building with a white pole in front of it across the track. The place is called the Serondela gate. It marks the start of the Chobe forest reserve.

Among the many ways of loosely grouping the larger Kalahari mammals, the most obvious is according to their dependence on water. Some, like the gemsbok, can survive without it indefinitely —obtaining all the moisture they need from the desert leaves and grasses. Others need water daily or at least at very frequent intervals. In the case of elephants, the average requirement is fifteen gallons every twenty-four hours. From the banks of the swollen Chobe River, water is constantly available. It is elephant country.

We see our first elephant within minutes of entering the reserve. The truck drifts around a bend, wheels churning in the sand, and suddenly a young bull appears in front of us. Huge, honey-colored from the layered dust, a swaying sack of baggy skin and grimed tusk. Almost before we register what we have seen, the animal has vanished.

We drive on. The bush is like an intricate maze. Flour-white tracks, patterned with immense oval hoofprints, lead off in every direction. Some end abruptly at the water's edge. Others meander sinuously for a mile before petering out in grass or reeds. Others still circle, weave, loop and wind back to their starting points.

Always on either side there are the walls of yellow-green mopane. The yellow a hot, bright buttercup and the green sharp lime. Spring colors except that the sky above is white, the leaves patinaed with dry winter dust, and the air in the narrow lanes bends with the heat.

We reach a track junction and Syd brakes to search for the supply truck's spoor. I stand up and look out. I can see nothing except billowing sand and the golden barriers of scrub, but suddenly there are elephants everywhere. I sense their presence, smell the drying mud, feel the pressure waves of movement through the air on my face.

The bush parts and a second young bull ambles by. A pair of calves follow him. They notice the truck, stop and inspect us warily. Then a shadow falls across the roof. I turn. The cow has emerged ten yards behind. She lifts her trunk and scans the afternoon breeze. The splayed nostrils are tulip-shaped on a dark wavering stem. She picks up the truck's stench and the trunk becomes rigid like a radar antenna locking onto a target.

I duck my head and call into the cab, "She's coming, Syd."

As I speak, the elephant's ears go back. She screams, lowers her head and charges. Syd lets out the clutch and the truck leaps forward. We slide through a corner and the cow breaks away. An instant later another is coming at us, this time from in front.

Syd slams the gear lever into reverse and we roar backward. For a few seconds the elephant gains on us, a towering, trumpeting mass of blackness shining with the still undried water-glow from the river. Then she too turns aside and disappears.

"We'll make straight for camp," Syd says. "We've cut it fine."

We move cautiously forward again. In the truck everyone is tense and silent. Immense shadowy shapes half-screened by leaves throng the bush round us. The air is thick with dust, and the constant screams drown the sound of the engine. Finally we arrive at the campsite, on the riverbank. Syd climbs out and glances at his watch.

"If we'd left it till ten minutes later," he says, "I reckon we'd have had to turn back."

I nod in agreement. What we had caught was the start of the second of the day's tidal movements to the water. We had become tangled in an elephantine rush hour.

From Serondela to Kavimba, at the western end of the reserve, is a distance of about forty miles, all bordered by the Chobe River. South of the river, a mile inland, is a low escarpment. Beyond the escarpment the forest gradually gives way to plain.

There is therefore a riverine forest strip of some forty square miles on the extreme northern battlement of the Kalahari. On the strip that year was a population of over two thousand elephants. To the zoologist numbers alone have little meaning. A more useful measurement is biomass—in essence, the total weight of an animal population.

A mature elephant can weigh ten tons. The Chobe herds contained a considerable proportion of calves and half-grown animals. On a very rough-and-ready reckoning, I put the average weight per elephant at five tons. It meant we were surrounded by something like ten thousand tons of elephant—a ton to every area of bush the size of a football field. How had such an awesome concentration arisen, and what did it herald?

Neither question is easy to answer, but the first is perhaps less difficult than the second. To the hunter the elephant is both the most dangerous of all animals and also the most intelligent. Its danger derives from its size, strength and speed. With a cold nerve and a steady hand, even a charging lion can be turned by a scattergun cartridge. An elephant can be stopped only by a high-velocity bullet to the heart or brain. The charges we'd faced—and would face again and again over the days to come—were no more than territorial clearances. We'd crossed the constantly shifting border of the animal's private space of earth. Our invasion had been repelled by the threat of force. Once we'd retired behind the invisible boundary we were safe.

But if our retreat was too slow, if the truck stalled, we were in trouble. A charging elephant travels at more than thirty miles an hour. In the African bush, nothing apart from the rifle can deflect it. Trees, scrub and thorn all crumple like tissue paper before the vast hooves. Even a rhinoceros can be left trampled to death in its wake. Pitted against an old enraged cow, a steel-frame Toyota is as fragile as an eggshell.

The charges, and the danger they represent, are a reflex action. They will happen whenever territory is invaded, even against a creature as harmless to an elephant as a jackal. The elephant's intelligence is quite another matter. It is formidable and still only partly understood. What is beyond doubt is that the elephant harnesses it for protection against its only predator—man.

"Declare an area a reserve," Syd said, "and they know. Many's the time I've spoored them out hunting. They cross into a reserve and the moment they're inside the boundary, they turn and look at you. There's nothing on the ground, no mark or fence or anything, but they know they're safe. Now, I've got a map and a compass. I can take bearings and reckon where the reserve runs. But how the hell do *they* figure it out?"

He shook his head. "No one's ever explained it. But believe me, they know."

I had heard the same story often from other hunters. Whatever complex mechanism teaches the elephant to identify and memorize the limits of a game reserve, there is no question that it happens. The concentration on the riverine strip was a classic example. The elephants had learned to recognize Chobe as a sanctuary against the hunter's gun.

So much, then, for the prime cause of the soaring numbers, the great biomass buildup. What of the consequences?

Theoretically, the Chobe area makes an ideal game reserve. Not just for elephants but for all the animals of the northern Kalahari. It is large and remote. It has water, forest and pasture. It is free of poachers. Even the rare visitor barely troubles the equilibrium of the wild. It satisfies, in fact, the most stringent criteria of the most dedicated conservationist. Theoretically.

In practice, all that has been sown on the Chobe's banks is honorable intentions. They are rooted in Kalahari wind. The reaping is yet to come. When it does, the harvest will be bitter.

To understand why requires understanding the metabolism, dynamic and family structure of the reserve's dominant creature. The very animal it was created to protect—the elephant. The giant herbivores are not only grazers but browsers. This means that virtually all plant life from ground-level grasses to the highest tree leaves is available to them as food. Requiring up to four hundred pounds a day each, the Chobe elephants roam the riverine strip and the plain behind, systematically foraging the landscape for their needs.

The litter of destruction they leave in their wake is apparently brutal, wasteful and wanton, resembling the aftermath of a B-52 bomber strike. Grass and bush are smashed and mangled. Tree branches are shattered and torn. Trunks riven and upended. Bark splintered, gouged and ripped away, leaving the pithy core to wither and die.

In that light the elephant is always rogue, an undiscriminating machine of havoc and devastation. But is it in reality devastation? The answer is no.

Scything, clearing and felling, the elephant herds open the land as they feed. They break the soil, unlock space for plants to root in the turned earth, eliminate pockets of life-inhibiting shade, allow the sun to penetrate and photosynthesis to operate. Slowly, behind them, the bush begins to flower. As it flowers, other animals can use the new growth, animals that in turn support yet more species, all the way up the food chain to the great Kalahari lion. The evidence of destruction is tainted and false. Elephants are not destroyers but engines of regeneration. Huge plows constantly at work in slow rhythms to till, seed and fertilize the earth. And of course, as they do, they breed.

As a society elephants are matriarchal. The young are suckled by their mother for up to six years. Not until fifteen are the adolescents turned away, and then only the young bulls. They leave and they have behind them fifteen years of instruction, of programmed experience and indelibly formed habit—the habit, above all, of survival.

Outside the reserve, they've been taught from birth, is danger. Inside, they are safe. So they and the maturing cows stay within the Chobe boundaries. It is the only world they have ever known. But neither they nor their parental generation can regulate what happens there. The dynamic of reproduction is irresistible.

The size of the reserve is constant, but the biomass within it is not. Every year it inexorably increases. Already the Chobe herds are too large for the area to support through the natural feeding patterns evolved over hundreds of thousands, even millions, of years. All the elephants can do is change those patterns. If they do not, they will starve.

So the ivory plows furrow on. No longer in the great, wide-ranging sweeps of the past, but in shorter, swifter, ever more intensive swaths. Where once a stretch of land was cropped every ten years, now it is happening ten times in a single year. Unable to support such demands, the habitat begins to crumble and degrade. The more it degrades the more fiercely and hungrily the plows are forced to work.

The process accelerates so rapidly that it is over within a few years. In several African elephant reserves the degeneration is complete. On the Chobe's banks it has just begun. Soon the riverine strip, the forest, bush, grass and plain will be gone. In their place the tusked harrows will have left a dust bowl. As the bitter climax approaches, the numbers of the elephant herds will suddenly crash. From several thousand the population will be reduced through starvation to a few hundred.

In other species under other conditions, a few hundred animals might be adequate as a breeding stock for the population to build back. Not in the Chobe. The Chobe survivors will be wrongly programmed. The habits and patterns of behavior they learned are artificial. The system worked only while the reserve worked. When the reserve breaks down, the animals will be helpless. Almost overnight, skills will be asked of them they do not possess. The young bulls and cows were never taught to search for new pastures. Even if, hunger-driven, they wander blindly out from the reserve's confines, they will find the ancient pastures gone.

Their parents were given the Chobe. The reserve was thought to have been enough for them, their offspring and each succeeding generation through to eternity. On that assumption, the land beyond was allocated for other uses. The Chobe is not enough. Without a mechanism to control the size of the population, it is not even a reserve. It is a death trap.

For a while those who survive the crash will roam the ruined landscape. Before, when the bush was healthy and whole, there was no competition for food between the elephants and the other herbivores that shared the Chobe. At different levels and in different kinds, there was abundance for all. Now the rivalry for the sparse remaining plant life becomes intense. It is not a contest the elephant is equipped to win.

In the struggle to meet the body's energy requirements under famine conditions, the advantage shifts dramatically from the large to the small. Suddenly size and strength are not assets but terrible liabilities. For every shoot or succulent garnered the elephant burns up more calories than it replaces. The energy debt mounts.

Emaciated, giddy, staggering and racked by disease, the last members of the once-great Chobe herds drop one by one. Within a generation there is not a single elephant left. But the elephants are far from the only casualties of their own biomass explosion. The community of plants that supported them, thousands of years in the making, has been wrecked beyond repair.

So the populations of buck crash too. With the buck gone, the predators dwindle and die—the lion, leopard and desert lynx. As the predators vanish, so do the scavengers and cleansers—the hyena, jackal and vultures. Nothing is unaffected; no animal, bird, insect or flower. The harvest of honorable intentions is finally home.

"Stand still."

The voice is quiet and close to my ear. I freeze. Ten feet in front of me, an immense black shadow glides silently through the darkness. For an instant it shuts out the stars. Then the shadow is gone.

"Good night, lady."

A chuckle and the voice again. Piet Maritz' voice. The old hunter is standing beside me with his hand on my arm. It is 9 P.M. After supper I'd walked away from the camp along the riverbank. Fifty yards from the fire, Maritz had suddenly materialized at my shoulder.

"Saw your truck's spoor," he says. "Reckoned I might find you."

It is ten days and five hundred desert miles since we met, but I'm not surprised to see him again. Maritz was also heading north. Like the Boteti, the Chobe bank is a favorite campsite for the Kalahari traveler.

"Come over and meet the others," I suggest.

Maritz glances in the direction of the flames and shakes his head. For reasons of his own—reasons I can guess at—he prefers the privacy of his fire. We move toward it. Another gliding shadow blankets the night sky, and Maritz checks me once more. The shadow passes without sound like the first, and we continue.

"The truce," Maritz says.

I frown. "Truce?"

"That's what I call it. You step into that old girl's territory by day and she'll see you off like a steamer out of hell. At night it's different. Almost like way back they made an agreement with us. Day we'll fight over, night we'll share. . . ."

He pauses and adds a caution: "Don't press the truce too far. Put yourself between a cow and a new-dropped calf and you'll still get hell."

Above us as we walk, the baboon packs plunge, wheel and leap through the foliage like dolphins through night surf. We reach Maritz' fire and sit down. There are many ways of constructing a Kalahari fire according to its purpose, the available wood and the preference of the builder. Maritz used the simplest and most economical of all. Two logs set end to end. Where the ends touch is a small patch of scarlet.

We talk. Inevitably, there on the Chobe with the great black shadows wheeling round us, the talk is of elephants.

"Easy to reckon you know them," Maritz says. "There was a hunter at Savuti ten years back, Rick Huysson he was called. Young fellow, good in the bush and one hell of a joker. Had a favorite trick. They'd set up a fixed camp on the edge of the channel. Plain, the tents, then the escarpment and sand on the water bed below . . ."

Maritz delves in his pocket and produces a length of biltong. He carves a strip for me and chews on the rest between sentences as he talks.

"There was an old bull near the camp, been there for years. Now, jumbo can handle anything except a steep drop. Put him on top of a big bank and he'll do everything to avoid climbing down. This old jumbo was the same as the rest. . . ."

Elephants to hunters are invariably known as "jumbo," just as lions are "pussy" and buffalo "buff."

"So what Rick did was this. Early evenings when they came back he'd search out that old bull and he'd provoke him. He'd draw him out of the bush, goad him, make him charge—hell, he used to drive jumbo wild. Then right at the end when jumbo was almost on top of him, he'd jump down the bank. Did it all to entertain the clients. Used to scare them half to death, but they loved it. Became quite famous, Rick did. . . ."

Maritz pauses. Time, in the telling of his stories, as I know from before, is of no consequence. He works through them as methodically as he chews the flavor out of the biltong.

"Well, middle of one season," he went on finally, "his tracker comes to Rick and says, '*Morena*, that old jumbo, I see him talking to a friend. You watch out, *Morena*.' He doesn't know why but he's scared, that boy of his. Rick laughs. He knows elephant don't talk.

He knows old bulls don't get together. Maybe a week later Rick does his trick again. Leads old jumbo to the edge, makes him charge and jumps. . . ."

Another pause. Another slow, considered bite at the hunk of dried meat.

"There's a second bull at the bottom of the bank, down where there's been no elephant spoor ever. He's waiting, this other bull. He picks young Huysson up and he throws him thirty feet. Then he kneels on his legs. The other hunters manage to drive him off before Huysson's killed, but he's never hunted since. He's in a wheelchair now down in the Cape. That old jumbo watched it all."

Maritz stops.

"It's like learning to read. Know the words and you can tell the story. I'll give you an example. 'Way back, I was hunting ivory under government contract in the Luanga Valley. One day a Yank walks into camp. He's a young man, a scientist, and he wants to see jumbo out in the bush. . . ."

Maritz agreed to take the American with him. I can see them both as they set off—the wiry little hunter with his amber-colored eyes, his strings of biltong and his tattered shorts, and the earnest young scientist.

"We go out some way and I sit this Yank down with me beneath a tree. A while goes by and I see a bull maybe a mile off. So I say, 'You get your notebook out and you write down what happens.' Then I whistle and call to jumbo. 'Over here, son,' I say. That elephant walks right across and up to us. When he's ten yards away I say, 'That's far enough. You stop right there.' Jumbo stops. Then I say, 'Shake hands like a polite fellow.' . . ."

Maritz stretches out his hand, miming the gesture he'd made.

"Jumbo lifts his trunk and waves it at me. Then I ask him, 'Aren't you going to give us good morning?' The bull lowers his head like he's nodding and gives a big low snort. Afterwards I tell him, 'Fine, you be off now.' And that jumbo, he turns, circles round us and moves on. . . ."

Maritz chuckles. "Shit, man, you should have seen the Yank's face. He really believed me and jumbo were talking. He figured he'd seen a damn great breakthrough between man and the animals. Hell, years afterwards he was still sending me letters about it."

As the chuckles went on, mingling with the baboon barks and the grunting of hippos from the river, Maritz explained what had happened.

From the way the bull was browsing Maritz knew he'd move toward the tree. Maritz knew too the sequence of behavior that would follow when the animal reached it. The elephant would stop and raise his trunk to identify the alien scent ahead. Satisfied it didn't signify threat or competition, he'd lower his head and snort to affirm his presence. Then he'd amble away.

"Trouble is," Maritz adds, "jumbo's book is as long as the Bible. Young Rick Huysson, he'd been through Genesis and he reckoned he knew it all. He forgot there's Judges and Kings and the rest to come. I've learned the words for some of them, but I won't reach the end before I take the tide."

Maritz leans forward to scratch the head of the ancient slumbering dog beneath his chair.

I watch his face in the fire glow. Crossing my mind are incongruous images of two students poring over the Holy Book for elephant lore. The one a feckless truant. The other diligent and scholarly. Jumbo and Deuteronomy. A rogue's territory written in Leviticus. A tusker's charges chronicled in the Psalms. Both study.

Huysson flunks. He drops out with shattered legs and begs now from that invalid carriage. The scholar, old Piet, wins cap, gown and a bachelor's degree in pachydermic arts. But a bachelor's only. Even three full generations in the bush are not time enough to earn a doctorate.

Incongruous images? Maritz carries the Bible with him always. What more natural than that it should provide him with his terms of reference, his simple metaphors, his measures of wisdom and value? And that strange phrase, strange above all in the citadel of the Kalahari, "before I take the tide," for his death?

Briefly it puzzles me. I wonder. Then I realize. Maritz grew up in a waterfront cathouse with sea and spume and storm beyond the jetties. Sailors mounting stairs to mount the whores above were his childhood companions. Their language, their boasts and tales and superstitions, his first bright coins in bartered talk.

Sailors die on the ebb tide. Maritz carries the knowledge, and the words in which it's framed, to the desert's heart. He has lived sixty years and more with jumbo, pussy and buff. But the print that outlasts them all is the print of the widow-making waves.

---

A hippo snorts belligerently and crashes through the grass at the water's edge. The animal wishes to graze the bank, but the patch of flame troubles and irritates it. As it moves upriver in search of another feeding ground it disturbs a group of elephants. A chorus of angry trumpeting calls rings through the darkness, and a splash marks the hippo's retreat into the water.

There is one solution to the threat facing the Chobe herds, one means of controlling the biomass explosion taking place all around us. I have heard it eloquently advanced in the past. I will hear it put forward again and again as we go on. It is as simple and economical as Maritz' fire, and it has the additional merit of being apparently foolproof.

I ask Maritz his views.

"You mean culling? . . ."

He pauses. Then he shakes his head. The rejection is emphatic and absolute.

"I reckon I know as much about jumbo as anyone alive. You give me a herd, you give me a little time and I'll tell you something different about every goddamn animal there. What I can't tell you is which ones to take—which bull, which cow, which calf. But the elephants know. They'll have decided that one's for seed, that one's to bear . . ."

Maritz' finger stabs out above the flames, selecting the breeding stock from the invisible multitudes of animals surrounding him.

"Hell, they go much further. They'll choose some for midwives. They'll rank the seeders five and six back in case of accident. They'll keep a barren old cow we'd kill out of mercy, let alone culling. And they'll have a reason. Maybe she's a teacher, maybe she has a nose for pasture, maybe she's a water guide. We'll never know, but they do, and they'll be right."

Maritz shakes his head again. To him the plausible solution of culling is specious. The natural process through which the elephants structure their herds is too subtle and complex for us to understand. Maybe with years of study we can unravel its mysteries. We do not have those years. To cull at random now is like using a meat axe for brain surgery. The Chobe herds may yet be culled, if only to check the gathering dust bowl. If they are, the stock will waste and degrade like the habitat.

"Do you still take ivory, Piet?" I ask him.

"When I get a permit, sure. . . ."

He stops. I was not asking about hunting under license, and he knows it. I was talking about the other major threat to the survival of the African elephant—poaching.

It is a delicate question to put to him, and I fully expect him to avoid answering. The penalties for illegal killing are severe, perhaps more severe in Botswana than anywhere else in Africa. By law a hunter's truck, guns—all his equipment—are confiscated. A heavy fine is imposed. Often he is given a prison sentence too.

Maritz considers the matter in silence for several minutes. Then, to my surprise, he does reply, not with evasion or denial but directly.

"Look," he says, "I've hunted all my life. I reckon there's not a bird or animal from the Rift Valley south I haven't taken one time or another. But for a hunter, jumbo's always different. Each time you hit a big tusker you hit a pot of gold. . . ."

He gazes out over the fire toward the river.

"Let's say this. Maybe somewhere there's a herd as I know of but no one else. Maybe following that herd there's an old bull. Finished, thrown out, replaced by a younger. So I look at him and I think, Your time's up, old man. You got nothing left except wander and grow blind and go to the hyenas. And if I don't help you out some kaffir's going to find you . . ."

Maritz breaks off again. He doesn't finish, and he doesn't need to.

What he's said is a rationalization, a justification. We both know that. There's no point in arguing that by taking those lonely and doomed old bulls he's helping build the pressure on the breeding tuskers. The pressure is there relentlessly anyway.

"Christ, man!" he suddenly bursts out in anger. "They took this country from us and now they're burning it. We hunted, sure, but we hunted straight. We took what we needed and left the rest. Now they're coming in with repeaters—not rifles but heavy-penetration machine guns. I've followed spoor and seen elephant cut in half. Elephant that have taken a full magazine, maybe eighty armor-piercing bullets, in a few seconds. That's not hunting nor culling nor even poaching. That's wholesale butchery."

As well as anger there was pain and confusion in his voice. He has been trying to answer the unanswerable. Poaching has become an infection. Maritz has been contaminated by the carnage of the organized gangs. He cannot rid himself of the taint.

"There've been suggestions," I say, "of a conspiracy to exterminate all elephants so the ivory hoarders will be able to set their own price."

I wait for his comment. Maritz twists the biltong between his fingers. The dark, leathery meat is the same color as the skin on his hands.

"No need," he says finally. "Jumbo's dying of his own accord."

The shuttered look is back on his face, and the dog is whimpering. I know it is time to leave.

Maritz walks back with me along the bank. The moon is high now, and the grass bright with dew. The baboon packs are silent. They have settled at rest in the branches. But on every side I can still feel the unseen presence of the elephant herds.

We stop twenty yards from our fire. Maritz stands for a moment frowning. He hasn't spoken since we left his camp. Now he glances up at me.

"Do I still take ivory?" He repeats the question I asked earlier. "You take a good look at the bush in the morning. You reckon you're seeing jumbo? Man, you're wrong. Jumbo's gone. There's no more elephant left in Africa. Only ghosts. Ghosts, that's all I take."

He turns and disappears as silently as the great moving shadows between the clumps of acacia.

Ten miles east of the camp, just inside the reserve on the Chobe's bank, was a modern brick-built game lodge. For forty-eight hours, six years earlier, the lodge had briefly made Botswana and the Kalahari the focus of the world's attention. It was there, among the Chobe elephants, that Miss Elizabeth Taylor married Mr. Richard Burton for the second time. In gratitude for the Tswana people's kindness to them both, a radiant Miss Taylor announced to the world's press that she was giving the country a hospital. Even now the Tswana remain quietly confident that she will return one day and fulfill her promise.

After their brief moment of fame, the lodge, the country and the plateau returned to obscurity. The lodge had been constructed to cater to visitors from Zimbabwe, but the civil war had proved catastrophic for the expected tourist trade. The sinking of the Kazengula ferry the week before was only the final nail in the coffin of a long-doomed enterprise.

When we drove up there on our last afternoon, the place was shuttered and deserted. We walked around and found a little general store close to the lodge that was still open. The European owner, an acquaintance of Syd's, had the lodge's keys. An hour later, we were heading back upriver in a small open launch that had been transported there for the use of visitors.

It was midafternoon. The air was utterly still, and the heat reflected from the water was even fiercer and more arid than on land. On our left was the winding tree-lined bank. On our right, the flooded plain stretching out into the haze on the horizon. The light beat down oppressively from above in a harsh, sterile glare. It sucked out tone and texture and color until the entire landscape was reduced to a series of gray metallic images.

The spits of sand that ran out into the water were gray. The clustering trees above them were gray. The river whirls and ripples, the floating clumps of grass, the branches raised above the submerged trunks and the dead leaves hanging from them—all were the same hot, barren gray of a smoking gun barrel.

We sat limp and sweating on the launch's duckboards. The only creatures that moved as we passed were fish eagles. There was a pair to every hundred yards of the bank. Once long ago, the boat had traveled the same way with visitors from the lodge. To entertain them the boatman used to bring a supply of dead fish which he'd toss into the water as the launch went by the eagles' perches. The eagles would swoop down and scoop the fish from the river by the boat's gunwales.

Every time we passed a perch, the birds launched themselves into the air and circled over us, waiting for the remembered gleam of silver and a splash on the surface. Often they followed the boat into the territory of a neighboring pair, where they'd be driven away by screams and diving attacks. Then the next couple would take up positions above us. All were disappointed. We had no fish. We moved on up the river trailing a chorus of puzzled and plaintive mews in our wake. Even the eagles were gray.

Once the boatman spotted something on the bank. Pointing, he angled the launch in toward it. I followed the direction of his outstretched arm and saw a mound of darkness at the river's edge in the shadow of a tree. We came closer. Fifteen yards from the shore he cut the launch's engine. As we drifted nearer still, the shape in the shadow acquired bulk and form and resolution. It was a huge solitary buffalo asleep in the heat.

Ten yards away, something in the buffalo's brain registered our presence. What happened then happened faster than anything I had ever experienced. One instant the boat was moving silently toward the shore. The next, the sleeping black mound exploded. Without warning, without opening its eyes to examine us, the buffalo surged to its feet and charged.

There was perhaps two yards of sand between where it was lying and the river. It lunged, hit the water with a detonation like a high-velocity rifle shot and drove forward. Spray soared upward like breaking surf. Waves thrust in front of the animal's plunging chest hammered against the boat and almost overturned it. Horns slashed down past the planks, and the stench of animal mucus and undigested grass, sweet and wet and fetid, billowed into the air.

Then, halted by the water's resistance, the buffalo broke away as abruptly as it had charged. It swirled around in the shallows, galloped back up the bank and vanished into the bush.

We picked ourselves up from the bottom of the launch. The boatman smiled weakly and started the engine again. As he pulled the starter cord, I saw that his hands were trembling. He steered the launch out into the middle of the stream and we went on.

An hour later the sun began to dip. Within minutes the pervading grayness changed to a still metallic but now dark and menacing golden-green—as if the smoke had drifted away from the landscape and the gun-barrel steel below had been filmed with oil. A group of elephants came down to drink. An old cow waded out toward us. Her wrinkled hide was wet and glossy, and water dripped from her yellow tusks.

On the sand beyond, a basking crocodile lifted itself and moved down to the river. In the trees above, cormorants were hanging out their wings to dry, holding them spread open like black tents around their bodies so that the water droplets in the tiny feather pouches which act as ballast when they dive could evaporate in the late sun. And then in a wedge of dry reeds I saw an iguana lift its head, gaze slowly around and waddle forward.

I looked at them all. In the gleaming golden-green light of the afternoon I was seeing the world unchanged as it had been millions of years ago. The grotesque armored shapes of the iguana and the crocodile, the silent mass of the elephants, the cormorants' angular predatory silhouettes—they belonged to creatures of prehistory. Nothing in the passage of the millennia had touched this northern rampart of the plateau. I was surrounded by the animals that had inhabited the riverine strip from the start. Tense, I watched for a long, black shadow which must have been here at the beginning of time too.

The sense of dislocation, of a time warp that had jolted the launch across the millions of generations, lasted only a few minutes. Then the angle of the light changed again. The overhead sun hadn't sucked out the colors and textures from the landscape. Pressing down on the river and shore like some vast weight, it had merely walled them in.

The sun angled away, the weight rolled back and instantly water and land were irradiated. Colors flooded out from every quarter. A stone-gray lily was drenched in lilac. A stiff, unmoving reed bed was turned to bending emerald. A gaunt tree was drowned in leaf-green and its branches sprayed with shining honey-bronze lichens. The river surface shattered. Instead of the gray hostility of a warrior's shield, it held flares and depths and transparent eddies where fish and dropped blossoms coiled.

On shore the animals began to call. An elephant trumpeted, a dog baboon growled, a nervous reedbuck barked anxiously. They could feel the cooling air and crisp, fresh sand beneath them. Responding, gaining in confidence like the animals as the deadening heat pressure lifted, the boatman increased the launch's speed. The bow lifted, and sparkling waves, bouncing fireflies among the foam, rippled out behind us.

It was almost dusk. The campfire shone like a beacon ahead. We turned and headed toward it. In our path was a group of trees. They were almost submerged by the flood; only their upper branches showed above the surface of the swollen river. In normal years the Chobe's banks provide a nesting site for a huge colony of one of Africa's most dazzling and graceful birds—the carmine bee-eater. That year we knew the birds would have deserted the river and tried to find a site for their nests elsewhere.

We circled the trees, and suddenly, as we passed, the branches flared with soaring fountains and rocket bursts of rose. The bee-eaters hadn't gone after all. They were still there waiting for the flood to subside. The birds thronged upward into the sunset. Their breasts were the color of the evening sky. They swept and tumbled round us, scarlet and crimson and vermilion. Then in a single climbing flock they vanished westward into the scarlet clouds.

Minutes later we bumped ashore at the landing place below the camp. The bank was crowded with drinking elephants. The boatman jumped into the water and shouted and clapped his hands to drive them away. He'd recovered from the charging buffalo, and he was laughing uproariously in the darkness.

# 7

WHENEVER SOMETHING goes wrong on a safari through the African bush, from a simple quarrel to a fatality—and the one can destroy an expedition as well as the other—the immediate cause is almost always a trivial accident or misunderstanding against a background of accumulated strain and fatigue. That day it almost happened to us. Yet the morning started well. By eleven, with the campsite cleared behind us and the supply truck on its way ahead, we'd reached the Ngoma gate.

Ngoma was nothing more than a bend in the Chobe River—or more accurately there, the Linyanti. Like every African river, the Chobe changes its name with each stretch of countryside it flows through. The gate was a wooden pole across the track with a little rondavel—a round, grass-roofed mud hut—beside it. Together they marked the western end of the riverine strip.

We stopped and got out. The morning was clear, crisp and sweet—a bright winter morning, chill in the shadow and warm in the sun. I walked up the track. Below the shelving riverbank an expanse of flooded plain spread out to the north. Across it ran the Ngoma bridge. The bridge was a low antelope-colored shaft of concrete and steel. On either side the water was veined by stands of quick green grass. Clouds of terns hunted the shallows.

The bridge was an artery to a South African military base in the

Caprivi Strip. Occasionally an armored vehicle rumbled over it. Through my binoculars I watched them both—the terns and the armored trucks. The terns were black-capped, with dazzling quivering white wings and bodies. They hung in the air, swooped and skittered away. The trucks were gray. Inside them the soldiers' helmets were as black as the birds' caps against the light.

Afterward I walked back to the Toyota. EBL was painting a baobab, a huge, twisted carcass of a tree looming over the rondavel. The foot soldiers were discussing life across a crate of Castle beer. Their voices were quiet, and from time to time they laughed. I lay down on the elephant-hoof-imprinted verge. White butterflies, white as the terns, lazily circled my head, and the sunlight was warm on my face.

I was at ease. The day was fresh and calm. In front of us was a swift one-hundred-and-fifty-mile run to Savuti. The road was graded and firm. There was no need even to leapfrog the supply truck. For once, time and scheduling were unimportant. I closed my eyes.

"Shit! I'm afraid we've got a problem."

The voice was Syd's. I sat up. He was standing above me. His face was clenched with frustration and uncertainty.

"It's George," he said. "I don't know what the hell's happened, but the bastard seems to have signed out for Maun."

Inside the Ngoma rondavel there was a register. Anyone passing through the gate was required to enter his next destination. On the fragile network of Kalahari roads it was a reasonable precaution. An entry didn't guarantee rescue in case of accident, but at least it gave a search party a date and direction reference.

Our destination was the Savuti channel. George had logged it as Maun. Maun was two hundred miles beyond Savuti. There were only two explanations. Either George had entered Maun out of habit—the village was a recognized staging post, while the camp at Savuti wasn't even recorded on the map; or, inexplicably, George had misunderstood his instructions and thought we were heading straight for the delta.

"I guess it's the first," Syd said, "but we can't risk it. If he's really got it wrong and he overshoots Savuti, we're screwed. We haven't got the gas to go on from the channel. We've got to catch him before he gets there."

We clambered into the Toyota. Syd gunned the engine and we

spun through the gate, past the startled face of the rondavel warden. Then we roared away south.

The run should have taken a leisurely eight hours. We did it in just over three. They were the worst three hours so far on the entire journey. The crispness of the morning air gave way to the torrid, scalding heat of midday. At speed, the graded track turned into a twisting, pitted obstacle course, corrugated with sand ridges and bands of rock.

Syd drove like a man possessed. In his mind he could see George vanishing forever into the heart of the delta with all our supplies, guns and gasoline. Behind him we clung grimly to the side struts. The truck careered, bucketed and plunged. Every few minutes it would strike a pothole or boulder, leap like a gazelle and then smash back onto the ground, sending the metal benches crashing against us.

The landscape rushed by in a juddering blur. It was impossible to talk, even to think. The sun beat unrelentingly through the open sides. Choking dust spewed up from the wheels. Bruised, sweating and shaking, we could only grip the supports and wait numbly for the journey to end.

It ended at three. By then the expression on Syd's face was haunted and fanatical. At the speed we'd been traveling, we should have caught up with George miles back. There was no sign of him —only the supply truck's spoor stretching out tantalizingly ahead. We surged through a ford in the Savuti channel and swung right to check the site Syd had chosen for camp before we raced on.

There, in an open space ringed by acacia scrub, George was placidly building a fire. The supply truck was parked carefully in shade behind him. Elvis and Mtimba were laying out the sleeping bags. The camp was almost ready.

"Why did you put down Maun, you bastard?" Syd shouted.

"Only place I can spell, *Morena,*" George answered.

He chuckled and put a flame to the heaped logs.

Syd said nothing. With an immense effort of will he controlled himself. He climbed stiffly down from the wheel, rubbed the crust of dust and sweat from his forehead, and walked around to the icebox in the back of the Toyota.

The icebox was Syd's pride and delight, his talisman, the one supreme and irreplaceable luxury he allowed himself on safari. He tended it like a capricious and demanding mistress, lavishing endless care on its leads and thermostat and power supply. A lifetime in the bush had taught him the crucial difference at a moment of crisis after hours of dehydrating exhaustion between a cup of warm muddied froth and a chill frosted bottle.

It was a moment of crisis now. Syd lifted the lid. Inside, the cans of Castle steamed in a puddle of scum. The icebox had been damaged on the run from Ngoma.

David peered over his shoulder. "Buggered I'd say, old bean," he commented helpfully.

Syd still didn't speak. He went over to the supply truck. Carried away by the sheer esthetic beauty of producing ice in the desert, Syd had fitted the second vehicle with an icebox too. He raised the lid again. Sparks flared from the power connection, water hissed and bubbled, and a stench of rotting fruit drifted up into the air.

David had followed him. He rocked back at the smell and wrinkled his nostrils.

"I stand corrected," David said. "Our one is merely shafted. This is truly and movingly buggered."

Syd leaned against the truck and swore.

The rest of us slept through what remained of the afternoon. Not Syd. He sat up obsessively tinkering with the mechanisms of the two iceboxes. At dusk, when he was forced to stop, both were still not functioning. He washed the grease from his hands and wearily joined us by the fire.

We were all dazed and aching from the hammering run from Ngoma gate. Before that there had been three days of the constant oppressive presence of the riverine elephant herds. They'd patrolled the camp at dawn and evening, charged the truck in furious trumpeting stampedes whenever we ventured into the bush, lurked always in silent menacing groups in the mopane that surrounded us.

Fatigue, dehydration and the remembered elephants. Those were what preoccupied us as we sat in silence over the flames that night. Syd had experienced them all. He also had the bitter recollection of another wasted day and the loss of his beloved iceboxes. Uncharacteristically, he reached for the whisky bottle. He filled half a tumbler and drained it.

"This is what we'll do tomorrow," he said.

He spelled out his plans for the morning. I listened until he'd finished. It wasn't what I'd had in mind.

"No, Syd," I said. "We'll start down the channel and work south."

I explained what I wanted. Syd glowered at me and shook his head.

"I know Savuti," he insisted. "We'll do it my way."

"I've just told you how we'll do it. . . ."

The argument raged pointlessly for half an hour. Finally I stood up. I told him to take the foot soldiers on the early run and said we'd discuss the rest of the day after breakfast. Then I dropped exhausted into my sleeping bag.

For a change, Bobby was the first up. I woke blearily to find him shaking my shoulder.

"Not coming up to the front this morning, Colonel?" he inquired.

Syd was standing behind him. He looked stubborn and resentful. Somewhere out of sight David was stamping around cursing.

"You're on your own," I said. "I want a reconnaissance and full report."

I pulled the sleeping-bag hood over my head. Moments later I heard the Toyota pull away.

The party returned at nine. Bobby briefed me on what they'd seen. Afterward we had breakfast. We ate in silence. When we'd finished, I beckoned to Syd and walked down with him to the channel.

We squatted on our haunches facing each other by the water. The sun was lifting, but the air was still cool. Upstream a solitary elephant, a young bull, shouldered his way silently through the bush, inspected us calmly and lowered his trunk to drink.

I gazed at Syd. As a young man he'd fought in the Second World War as a tail gunner—an "arse-end Charlie" in his contemptuous but proud description. Pride to Syd is almost everything. He has much to be proud of. He is brave, resourceful, resilient and learned. Here in the Kalahari he can demonstrate all the hard-won skills he has acquired across the years. He is at home.

Yet his face is clouded and angry. The sequence of tiny irritations, from George's entry in the Ngoma register to the failure of the iceboxes, has built up like an overload on an unfused circuit and burst into flame. What's been burned is Syd's pride. He tried to repair it by asserting himself with me and was rebuffed. I feel for him deeply. His authority has been called into question on his own hearth. But a moment of reckoning has come—and the reckoning can only be mine.

"Syd," I said, "you know the desert better than I ever will. You know the pans and Chobe and Savuti and the delta. You know Maun and Ngami and your great clean country to the south. You know it all. I accept that. But this time we're going to travel as I choose, along the tracks I pick, across the country I decide. . . ."

I stopped. I was going to add: because if not, I would take the expedition straight to Maun, disband the safari and continue without him. There was no need. Syd knew what I was thinking.

He broke off a grass stem and shredded it between his teeth.

"We'll do it your way," he said finally. "I just wish to God we weren't making the run south. Would you compromise and change that? We could do it another time, another year. If you push on like this, you're just going to break everyone to no purpose."

I picked a frond of grass and chewed it too. The issue of how we traveled had been conceded without a fight, but suddenly the ground had changed. Syd had voiced the reservation he'd harbored from the start. The route was too long and difficult. Logically we should break the journey at Maun and then wind our way slowly back to Gab's from there, missing the great swing through Ngamiland, Ghanzi and the southern desert.

Briefly it was a tempting thought. The pressure would come off the safari. Syd could restock and repair the trucks at his leisure. EBL would have more time to paint, the foot soldiers to drink, laugh and read, I to watch and listen and write.

And then another time, another year, we could return and make the southern crossing. Another time, another year. How many more years were there left for the stone citadel? Fifty yards away, the young bull elephant had finished drinking. He snorted contentedly and paced off into the bush.

"There's no more elephants," Maritz had said. "Only ghosts."

I looked back at Syd. "I'm sorry," I said. "We're going on."

Syd stared unhappily at the water. Then he shrugged, stood up and walked back to camp.

The Savuti channel is a waterway running southeast from the Chobe River down the tilt of the plateau into a huge oval basin called the Mababe depression. Once it was a great lake, flooded in this century; now the depression's floor is covered with grass plain and trees. The flow of water down the channel is intermittent. For years it was totally blocked, and the plain dried out. Then one winter the channel opened again and the Chobe overspill pushed through—spreading out across the depression not as a lake but as a marsh. The original lake covered the entire bowl; the new marsh, only a fraction of its surface. Yet it still held water, and for the animals that was all that mattered. The game returned.

The areas surrounding our camps had each been "dominated" by animals adapted to the successively changing conditions, the different habitats along the route. At Boteti they were springbok and gemsbok, true desert creatures able to survive almost indefinitely without water. On the pans there were the migrant clouds of flamingos. Along the Chobe's bank the elephant herds held sway. Here at Savuti the community was mixed. In the days that followed we traveled among it.

There were elephants again, but no longer the thronging, tightly packed groups of cows with calves. Instead, young bulls scattered grazing across the plain or standing alone at rest in the tree shadows. They too charged often, but their charges were more tentative and less angry than the Chobe cows'—a testing-out of their growing strength in preparation for the day when they'd dispute the herds' supremacy with the aging seed bulls.

Then there were herds of impala, swift and fragile and slender, the same glowing chestnut-gold as the springbok but smaller and more graceful still. The does were marshaled in harems fifteen to twenty strong by a single breeding ram. Around them circled patrolling groups of immature males. Occasionally, with the guarding ram's attention distracted, the young males would race forward and attempt to nuzzle the does. Then the ram would notice them, whirl round aggressively, and they would gallop away again.

Like an elaborate game played out by every harem, its ram and the satellite herd of males, the ritual of challenge and chase was repeated again and again from dawn to dusk across the plain. It swirled not only among the bull elephants but around zebras, wildebeests, sable antelope, slow-pacing giraffes and wandering tsessebes—strange, ungainly creatures with the faces of puzzled cattle and the dusty-violet hides of the desert gemsbok.

Wherever wildebeests, zebras and antelope congregate, so inevitably do the predators. The presence of lions had been with us from the start. Within an hour of landing at the Tsoe airstrip we had come across the first kill. Rising next morning, I had found the print of pads in the sand a few yards from Bobby's sleeping bag. During the night a large male had walked into the camp, examined him and turned away. Afterward we heard their roars every evening. Once, on the Chobe's bank, we had glimpsed a group of three, a lion and two sleek lionesses, against the setting sun. They had examined us and moved off into the night.

On the Savuti plain we saw them clear and close for the first time. We were pushing through thick bush when Syd's head jerked up and his eyes narrowed. A tiny black shape had whirred past the open window. It was a dung beetle. To a hunter a dung beetle's urgent flight means that an animal has dropped fresh excrement only moments before somewhere just ahead. We were beyond the territory of the elephants, bucks would have scatted in front of our approach; only lions in the midday heat would have chosen to ignore us. We drove slowly on. Then we stopped.

There were five of them. A lioness, two cubs, an old black-maned male and a younger lion. The first four broke from cover as we reached them. They cantered away disturbed and rumbling and irritable, pausing at intervals to snarl back at us. The younger male didn't move. He lay quite still in a half-shadowed nest of winter-dry thorn and grass. His eyes, hooded, sleepy and remote, were pale as the desert sand. Like the bush, they were colored agate.

As I watched, the eyes filmed and focused and then filmed over again. The lion was alternately registering and losing something. We were totally excluded. A trawl net had been drawn over its brain. We had been sifted through the meshes and discarded. Somewhere far beyond us the animal was seeing or remembering another silhouette against the horizon.

After a while it stood up and padded forward. As it passed us, so close in presence I could have touched it, so distant in concentration it might have been treading another planet, the bush seemed to move with the lion. I thought again of the Boteti's rose-red zebras and stone-colored jackals. Once more an animal had taken on the tones and texture of the plateau, the two blending in such a fusion that each was inseparable from the other.

Thorn and talon and grass and hide traveled by like the passage of desert wind. For an instant the agate eyes, still distant and impenetrable, monitored my face. Then they and the animal were gone. All that was left was bending stems and briefly on the air, as fugitive as the aftertaste of wine, the scent of blood. The pride had killed that morning.

We drove on. The kill was a wildebeest. Spiraling vultures—the soaring birds of life riding the Mababe's thermals—signaled its location. As we approached, hyenas and jackals broke away, and a flock of marabou storks climbed laboriously upward. Like the vultures, they were all links in the life pattern of the Mababe plain. The lions killed and fed. The hyenas cracked open the carcass. The jackals scoured it. The marabou trimmed and cleaned. The vultures tidied up behind.

What the vultures couldn't reach, the flies and insects stripped—leaving at last a white bone-scatter on the sand. Even then the sequence hadn't finished. The hyenas returned, broke down and digested the dry bones—sucking the trapped marrow, the iron and protein and vitamins that remained. I had picked up hyena droppings near each of our camps. They were as pale and hard as the bones from which they'd been converted. They smelled not of excrement but of wild thyme—clean and sweet and fresh.

Turning back, we headed for the marsh again. We reached it in the late afternoon and stopped. An hour afterward, as the light began to fade, a small wind rose. There are few smells anywhere in the Kalahari. The cleansing sun scorches out and destroys almost any scent as soon as it begins to form. The blood from the lion kill and the lingering trace of thyme in the hyena droppings were rare exceptions. Now there was another, and again it was herbal.

Rolling over us on the wind were waves of freshly cut sagebrush. We stood up. The surrounding bush was thick and tall. Moments afterward, there was a rumble from the south like far-off Atlantic breakers pounding a rocky headland. The sound came closer, a moving wall of dust enveloped us and suddenly on either side columns of buffalo were galloping by.

There were animals of every size, from huge old bulls to young calves, all pressing toward the marsh water. Canopied by dust in the gathering darkness, they blended into two unbroken black streams. For five minutes they surrounded us. Then a last group of bulls passed, the rumble faded and the herd vanished. It was impossible to estimate how many there'd been, but in some years at least six thousand buffalo drank from the Savuti marsh every evening.

---

The fresh sharp scent of the trampled sage stayed with us all the way back to the channel.

As we drove alongside it, I looked down at the water. The depth varied from a few inches to perhaps five feet, and the width from ten to twenty yards. The flow would be greater at certain times of the year, but even when the water was running at its strongest the channel still seemed an absurdly narrow and fragile lifeline for what it supplied. On Savuti water depended almost every animal in the entire Mababe depression—an area of some three thousand square miles. If the water failed, the herds of antelope, buffalo, zebras and wildebeests would collapse. As they vanished, so would the elephants which seeded the plain and the predators that cropped it—and once more the entire life chain would unravel, down to the last dung beetle.

The channel had silted up naturally before. The process had taken years, and the game populations had at least had time to adjust. Looking at the waterway now, I remembered childhood holidays in Scotland when I had devoted my days to damming the moorland burns. I was never much of an engineer, but diverting Savuti's water wouldn't have been beyond me even then.

On the stone plateau there are considerably more sophisticated engineers than a small boy on a Hebridean island.

As we drove toward camp, we passed some fresh tire spoor on the sand. A few minutes later, we rounded an acacia bush and stopped.

A guy rope was stretched across the track in front of us. Beyond it, a large burly man with the belly of a Welsh darts professional was erecting a tent with the assistance of some Tswana camp hands. Syd climbed out.

"You fat slob!" he shouted.

"You drunken bastard!" the man bellowed back.

"Get out of my way or I'll run you down!"

"Come any closer and I'll knock your nut off!"

"You son of a bitch!"

"You great arsehole!"

After the ritual exchange of civilities between two old friends meeting unexpectedly in the desert, Syd greeted the man beaming and introduced him. He was Ted Morgan, and he was taking two South African engineers up to Kazengula.

I invited the three of them for a drink at our fire after supper. They arrived on foot at eight, from their camp half a mile downchannel.

"I want you to meet Hendrik and Dawie," Morgan said.

Hendrik was about fifty, thickset and powerful, with a granite-colored face and cropped graying hair. Dawie was darker, thinner and smaller. Both were intelligent, articulate men who laughed easily and often, but Hendrik was unmistakably the leader and spokesman.

We sat down with cans of beer and talked about South Africa. It's impossible to talk about South Africa without discussing apartheid. I asked Hendrik.

"I'll tell you a story, man," he said. "We've got a bloke in the office in Jo'burg. Colored boy. He's bright—shit, he's bright, man. Hardworking, conscientious, keen as hell. This year we had a vacancy in the admin section. I appointed him to fill it. Never happened before. Always white until then. But this boy was worth it on merit. Only as he's colored, I have to submit a report. . . ."

Under South African race laws there must be separate toilet facilities for white and black. An inspector was sent to Hendrik's office to see that the law had been complied with.

"I take him to the toilets," Hendrik said. "Damn great room with urinals and all. I say, 'Here at the end I'm going to build a partition to shut him off.' The inspector says, 'That's excellent, man.' Then I say, 'Look, it's a high room. For what do we waste good taxpayer's rand in taking the partition up to the ceiling? Why don't we cut it off here seven feet from the floor?' The inspector thinks. Then he says, 'Fair enough, man.' So we lose the top two meters. . . ."

Hendrik opened another can of beer. Like Morgan, he had a great beer drinker's belly. He balanced the can on it.

"Then I say, 'Listen. We're living in a siege economy, man. This colored boy's whanger, it doesn't reach to the floor. Why don't we start the partition knee-height?' The inspector thinks again. Then he says, 'You've got a point, man.' So we strike off another meter. Remember, Dawie?"

Dawie nodded, chuckling.

"Well, I go on. Slowly I whittle away at this guy. Know what we end up with? A goddamn string across the room, that's what! I put up the string. On the way out, the inspector accidentally knocks it down. He's so embarrassed he doesn't know what to say. He just laughs and leaves."

Hendrik shook with laughter. Then, abruptly, he stopped. He picked up a dry acacia pod from the ground. The pod was large and gray and hollow.

"There is no apartheid, man. Sure, the Church, the *verkrampte*, will go on fighting for it. But they've lost already. It's gone. All that's left is a shell. . . ."

He crushed the pod between his fingers, and the broken flakes spiraled down.

"Listen, Dawie and I belong to the same political party—right? . . ."

Dawie nodded again.

"Can you guess which?"

I looked at the two faces. One rugged and pale, the other lean and dark. Both strong, challenging and obdurate, with the grim features of classic pioneering Boers. They were certainly not liberals, Hendrik and Dawie. They could only be members of the National Party, the stubborn rearguard defender of white supremacy.

I say so, and I am right.

"And for why?" Hendrik asked. "Not for apartheid. No. But for good, sound financial policies, good policies for South Africa. We'll never give the country to the blacks. But we need them and they need us. So together we'll share it."

"We've got no choice," Dawie agreed. "And it's going to happen soon."

For a moment I said nothing. There in the Kalahari darkness I had heard, from these two staunch nationalists, the most terrible of all heresies—that apartheid was dead, that South Africa could be shared by white and black. I believed them, too. They were nationalists and conservatives. They were also pragmatists.

They knew their economy couldn't continue to expand without creating purchasing power for the blacks. That meant education and jobs. Education and jobs in turn meant freedom. Freedom meant sharing in the Republic's riches. It wasn't a question of sudden moral enlightenment, of belated repugnance toward the vicious and death-driven philosophy of the Reformed Church.

Something much simpler was at issue. Self-interest. Their standards of living were at hazard. The threat was so great it could be turned aside only by a traumatic and radical break with their country's entire past. They accepted the trauma, the magnitude of the rupture. As tough, hardheaded businessmen, they had, in Dawie's words, no choice.

Yet how far in personal terms, I wondered, did their acceptance go?

I asked the oldest, the most simplistic of all racial questions. Sometimes, as over lonely desert campfires at night, the answers to the old and simple questions reveal more than anything agreed by consensus in the spotlit forums of public debate.

"Would you allow—" I started.

"My daughter to marry a black?" Hendrik finished the question for me, chuckling. "Hey, why don't you stick to the sophisticated intellectual issues like economics, man? Why do you have to go for the gut? . . ."

He paused. "It won't happen in my time. Not on color, but on culture. For my grandchildren maybe. I don't know. But not yet."

"But if it did," I said, "what then?"

Hendrik was silent for a long time. When he finally answered, he spoke very quietly.

"If it happened," he said, "I would accept it. My daughter and her husband would go to prison. That I would not accept. I would go to the prison too. I would hammer on the doors and say, 'What you've got inside is the future—our future. It's come sooner than we thought, but you can't lock up the future. So let them out. If you don't, they will burn it to the ground. And I will throw matches over the walls to help them start the fire.' That is what I'd do. . . ."

He paused again. "And I would not go there alone, would I, man?"

Dawie shook his head. "Shit, man, you'd have an army with you."

There was another silence. A tense, awkward silence. I glanced from one to the other.

South African whites—and the middle-aged conservative nationalists are the worst—are violent, mindless and incorrigible bigots with incurable tunnel vision and the greed of Midas. All the liberal Western world knows that as a scientific certainty. And here once more were these two, archetypes of their race, not only turning that certainty on its head with Copernican perverseness—but offering to bring flame and an army to wage a crusade in support of their blasphemy.

"I find this rather jolly." I heard Big David's comment at the Boteti River again. "Are you sure you've read your maps right, Colonel?"

Then Dawie added, "If you're going to let him go for the gut, Hendrik, for Christ's sake why do you give him such a damn great target?"

Everyone laughed. Hendrik lifted the beer can from his belly and drained it. The tension had gone. For that evening South Africa and its future had been stamped, sealed and put away.

"So what brings you to the Kalahari, gentlemen?" I asked.

"I can tell you," Morgan interjected. "These two bastards are here to bugger up the bush."

"Bugger it up? Hell, man!" Hendrik protested. "We're just simple engineers. We're here to take a look at the roads and maybe come up with a few ideas for government. . . ."

Hendrik and Dawie might have been many things. Simple engineers looking at the desert tracks under the escort of a man like Morgan they were undoubtedly not. I remembered the fenced diamond mine at Orapa. The bulldozers at Kazengula turning a brushed earth strip into a modest-sized airfield. The geologists at the bar of the Holiday Inn listing the mineral treasure below the Kalahari sand.

I thought of questioning them further, but knew it would be pointless. A man might bare his soul over a desert fire. To professionals like these, there were more important matters than souls. Industrial and military secrets ranked high among them.

We talked for a while longer. Then they left. Syd and I accompanied them halfway to their camp. Syd walked ahead with Morgan and Hendrik, I behind with Dawie.

"This is one hell of a fine country," Dawie said.

He stopped and looked out over the plain. Under the starlight the bending grass was silent and silver-white. An owl called, and distantly up the channel I could hear a pack of wild dogs hunting the shallows.

"Will you share it with the blacks too?" I asked.

"Sure, man, all of it. You just give us a few years and see what we can do." He paused and smiled. "Hell, you really mean are we going to bugger it up? We'll try to leave you a few patches."

He laughed. Then he joined Morgan and Hendrik, and the three disappeared into the darkness. I walked back with Syd.

"What's that?" Syd asked.

I'd been muttering under my breath. I wanted to send a shout of encouragement to the Kalahari ringing through the night: "Don't worry, old stone citadel, you're going to be shared. And because they're sane and honorable men, they're going to leave a few patches."

Something to stop the owl cries and break the silence of the silver plain. But the desert was listening to its own sounds—not mine. "Bastards," I said.

Syd glanced at me surprised. "Shit, Colonel, they're good, regular guys, all three of them—"

"No, Syd," I interrupted him. "You've got me wrong. I meant it would have been easier if they had been bastards."

Syd frowned. But I was right. They should have been bastards and they weren't. They were decent, sane and honorable men. That made it worse. Except that in the end, of course, it made no difference either way.

We warmed ourselves by the flames, and the owls kept calling. But I listened in vain for that singular cough. I went to sleep with the scent of buffalo-trampled sage in my nostrils, and the memory of the small boy damming a Highland burn.

Early next morning, George, as always, brought me a scalding mug of tea. We were moving on from the channel southward to Maun. There we'd make a halt for a few days. It would be a welcome respite. The worst of the journey still lay ahead, on the sweep south again across the desert from Maun.

After the flare-up three nights earlier, Syd and I have made our peace. He still wishes that we'd take the alternative route back over the plateau, and his arguments are sound. But he has accepted that I'm committed to the long trek down the Road of Death, and he will do all he can. I have no more worries about him. Nor about Big David.

"Beans, beer and pachyderms," David remarked happily on the Chobe after a furious cow elephant had pursued us screaming in rage for half a mile. "My idea of Paradise." The elephant herds are behind us. He still has his beer and his lunchtime beans—and the mention of the Road of Death sets his nostrils twitching in anticipation. He is confident it will be another deeply moving experience.

It leaves me with EBL and Bobby. Sipping my tea, I glance at EBL. It is not yet 5:30 A.M., and she has been out of her sleeping bag ten minutes. The air is still gray and chill. Yet she is already at work, hunched on her stool with a sketchbook open on her knees, frowning concentration on her face. She will continue working almost without interruption for the thirteen hours of daylight that lie ahead.

She travels beside Syd in the front of the lead truck, her eyes constantly scanning the landscape. Whenever she sees an image she wants to record—a dew-hung spiderweb, a twisted baobab, the flare of a crimson-breasted shrike in a barrier of thorn—she taps his arm, and the truck stops. Before Syd has cut the engine the book will be propped in front of her and the paintbrush dipping in the water jar taped to the instrument panel.

"The dark fringe to the white stomach bar . . ."

Ten days earlier. She is painting a young springbok doe held motionless by fear and curiosity in a coil of dust on the Savuti plain. She has studied the animal through her binoculars. Now, as the brush flickers over the paper, she wants Syd to check the details of its coloration.

". . . does it stop at the haunch or run down to the knee joint?"

Syd has hunted springbok for half a century. He has watched millions, killed or guided other hunters to the kill of thousands, skinned and tanned the hides of more than he can remember. He doesn't need to check a coloration detail with his glasses. He already knows. He opens his mouth to tell her—and suddenly he stops. He doesn't know the answer, and he shakes his head in disbelief. He would have staked his life that on springbok he was faultless. But the probing painter's eye has snared an element in the creature's physical presence he has never even considered. Syd lifts his own binoculars, peers through the heat haze and reads out the bars and colors and patterns.

For EBL the work, the visual record of the journey, is everything. It dominates her existence, insulating her from the sun, the dirt, the endless grinding hours of movement. It does not end with the onset of night. She paints until the last stray beams of light have gone. Then instantly she switches. The sketchbooks are tossed aside and out come the gatherings of the day's travel. The golden leaves and parchment grasses, the scarlet and amber berries shining like plunder from a child's jewelry casket, the white, bone-hard, bone-dry hyena droppings with their scent of thyme, the broken flight feathers from a stooping eagle. All to be labeled, catalogued and stored by firelight. She labors until the rest of us are asleep, sifting and sorting the fragments that with her diaries, her swift sketches, her scrawled-on and annotated textbooks are what she will take away from the desert.

Syd finds her energy and dedication awesome. They are nonetheless qualities he can understand. What baffles him is her bawdiness, her laughter, her raunchy dialog with the foot soldiers. In southern Africa one does not talk dirty in the presence of ladies.

Syd will remain perplexed. EBL, unconcerned, will continue as before. I have no more doubts about how she will last the journey than I do about David.

In a different way the same applies to Bobby. If Bobby were Chinese he would be described as inscrutable. He speaks seldom, sleeps long and deeply, regards the world through lazy, unexpressive eyes. It is easy—and unwise—to underestimate him. A week ago, at the Makgadikgadi pans, Syd asked innocently if he would care to shoot a brace of guinea fowl for the next evening's supper.

Pursuing desert guinea fowl on foot with a shotgun is one of the most difficult and frustrating activities the Kalahari has to offer a hunter. The apparently languid birds are fast, cunning, evasive and as hard to drop as a twisting woodcock. Bobby picked up the gun and ambled away. Syd, who had been told of his exploits among the Scottish red deer, chuckled.

Half an hour later Bobby sauntered back into camp. He tossed George a pair of plump birds and returned the shotgun to Syd. "As we seem a bit low on ammunition," he said, "I thought it sensible to use only one cartridge."

He sat down and picked up his book. Syd gazed at him dumbfounded. Then he examined the gun. Only the right chamber had been fired. Afterward, without chuckling, Syd passed him the gun whenever we found ourselves short of meat.

Whatever Bobby felt about the plateau—unlike David, with his sardonic chuckles and caustic commentary, Bobby kept his reactions to himself—there were his books to retire to. Bobby read with a voracity and a concentration I had never seen in anyone before. Perhaps he had been starved of reading matter in the Amazon jungles and had been compensating ever since. He could read anywhere—in the dawn light before breakfast, at rest stops in the midday heat, in the back of the jolting truck, by star or fire glow after supper. He even managed to read throughout the hammering run from the Chobe to the Savuti channel.

Big David brought a cellar with him as essential equipment for the journey. Bobby brought a library. It consisted principally of nineteenth-century French novels and treatises on Scottish ecclesiastical history. His dreams, I imagine, interwove Zola heroines, brimstone sermons in Edinburgh dialect and the night roars of Kalahari lions. Whatever the blend, Bobby seemed to be thriving on it. Provided the books held out, he would be content to the end too.

# 8

"MAUN, YOU OLD BUGGER," Syd said. "You write down Johannesburg, Hong Kong or London and I'll tan your bloody hide."

George chuckled and drove off. An hour later we followed. In contrast with the run to Savuti, there were to be no disasters that day.

The track south from the channel was sandy but passable. We drove steadily all morning through mopane scrub and woodland. As at Chobe, the colors were bright green and buttercup-yellow, but there were no trampling elephant herds to layer the leaves with dust, and the bush glittered. Sometimes the scrub gave way to rolling grass meadows set with clumps of trees. At moments then we might have been traveling through the park of some great English country house in the heat of a far-off August day. The landscape had been painted by Turner and Stubbs. Only the distant roofs of Petworth or Longleat were missing.

In the early afternoon we came to a Tswana settlement and a tsetse fly control post. The tsetse areas were to the west of us, but we'd passed tracks leading into them as we headed south. Every truck using the road had to pass through the post in case it was carrying flies trapped in the cabin. We drove into a corrugated-iron shed and got out.

"Good morning," said an old Tswana.

He closed the doors behind us and picked up a hand-operated spray gun. Then he moved around the truck pumping at it in the darkness.

"One, two!" He chanted rhythmically.

Each chant was followed by three sedate pushes at the gun's rusting handle. When he'd finished, he put the gun down, opened the doors at the front and beckoned us out.

"Good morning," he said politely again.

As I climbed back into the Toyota I lifted the spray gun, shook it and sniffed at the nozzle. The little tank was empty and there was no trace of any chemical smell. Only rust.

We drove away. The old man had been there three years before. The spray had been empty then too. Perhaps the colonial officer who'd taught him how to use it had forgotten to replace the original drum of pesticide. I had no idea. I did know he was very proud of his chant.

"And a very good morning to you, old bean," Big David turned and called back as we left.

The old man thought for a moment. Then he smiled and shouted confidently, "One, two!"

He waved.

We rocked and bumped on through the mopane. Increasingly there were signs of cattle and people—dry dung pats in the sand; little clusters of rondavels; once a cantering horse, a glossy, well-muscled stallion that paced us in the roadside shadows. Occasional groups of children appeared. One group of small boys was guarding a pile of melons. As the truck passed they spun around, dropped their tattered shorts and derisively flashed their bottoms at us.

"Big white Bwana fancies little black bum," David said. "I remember once out East—"

"No time for reminiscence, Dave," I interrupted. "We're almost there."

The sunlit buttocks and the sunlit melons vanished. Five minutes later we drove into Maun.

According to an early African hunting guide, Maun is

> a lonely Kalahari outpost on the banks of the Thamalakhane river ideally situated for the game of both the delta waterways and the desert plains. The journey of approach, how-

ever, is notoriously arduous, dangerous and lengthy. The traveller is further warned there is nowhere to go beyond.

The description is no longer accurate: the track now continues north to the Chobe, and Maun has an airstrip; but the village still retains a feeling of remoteness and isolation. Like one of the strangely named stations on the London subway network or some distant Pacific island, Maun seems to mark the end of a line—the place where everyone gets out because there is nowhere to go beyond.

Originally a Yei settlement, by the late nineteenth century it had developed into a trading post and local administrative center. Today it has a fluctuating population of some one hundred whites and one thousand blacks. They support a post office, a little hospital and, with seasonal visitors, three lodges. They also support Riley's Bar, Riley's Garage and Riley's Store. Maun is dusty, sprawling, unplanned, gimcracked, windy and impermanent—a casual scatter of saloon, store and shelter at the meeting point of desert and delta. It also has the bite, wit, vitality, steel and laughter of a frontier stockade. For the end of the line Maun is a very fine place.

We had been traveling for three weeks. Now it was time for a halt. We set up camp in the grounds of Island River Lodge on the edge of the Thamalakhane. The lodge was owned by Tony and Yoey Graham. Tony was South African, stocky, tough and shrewd, a straight-shooting, hard-grafting former hunter, mercenary and much else. Yoey was a London lady from Kensington. She spoke with the high, clear voice of Kensington ladies, and like all her kind she was just as shrewd and strong and hardworking as her husband.

They made an excellent couple and they ran an excellent lodge. There were neat, clean rondavels, good plain food, cold and generously measured drinks in the bar above the river. They had sweated blood to build a success in the wilderness. They had won.

We settled in. For a while there would be no more jolting days of travel across sand and stone. Instead, briefly, we'd have the space and silence of the Okavango waters.

The inland delta of the Okavango basin is the second of the two great natural features that dominate the northern Kalahari. Covering some ten thousand square miles, it owes its presence on the stone plateau to the idiosyncrasies of the Okavango River flow.

Rivers, by convention, rise inland, flow to the sea and form their deltas on the coast. The Okavango's pattern is the reverse. It rises in the highlands of Angola not far from the Atlantic. Then, instead of winding down toward the ocean, the river pours eastward across southern Africa. One thousand miles from its source, almost in the middle of the continent, it suddenly spreads out in the shape of a huge funnel on the Kalahari. Maun lies at the center of the funnel's base.

South from Maun, what's left of the river drains away into Lake Ngami or down the Boteti to the Makgadikgadi pans and the vanished Lake Xau—now the boreholes of the Orapa diamond mine. But the true delta—the triangle of water and green resting like an immense oasis on the citadel's battlements—lies to the north of the village. Not all of it floods every year. The distant rains which feed the river, and which months later create the delta itself, are erratic and unpredictable.

Some years, if the Angolan fall is heavy enough, the whole Okavango basin fills, and the overspill floods both Ngami and the pans. In other years, and they can run in succession for decades, only the northern quarters of the delta are replenished. When that happens, Ngami becomes a dust bowl and the Makgadikgadi dries out in glistening bands of crusted salt. Every year the determining moment comes at the start of the Kalahari winter when the press of water reaches the funnel's mouth and begins to ripple out across the plateau.

In May that year, the southward pouring was still a month away from Maun. By unreliable report from the north, the fall had been heavy, and in due course the whole basin would be irrigated. That lay ahead. Meanwhile, we would fly up to the permanent lagoons at the delta's center before the coming rain-feed reached them.

It was midday before we took off from the Maun airstrip in a small Piper. Our destination was a tented lodge one hundred miles to the north. As on the afternoon we'd spent on the Chobe River, the sun was bearing down directly from above. From the air the ground below was obscured by thick heat haze, and the colors wavering up were pale and indistinct. Yet even through the blurred and grainy light the change on the plateau's surface was startling. Before there had been only barren sand and stone and thorn. Here there were endless streams, channels, oxbow lakes and long, gleaming expanses of grass plain, low islands and winding banks ridged with trees.

For an hour the faded patchwork unrolled beneath us, the lagoons gray, the earth a sun-bleached umber, the trees drab and misty. Then we banked and dropped down. We landed on a grass strip where the water level had already begun to rise. Little fans of spray lifted from the wheels as we bounced to a halt, and the ground rustled damply when we jumped down. There was a boat waiting for us in the nearby channel. Five minutes afterward, we stepped ashore at the Xugana Camp.

Like the forlorn lodge on the Chobe, the camp had been created for the Kalahari's few visitors—in this case for the clients of a safari company, who could rest and fish there when their hunting trip was finished. It had comfortable tents for sleeping, hot showers, a well-stocked bar and a fine eating area under the trees above the lagoon. It was also superbly run. In every way as a luxury retreat in the wilderness, the camp was peerless.

Yet it too was melancholy. A magnificent site had been chosen. Care and thought and imagination had been applied to its use. Every facility had been provided. All it lacked was people. The stone plateau was still too vast, daunting and remote. Only the rich and the bold came to the desert. By and large, the rich like company; the bold lack money. So the camp stood there, a private and empty realized dream at the delta's heart.

Xugana was managed by a young South African woman named Ursula Wilmot. She was tiny and trim, a little waiflike figure, with a pale face, piled dark hair and a long flowing skirt. In the middle of the Okavango she looked as incongruous as a crinolined young lady from a Victorian children's book. Inevitably she was also tough, resolute, experienced and competent. Living alone with the staff for months on end, she had made herself an excellent naturalist.

I wanted to stay at the camp and talk to her, but by chance the same day another pair of guests were expected there. Ursula's time was taken up preparing for their arrival. Instead, we took the boat and set off through the delta's waterways.

At ground level, just as on the Chobe when the light revolved, everything changed. The water, oily and leaden from the air, was clear and translucent—so clear that whatever the depth, every detail on the bottom, every sunken leaf and frond, was as crisp and vivid as if it had been on the surface. Unlike almost any other delta, the Okavango spreads out not on silt but on sand. By the time the streams have penetrated south, the last minute impurities have been filtered out.

The water that reaches the central lagoons has the absolute purity of blown Venetian crystal. The sand filters have even removed the invisible nutrients from it, so that few fish survive in the channels. What's left is a brilliant limpid flow colored gold and white and amethyst according to the light's fall and the composition of the channel banks. On the banks, their roots reaching deep beneath the surface, grow great stands of phragmites and wavering papyrus.

All that afternoon we traveled the lagoons and channels around the camp. For half an hour without break we'd press down some narrow stream walled in and shadowed by papyrus fronds and the long, slashing blades of delta reeds. Then we'd break out into an oxbow lake. Floating lilies, violet and saffron and rose, dazzled on the surface, and malachite kingfishers—sudden emerald-green flashes—arrowed through the air. The heat then was searing. Everything—water, reed and papyrus stem—hurled the light back in dizzying reflection against our faces.

The blinding glare lasted until we entered another papyrus tunnel. Sometimes we'd emerge to find an island nestling by a lagoon—a low whaleback hump covered with sparse winter grass and studded by clumps of trees. There would be the clamor of flighting egrets from the high branches, the grunt of unseen hippos and the plunging rush of a buffalo herd through the shallows. Afterward, silence and heat and the bending papyrus over the transparent drifting waters again.

In the late afternoon we returned to Xugana. The plane was due back at six to collect us. Ursula had settled in her guests, and I had just enough time to walk with her across the island on which the camp had been built. We strolled under the trees watching and discussing the birds that thronged the branches. EBL was perched on her stool by a pond in the shallows, her head bent over her sketchbook. Ursula moved on. As we approached a towering hardwood, something crashed down from above and into the bush on the far side.

Ursula stopped. I came up to her shoulder and stopped too. The birds were suddenly silent. I could hear water lapping against the reeds in the lagoon and the grass stirring in the evening wind. There was something else. The slow, quiet ripple of breath as a pair of lungs filled and emptied a few yards ahead of us. We waited. Then a furious bark rang out, the bush parted and an old dog baboon bounded away—almost trampling our feet.

Ursula turned to me and smiled with relief. "That happened right here a week ago. It was a leopard then."

"A black leopard?" I suggested, smiling back.

She shrugged. "It vanished so fast I don't know. I thought it had spots, but at dusk, how can you tell?"

We walked back to the bar to collect the foot soldiers. The Tswana barman was beaming with pleasure. I had no doubt they had doubled his annual takings in a single day.

The returning plane buzzed us to announce its arrival, and we left for the tiny, sodden airstrip. The pilot was in his mid-twenties, but he flew with the easy, practiced nonchalance of a delta veteran. Now that the haze had gone, the landscape beneath us was bright and clear. He took the Piper down low and we skimmed the lagoons at treetop level. On the grass plains between them, buffalo, elephants and bucks raced before us.

Once as the evening closed in we spotted a sitatunga ram standing in a cone of late sunlight at a stream's bend. The splayfooted, marsh-dwelling sitatungas are the rarest and most elusive of the delta's antelopes. We banked and came down over the ram again. The animal never moved. It stood there, antlers raised, frozen in a circle of glittering lilies with the light pouring away up the river behind it.

When Livingstone reached the edges of the delta there had been sitatungas on every waterway. They were so common they ranked among the favorite prey of leopards—perhaps the Kalahari black leopard. Livingstone was sent to the Kalahari on God's instructions. When the doctor finally reached Lake Ngami, he found possibly one of the largest and richest communities of wildlife that have ever existed. From horizon to horizon the plains rippled with moving antelope. Lions bounded across the backs of the herds, unable to touch ground without being crushed. Leopards hung drowsily from the trees above. Columns of elephants shouldered their way through to water. Hyenas, jackals, foxes, genets and honey badgers darted in hundreds of thousands between the pressing flanks. Over them all circled birds—flamingos, pelicans, swallows, bee-eaters, kingfishers, eagles, falcons and countless others—in such immense rainbow-colored concentrations that they darkened the morning sun.

As soon as he returned, Livingstone sent out word of his discovery. What he'd seen was one of the miracles of creation. It deserved to be admired and celebrated. But now that the road to the interior had been opened, the hunters and traders forced their way across the plateau to loot the reported treasure. The slaughter that followed was swifter, bloodier and more frenzied even than the massacre of the American bison. No one had dreamed game could exist in such awesome numbers. The land was a wildlife El Dorado, an inexhaustible cornucopia of hide, flesh, ivory. By night, campfires blazed far into the bush beyond Ngami. By day, smoke and dust hung above the desert. Always there were the stench of rotting meat and the crackle of gunfire on the Kalahari wind.

Some idea of the scale of the killing can be obtained from the records of the game-exporting companies that set up in business around the lake after Livingstone's expedition. At the height of the trade there were ten principal concerns. Among them, the average annual kill from 1865 on was 5,000 elephants, 3,000 lions, 3,000 leopards, 3,000 ostriches, 250,000 of the smaller fur-bearing animals and countless meat animals—certainly not fewer than 100,000 every year.

The slaughter was maintained at that level for ten years. In a single decade four million wild creatures were slain. The figure is difficult now to comprehend. It becomes almost unimaginable if one considers that the deaths were inflicted by relatively few men using slow and cumbersome weapons in an area restricted by the lack of water.

In 1875, for the first time, the annual total dropped. Within a few years it had plummeted. The reason was simple. The cornucopia was not, after all, inexhaustible. The wild could not sustain the carnage. It had been bled almost to death. There was a final orgy of shooting. Then the hunters and the traders departed. Ngami had nothing left worth the powder and shot. The animal multitudes had gone. Their tusks, skins and plumes had been converted into the raw material of human ornament and shipped overseas.

Ivory is durable. Fur and feather are not. The vast bulk of the cargo that the ships carried away was in effect dust, and soon it became so.

To the wild, the Ngami slaughter stands like Deir Yassin or Wounded Knee—an enduring symbol of greed, brutality and treachery. The numbers of the deaths were awesome. More leopards were killed each year of the carnage than exist in all Africa today. Yet the killings involved more than numbers. On the lakeside plains an entire world and an order were destroyed as the animals were scythed down.

On the rare occasions now when it's possible to see a gigantic wildlife concentration, the observer tends to watch it almost disbelieving. The sheer, dizzying magnitude of a migrant flock or herd is such that it seems it can only be an aberration. The wild is fecund and generous, but surely not as lavishly, recklessly prodigal as that. The assembly must be a random explosion of life without precedent. The congregation of creatures seems to be a freak of nature.

It is not a freak. It is the reverse—the wild functioning at its most logical, efficient and economical. It happened at Ngami little more than a century ago, when not one but hundreds of species of bird and animal were gathered in far vaster quantities round the lake. Every single individual in those teeming millions, from the smallest lark to the largest tusker, was there because the lake had the resources to support it.

There was not one lion, one jackal, one springhare, even one sparrow too few or too many. The populations had adjusted with slide-rule precision to each other and to their surroundings down to the yield of the last blade of grass, the last drop of water, the last unit of the Kalahari sun's energy. They utilized Ngami's resources and in return they maintained them. If the rains failed one year and the pastures shrank, the antelope herds contracted in compensation. As the herds contracted, so did the packs of predators and the scouring vulture flocks that followed them. The balancing effect traveled effortlessly up and down the food chains, so that the equilibrium never varied. The lake functioned like a huge pair of lungs, breathing in response to season, drought and flood but always pumping a strong, bright stream of life through the birds and animals that constituted its veins.

---

And then the hunters came. The animals were destroyed individually, and with them the order. It could never be re-created. By the time the guns left, cattle had started to move into the bush. Ngami's resources were no longer replenished every year, but progressively depleted until the change was irreversible. The veins had been leeched. Now the lungs emptied and collapsed. Both the wild and the place had gone.

The greed that wrought it all is patent. So too the brutality in the methods by which the destruction was carried out. To save ammunition, wounded animals were left to die of their own accord. They could be seen days after they'd been shot—starving, blinded, dragging shattered limbs in blood-spoored circles round the plain. That there are any animals left at all is due to a miracle called tsetse. For the wild, tsetse is a very old, very potent and very fine miracle. It has served admirably for millions of years to keep hunters away. If it hadn't been for the arrival in the Kalahari of another of God's creations, it might have lasted forever. There was, however, Carruthers.

He was waiting for me when I returned to camp, his Land-Rover parked beside the Toyota. As I walked toward the fire, he strutted across and held out his hand.

"Carruthers," he said confidently.

He was short and stocky, with sandy hair, a brick-red face and a majestic belly. His eyes were angry and unblinking, his voice a truculent bark and his boots immense. They enveloped his feet like barges, mahogany-colored, polished to brilliance, brass eyelets glittering.

I stared at him.

"Met before, old boy," he added. "Heard you were back. Thought I'd pass by and see the state of play."

Slowly it came back to me. He was a tsetse fly control officer based in Maun, and we'd been introduced three years ago. I hadn't caught his name then. Carruthers. It delighted me even more than his appearance.

"How about a chota-peg?" I suggested.

I wasn't altogether sure what a chota-peg was. I did know it was what men like Carruthers drank. He studied his watch and nodded.

"Sun just over the yardarm," he said. "Sound thinking. Whisky and splash for me."

I poured him a drink and we sat down. Carruthers began to talk. I gazed at him as he spoke.

He was the sort of man to bankrupt the practice of psychiatry. In a world tormented by identity problems, he had not the slightest doubt who he was. Carruthers was English. He believed devoutly in Her Majesty and, only slightly less, the Almighty. He believed too in the Marylebone Cricket Club, the House of Lords, the London *Times,* Rolls-Royce motorcars and roast beef.

"Home leave by July, then?" he said after asking my plans. "Lucky fellow! You'll catch Boycott opening against those Indian johnnies. Off the front foot they say he's the best since Compton."

He leaned forward, drove a ball hard through the covers of the bush and shook his head wistfully.

Carruthers hadn't been home for seventeen years. I could have said that in England *The Times* had been crippled for four months by a strike. That Rolls-Royce had gone bankrupt. And that beef, freeze-dried and steroid-tenderized, was being imported from Iceland.

I said nothing. To Carruthers any state-of-the-nation report would have been irrelevant. Home was a state of mind formed a generation before.

I asked, "How's the control program coming on?"

"Great strides," Carruthers said. "Great strides. This new Endosulphan compound's a corker. . . ."

He began to speak about his work. On his subject Carruthers was crisp, lucid and articulate. The choleric face masked a first-class mind.

Three years before, huge tracts of the delta and the surrounding plain had been infested by tsetse. Rather smaller than a housefly, iridescent black in color, utterly silent in flight, the tsetse has one most obvious characteristic: a bite like the sting of an enraged wasp. Travel through tsetse areas was invariably torment; even in the midday heat George preferred to wear a heavy woolen balaclava to protect his head from the jabs. But much more inhibiting than the constant stabbing pain was the threat of the disease tsetse transmits.

The fly is a carrier of trypanosomiasis, more commonly known as tryps or sleeping sickness. Harmless to the animals of the wild, tryps attacks man and domestic stock. In man for a long time it was fatal. There is still no prophylactic against the disease, but human infection can now be cured. For cattle it remains lethal.

The blacks and, after Livingstone, the whites who reached the delta gazed at the rich pastures of the Okavango with covetousness and bitterness. The ten thousand square miles of the inland basin were a pastoralist's El Dorado. There were permanent tree shade, year-round water, lush waist-high grass. And all of it, because of the presence of tsetse, was useless. The delta was a mirage, a death trap. To the animals, by contrast—the antelope, lion, leopard, elephant and buffalo—it was a sanctuary. The tiny flies protected it more efficiently and completely than the strongest enclosure the most dedicated conservationist could have devised.

Or so it seemed. Then in 1896 the sanctuary was violated. Rinderpest swept down from the north. A disease primarily associated with cattle, rinderpest is also deadly to all other cloven-hoofed animals. The cattle around the delta died in thousands; so did the wildlife inside.

As the antelope, buffalo and warthog populations were devastated, the predators began to vanish. Once again a ruinous ripple effect had been set in motion. This time the tsetse were a casualty too. They were nourished by the very animals they protected—the wildlife off whose blood they fed. When the wildlife disappeared the flies starved. Soon vast areas of the delta, plagued for thousands of years by the tsetse curse, were declared clean. They were clean, of course, of everything else as well.

When the rinderpest burned itself out, the citadel's herders acquired new stocks of cattle and exultantly invaded the long-defended pastures. Fortunately for the wild, a few remote pockets of tsetse and a few animals had survived the havoc. As the herders moved forward, the tsetse launched a counterattack. The engagement lasted fifty years. At the end, the flies controlled most of the delta again, the cattle had been expelled and the wildlife had re-established itself.

Yet the battle wasn't over—it had merely entered a new and more vicious phase. The cattlemen had had one tantalizing experience of the delta. Now they wanted it more than ever, and they wanted it permanently. Studying the enemy, they found that tsetse needed not only animals but a special habitat to survive, a two-tier structure of bush and tree cover. Destroy the habitat and the flies retreat.

Clearing stubborn Kalahari bush is arduous and time-consuming. Trees are a different matter. Trees can be felled by axe or destroyed even more simply by ring-barking. The settlers set to work with gusto. Mile upon mile of woodland was ringed. The trunks withered and died, the cover wasted away, and the tsetse and the game withdrew. Afterward, cattle were driven in.

By then the cleared areas resembled the saturation-bombed plains of Flanders or Vietnam. The ranchers weren't interested in the shattered trunks or the communities of birds, plants and animals that were dying with the tree cover. They were concerned only with whether defoliation worked. It did work—in the worst of all possible ways.

When an area was tsetse-free, cattle were brought in. Then the ranchers started clearing the next belt. The problem was that even ring-barking is a slow process. By the time a second area was clean the cattle had not only exhausted the pasture in the first: through overgrazing, they had destroyed it. The herds moved on, leaving behind land that was now useless both to man and to the wild. And so it continued. The number of cattle remained constant and the tracts of degradation widened. Slowly but systematically the delta was being gutted.

Then in the 1960s the first pesticides reached the Kalahari. Within ten years they were being applied to the delta from the air. Suddenly the besiegers had been given a Doomsday weapon.

"Made a few mistakes at first," Carruthers said. "Got to admit it. Using DDT and dieldrin wasn't too bright, although we weren't to know that at the time. But everything's changed now. The new systems are bang on. Ecologically sound and damn near a hundred percent effective. . . ."

The latest technique was to spray from low-flying aircraft by night. The pesticide was a highly concentrated compound, free of chlorinated hydrocarbons and carried on a gasoline base. It spread out in tiny ten- to thirty-micron droplets which were drawn to the ground by inverse night heat reaction. A flask of only three kilograms was enough to saturate a square mile—and kill by overspill up to five miles away.

"Well, you've seen the results," Carruthers added. "Take Moremi. Clean as a whistle. We've snuffed the little buggers right out."

"Any side effects?" I asked.

"None to speak of," he said. "Fish go on the tilt at certain dosages, but we keep it good and diluted to avoid that. Lovely stuff. Mother's milk almost—take it from me."

"What about the long-term consequences?"

"For the delta? Good God, man, I don't read the entrails. I'm not a bloody soothsayer," Carruthers snorted. "I'm just here to do a job. New bosses say get rid of Brother Tsetse. So I boot him up the arse and kick him offside. Afterwards it's up to those dusky lads in Gab's. . . ."

He paused. "They've declared Moremi a reserve, but you've got to remember this country *is* cattle. Not mining, not hunting, not industry, not agriculture, just cattle. That's all. Anything else can stop and life goes on. But when the cattle die the people die. *Finito!* Now, Johnny Tswana and Joe Bushman don't fancy that idea any more than you or I. So if their cattle start to topple and there's grass and water in Moremi, it'll be bugger the government, how's your father to the reserve, let's get at the pasture. . . ."

Carruthers' glass was empty. I refilled it and he nodded approvingly.

"That's what's going to happen," he continued. "Not that one can blame them. I mean we'd do exactly the same in their position. It isn't a question of color or anything like that. . . ."

Suddenly Carruthers stopped. His glass was midway to his mouth. He gazed at me fiercely over the rim.

"Never occurred to me before," he said, "but this fellow Boycott—not black by any chance, is he?"

For a moment I stared back at him in amazement. Then I shook my head.

"Not as far as I know," I said.

"Good for him." Carruthers relaxed. "Nothing against them, mind you. Lived alongside the blighters most of my life. Trouble is, nowadays you never know where they're going to pop out of the woodwork next. Running a country's one thing, but opening for England—well, not quite a choco's ticket, is it? Hope he stays that way."

"I'm sure he will."

I couldn't think of anything else to say. I wasn't personally acquainted with Mr. Boycott. From what I knew of other Yorkshiremen a color change seemed unlikely. Perhaps Carruthers meant something else.

Before I could find out, Carruthers finished his whisky and stood up.

"Time to make tracks," he announced. "Little woman waiting and all that. Nice to have had a chat about home. Drop by and see us again soon."

I promised I would. Carruthers made a visit to the Kalahari sound like a Sunday-morning stroll down the street. We shook hands. Then he marched over to his Land-Rover and drove away.

Later I took the Toyota and drove north to Moremi. A few miles inside the reserve I stopped and got out. It was early evening. Ahead of me a pair of elephants wandered up to a water hole, drank and ambled off. A hyena followed in their tracks, watched by a herd of impala. The hyena turned and barked, and the impala bounded nervously away. A flock of saddle-billed storks planed down against the lowering sun, and a baboon pack began to call.

I walked forward. Three years earlier I'd stopped at the same place. As soon as I'd stepped down from the truck then I'd been enveloped by tsetse. They emerged from the trees in clouds, settling on my hands, my face, my hair, on every inch of my body that wasn't covered, and stinging me to mindless fury with their agonizing needle-sharp bites. Now there was not one. Carruthers and his mother's milk had annihilated them all. I could walk through the delta untroubled.

At the water's edge I stopped and sat down. The light was gold and the air still. From the middle of the pool a group of hippos inspected me, only their eyes, ears and nostrils visible above the surface. Occasionally one of them would lift its head and "yawn," asserting its right to the water by showing me its great curving teeth. Slowly they began to advance on the shore. My presence disturbed them. Moremi was the traditional hunting ground of the Tawana, nineteenth-century settlers of the delta whose favorite meat was hippo. Conditioned by years of predation, the animals found my very silhouette a threat. Unlike the Chobe elephants, the hippos hadn't yet learned that the area had been declared a reserve.

It had been named Moremi after a Tawana chief, and it occupied almost one-quarter of the Okavango basin. The decision to make it a reserve had been taken by the Tawana themselves with a little prompting from the district officer. Judged by every normal criterion, the decision was an excellent one. But Moremi met far more than the usual requirements for a wildlife haven. Moremi had tsetse. And then came Carruthers.

Conservationists like to compare the wild to some irreplaceable man-made work of art—a Botticelli, a Michelangelo or a Rembrandt. On their analogy, what had happened at Moremi was rather as if not one masterpiece but a whole gallery had been gathered together in the delta. And then very carefully and deliberately, every tack that held the canvases safe on their stretchers had been extracted, leaving the priceless artifacts vulnerable to the lightest gust of air.

On the face of it, the contradictions were so bizarre as to be incomprehensible. Spraying wasn't for the comfort of visitors—their number was negligible. It wasn't to safeguard cattle—they were banned from Moremi. It wasn't to protect the Tawana dwellers—few contracted tryps now, and treatment was available if they did. It wasn't even part of some overall plan to clear the delta and divide the area between reserve and grazing land. There was no overall plan. The country's resources simply didn't permit one.

What was the reason? Carruthers hadn't been able to tell me. He was merely acting under orders. In Maun I asked his colleagues in related departments. I got no farther forward. Later I questioned government officials in Gaborone. When I left I was still no closer to an answer. Finally I realized that there was no reason. Instead, there was a good idea. The tsetse had been eradicated because it was a good idea they should be eradicated. That was all. That—and the availability of the means to eradicate them.

So the tsetse were dispatched. In due course everyone would assess the likely consequences of their disappearance and make the appropriate ecological decisions. Except that by then, such being the nature of good ideas, in place of likely consequences there would be only irreversible results and the decisions would already have been taken of their own accord.

I gazed across the pool. On the far side, thickets of grass stretched away between the trees into the distance. The grass was tall and strong and ripe. As the sun set, its color changed from wheaten yellow to rose to a deep translucent crimson. Reflected in the water beneath the smoky pennants of evening cloud, the thickets appeared to be on fire.

For the moment, Moremi's grass belonged to the wild. Because the Tawana were an honorable people, it would be reserved for the wild as long as the rains held. One year the rains would fail. The following year they would fail too—and two years without rain was unendurable. Johnny Tswana and Joe Bushman, accompanied no doubt by Heinie Afrikaans and Roger European, would at last claim their long-coveted inheritance. From every side cattle would be driven into the reserve. This time there would be nothing to stop them. Rinderpest is cyclical. It exhausts itself, returns and vanishes again. But when the tsetse are gone they do not return.

For the wild, the pastures of Moremi would be truly in flames then. The cattle-cropped grass would be set ablaze to force new growth. Nothing would be given back when the drought and the fire passed. There would be nothing to give, nothing to be given to. Like the tsetse and the wasted grass, the wild would have vanished.

The hippos were close to the shore now. Still submerged, they faced me in a ring twenty yards away. An old bull raised its head, opened its jaws and roared defiantly. A cow copied him, then another, then a third. Green algal mucus dripped from their teeth, and the air was loud with angry bellows. I stood up.

During the Kenyan Mau Mau rebellion of the 1950s, the guerrillas retreated to a stronghold in the Aberdare Mountains. Unable to follow them, the colonial authorities strafed the mountains from the air with rockets, bullets and bombs. No terrorists died, but the carnage inflicted on the animals was devastating. Thousands were killed. Many more were wounded, mutilated and crippled.

Before the fire raids the Aberdares were tranquil. Afterward, they became the landscape of Bosch and Goya. They were turned into nightmare. Blinded elephants with shattered tusks and amputated trunks roamed the slopes trampling in rage and agony every creature they encountered. Maddened buffalo, their jaws and udders scythed off at random, charged trees and stones. Rhinos, lurching, choking, dragging mangled legs, stalked and crushed egrets, the very birds that cleansed them. Even the tiny vervet monkeys dropped from the trees in shock, cowered with the terrorists on the ground as the planes roared overhead, and then turned and savaged their companions.

Like Carruthers' corking Endosulphan, strafing the Aberdares had seemed a good idea at the time. I had no idea what effect the spray had had on the hippos. At that moment I had no wish to find out.

I walked back to the truck. Just before I got there I felt a piercing pain on my wrist. I shook my arm and swore, thinking I'd been stabbed by an acacia thorn. As I did so, I saw a tiny glistening insect soar upward. I glanced down. There was an oval puncture on the skin, and the surrounding veins were already bruising and swelling.

I sucked at the bite, spat out the blood and climbed into the Toyota. Then I started to laugh. I laughed helplessly and uproariously until tears flowed and blinded me and I was forced to stop. The delta's sharpshooters hadn't been totally annihilated after all. In spite of Carruthers there were still a few snipers left.

That evening I met Cameron Lyle in the Island Safari bar. And though I listened carefully I heard no whispers, no tinkle of coins. Lyle was a rawboned Scottish zoologist in his early thirties. He had freckled skin, tousled red hair and the long determined stride of the hill-bred Highlander. Taciturn, even dour, by day, he became almost lyrically eloquent after dark as he discussed his work over a tumblerful of whisky.

"Imagine taking a chopper down six feet above a herd of a thousand buffalo," he said. "They're all galloping and there's nothing but dust and horns and eyes and those great black backs plunging like waves. It's magic, man—magic!"

Whisky splattered the floor as his hand traced the movement of the racing herd.

Lyle was heading a U.N.-sponsored team to assess the likely consequences for the Okavango wildlife if the basin's waters were tapped for mining and irrigation. One of his tasks was to estimate the current buffalo population of the delta. He invited me to visit the project's headquarters next morning to see how the study was progressing.

Lyle and his group worked out of a low-roofed one-room building in the center of Maun. The room was crowded with filing cabinets, desks, sample racks and cluttered worktables. Plastic overlay grids glittered in the light from the open windows, and coils of computer tape trailed down from the tabletops, stirring slowly like wet reeds in the dusky air.

I arrived at 10 A.M., and Lyle introduced me to two of his white assistants. Both, like him, were highly qualified and experienced British zoologists. We all stood for a while discussing the delta's ecology and the techniques they were using for the buffalo count—marking chosen animals by dart gun from helicopters and charting their movements across the islands and waterways.

Then the other two excused themselves and left for a field trip. A few moments later Lyle, who'd been searching for a map he wanted to show me, remembered he'd left it at his house. As he needed the map that afternoon himself, he went off in his truck to collect it, promising to be back in ten minutes.

I waited by the door. When I came in I'd vaguely registered a figure sitting behind a desk at the rear of the room. None of the three had paid any attention to him, and I'd assumed he was a Tswana clerk. Now I saw that he was white.

I threaded my way through the clutter and introduced myself.

"Dale Koszinski," he said as he shook hands. "Peace Corps. Richmond, Virginia."

He was the same age as the others. Tidy, crew-cut, dressed in sharply pressed khaki shorts and shirt. A trim all-American boy with an attractive Southern drawl—and something strangely evasive in his eyes.

He sat down and hunched himself over a pile of papers. I stood in front of him. Apart from an occasional rustle as he shuffled the papers there was silence.

Peace Corps. It came back to me. The study team, Lyle had explained, consisted of four members. Under the terms of the aid program the U.N. agreed to fund two and Botswana was required to pay for the other two. The government had gone to Britain for one and the United States for the fourth.

Koszinski was the American contribution. Lyle had said nothing about him.

"You complete the team?" I asked finally.

He nodded without speaking. There was another silence. I waited. Then I tried again.

"What's your particular field?"

"Crocs."

The answer came grudgingly, but at least it was an answer. I thought for a moment. I knew little about the ecological role of the crocodile, but in a water system as large as the delta it was obviously significant. I wondered how a trim young man from Richmond, Virginia, had become an expert in the subject.

I asked him.

"What do I know about crocs? Shit, man, nothing. . . ."

He shuddered. "You ever seen a croc? I tell you, they're the goddamnedest meanest bastards ever. They give me fucking nightmares."

I gaped at him. "Then how come you're up here in charge of them?"

"Chickens," he said. "Chickens and my ma."

I tried to work out a connection between Koszinski's mother, chickens and crocodile studies in the Okavango. For an instant I wondered if it was some elaborate practical joke, but the intensity in Koszinski's face ruled that out.

He was staring up at me with the look of a cornered wild animal wondering if it had been trapped by a predator. He must have decided he was safe, because he suddenly started to talk.

"I've got this terrible fear of chickens," he said. "I just need to see one and I scream. I worked on it five years with my analyst back in Richmond. We finally figured out it came from my relationship with my ma. That got screwed to hell when I was a kid. She kept chickens and I associate them with her."

He paused. Still bewildered, I asked, "But what's that got to do with crocs?"

"Well, it's like this," he explained. "My analyst reckoned if I could learn to handle a really dangerous animal I'd be okay with chickens. Also I'd straighten out this love/hate thing with my mother. So I joined the Peace Corps and put my name down for a wildlife project. I was hoping to take it by degrees—maybe beavers or something first and then working up. But all they had was these goddamn crocs."

Koszinski shrugged gloomily and stopped. Then I heard Cameron Lyle's voice behind me.

"So you've met Dale?"

I turned. Lyle was trying to look cheerful, but his face was grim.

"Yes," I said. "We were discussing—"

"That's great," Lyle cut me off. "Now come and look at this map."

He gripped my arm and guided me firmly across the floor like a bouncer removing a drunk from a nightclub.

"Did he tell you some crazy story about his mother and chickens and his analyst?"

We'd passed straight through the door and were standing outside in the shadow. I nodded. Lyle clasped his hands to his head in anguish.

"What the hell's going on?" I asked.

"It's true, God help me!" Lyle answered. "Every single word. The day he arrived I heard a caterwauling down the road. I ran out. He was up a tree sobbing like a child with a bunch of chickens scratching round below. For Christ's sake, you ever heard of a man treed by a hen before?"

I started to laugh, but the bitterness in Lyle's voice stopped me.

"Listen, I've been stuck with this maniac for six months," he went on. "I tried putting him out in a delta camp with measuring sticks . . ."

Lyle had equipped Koszinski with three-meter black-and-white-striped poles. Koszinski's job was to locate crocodile breeding sites and lay a pole on the ground beside each one. Then, using low-level aerial photography, the team could assess not only the crocodile population but the size of the breeding individuals.

"We overflew his area three times a week for two months," Lyle said. "Not one bloody pole on the photographs. So I went up there. Know what he'd done? He was too frightened to go near the sites, so he'd tied five poles together and was trying to push the sixth across from the other side of the stream. And that wasn't all. . . ."

Lyle's voice rose in outrage, and the Highland burr thickened.

"We'd been visited by the Peace Corps director for Africa. Naturally the laddie's a black American. He insists on coming with me. I try to keep him away, but he wants to know firsthand how Koszinski's doing. He asks, and Koszinski says straight to his face, 'Not so good, because the nigras aren't cooperating'!"

For a moment I thought Lyle was going to emulate the chicken-treed Koszinski and burst into tears.

"I think you could use a drink, Cameron," I said quickly.

"Let's see if we can find some strychnine," he answered.

He gave a glance of loathing at the doorway, and we headed for Riley's Bar.

Soothed by several beers and a discussion about the likely fortunes of Scottish rugby in the coming season, within the hour he'd forgotten Koszinski and was talking about what he knew best, the delta.

The buffalo census was only the spearhead of his program. At issue behind that lay the future of the entire Okavango basin. Lyle's forecast was bleak.

"Look at it," he said. "Ten thousand square miles of water and no one uses it worth a tinker's fart. Know how much even seeps down to the delta's base? Only three percent of everything that comes in through the neck, that's all. The rest goes to waste. Think of what you could do with just a fraction of what's lost. . . ."

He emptied his glass, and I bought him another.

"Well, they'll take it," he went on. "They'll take it all. What I'm doing is just a bloody charade. I'll tell them there's so many buff and so many buck and so many lion—even, God help me, so many crocs. I'll put in a report showing them how it all holds together. And then I'll get a letter of thanks. Goodbye, and I'm on my way, and when I'm gone they'll tear it all to buggery. . . ."

Lyle hammered his glass on the counter. "Look, man, I'm not a priest," he said. "I just write out the words the bush and the water tell me. I try to put it down for true. Afterwards it's up to them—and they'll bugger it good."

"The Tswana?" I said.

Lyle chuckled sourly. "Ask those poor sods who honor the checks. If they tell you, then ask the laddies in the gray suits from the World Bank. If you get as far as them, ask for Geneva's market price on a cheetah or an eagle. Whatever they quote you, don't buy—you'll lose your bloody shirt!"

He stopped. He didn't want to talk about the delta anymore. Instead we returned to the subject of Scottish rubgy. Much later, I left him and headed back to Island River Lodge.

I had entirely forgotten about my last foot soldier—the long-delayed Little David—until one day on the Chobe when Syd was radioing south on the shortwave transceiver in the lead truck. Reminded by his namesake that we'd be late for Little David's arrival in Maun, I passed on a brief and cryptic message: "Delayed by fog —await orders."

Walking into the saloon at Island Safari Lodge I received the first word of him in a month.

"There's a phone message for you," the girl behind the bar said.

She handed me an envelope. I opened it and read the laconic communication inside.

"Where is he?" I asked.

"Across the river. I can call and say you're here. . . ."

She hesitated. She was young and pretty and wide-eyed.

"You won't be leaving yet, will you?" she added.

"No," I answered. "Why?"

She lifted a bundle of signed bar chits from a spike and smiled nervously.

"I'm sure these'll be all right," she said. "It's just that he's only been here two days and we've never had so many before."

I glanced at Big David and Bobby. They were standing side by side with a tumbler in each hand. The four glasses were filled to the brim. They looked back at me impassively.

"Miss," I said, "I'm afraid it hasn't even started. Tell him to come over."

We walked down to the landing point on the river's edge. Immediately opposite was a broad marshy meadow. Half a mile downstream the far bank curved in toward the water. Lights gleamed in the darkness, and behind them an occasional pair of headlights wavered along the Savuti track. The air was soft, and the night echoed with the lowing of cattle and the calls of herdsmen.

Fifteen minutes later a song drifted across the water. It was an Afrikaans battle hymn, and it was being rendered by two voices. One of them interjected a sustained passage of English invective between each chorus and the next. The sound came closer, and a canoe with a lantern in the bows appeared. There were three figures inside. A Tswana paddler at the stern, a lank and grizzled white lying with a bottle clamped to his chest in the center, and the elegant silhouette of Little David leaning against the front thwart.

The canoe bumped ashore. Little David stepped carefully out. He adjusted his shirt collar and drew on a cigarette.

"Evening, Colonel," he said. "Fog lifted, I trust?"

Before I could answer, the man behind clutched the canoe's gunwale and jackknifed himself over. Instantly he lost his footing in the mud. There was a terrible oath, his arms flailed wildly and the bottle shot into the air. Then he suddenly plunged forward and lay quite still.

I gazed down. The man seemed to be unconscious. At his feet the bottle bobbed gently in the shallows.

"Who's your friend?" I asked.

David frowned. "A graduate of life's university whose name for the moment escapes me. We've been discussing art and politics. It appears to have left him a little tired. I think he should be allowed to rest. Sambo!"

He called to the paddler. The Tswana vaulted out, rescued the bottle from the water and placed it in the man's hands. For a moment the man came back to life. He gulped from the neck and howled like a gun-shot hyena. Then he slumped down into the mud again.

"You look after him good, you idle black swine," David said. "Because if you don't I'll fill your butt with lead. Understand?"

"Yes, sir." The paddler beamed happily.

"Right." David turned to me. "Reporting for duty, Colonel. What are the orders?"

We climbed the bank toward the lodge.

"No toto talk," I said. "No talking dirty in front of ladies. Alcohol only on Sundays and then in moderation. You've joined a very tight ship."

The lights of the bar were flickering in front of us through the leaves of the trees that screened it against the day's heat.

"Absolutely." David nodded in agreement. "Now if I can find some benighted black to serve us a few beakers, I'll make sure the others have got the message too."

He barked out a laugh and strode away, with Bobby and Big David behind him. I thought of the pretty young girl behind the counter and shuddered.

The delta's traditional transport is a *makoro,* a shallow canoe hollowed out from a hardwood trunk. In the morning I took one and paddled downriver. Half a mile away, on the far bank, was another lodge. I tied up at the landing stage and walked to the bar. I was looking for Luke Carver, a former hunter who'd started a game-viewing operation, but the bar was deserted. I waited for five minutes. Then, as I turned to leave, a girl appeared behind the counter.

"Can I help . . ."

She recognized me and broke off. I recognized her at the same moment too. She was named Gail, and we'd met at Island Safari the night before. Luke was away setting up a fixed camp in Moremi, but Gail offered me a beer. She poured a Coke for herself, and we went outside.

We sat in a pool of tree shadow on the edge of the river. Gail slipped off her sandals and trailed her feet in the water. Beyond, in the sunlight, the water looked deep and black. Here in the shade it was bright and clear and flecked with peat-colored grains of light. Shoals of tiny fish nuzzled her toes.

Gail was nineteen. She was wearing jeans and an orange T-shirt printed with the name of the lodge. The jeans were faded almost to whiteness, and she'd cut off the legs above her knees. She had long, very fair hair, pale gray eyes, a slim body and a heart-shaped, almost childlike face that was at once both wistfully vague and dauntingly self-assured. Gail was a wilderness groupie.

"How do you come to be here?" I asked.

"I got a dose." She grinned at me. "Well, I guess that's how it started. I was in Hawaii and I had clap and for some reason I couldn't get rid of it. So I came home to get it fixed. And then one day I heard someone talking . . ."

She paused.

Home to Gail was Cape Town, where she'd grown up. At sixteen she had left school. For a while she had trained as a stenographer, but the prospect of nine-to-five office work had become more and more suffocating. After a few months she had had a furious row with her parents and walked out of their house and the secretarial college on the same day.

She had moved to a nearby beach resort, got a job as a waitress and joined the vacationing student community who barbecued, laughed, sang and made love by night and surfed by day. Whatever else she learned there, on the beach Gail discovered breakers. She drifted first east and then west, moving wherever the great waves were running. Finally, with a boyfriend, she had set out for Hawaii.

From the cold and towering foam-ridged walls of Pacific water through venereal disease to the heat and loneliness of the Okavango delta. I waited.

"Hell, you know how it is," she went on. "People talk about the places they've been to. You hear of somewhere. It sounds good. So you go. Right?"

I nodded. "Just as soon as the clap's cured."

She smiled again. "That was fixed. I met this boy and he'd trekked up here, and the way he told it, it was magic. Waves run and break and run again. They're beautiful. But in the end they're all the same. Not animals. They shift and change, and there's sun and rain and drought and stars, and all the time it's different. . . ."

Gail borrowed some money. She flew to Gab's. From Gab's she hitched a ride on a cattle truck to Ghanzi. She stayed for a week in Ghanzi. Then she found another truck heading north for Maun. Gail hitched again. She was no longer following breakers—she was trekking after animals now.

"I made it here and then, shit, I realized I didn't know what the hell I was going to do," she said. "I washed a few dishes, I did some baby-sitting the nights they were showing movies at Island, I did anything that was going. Then one day the kid running this place got sick. She had spinal meningitis. They flew her down to Jo'burg. I said I'd take over. They gave me the job. . . ."

Gail became manager of the lodge. That was just after Christmas. From Christmas until June, Maun had relatively few visitors. From June on, the lodge catered to tourists, mainly South African, who ventured into the delta to fish or watch the game and the birds. The lodge was still empty, but the season was about to begin. Its success would depend not only on South Africa but also on what happened over the coming months in Zimbabwe-Rhodesia.

"I'm on a percentage, but I don't really mind." Gail shrugged. "Just so long as enough people come to pay the wages, that's fine by me."

It was 11 A.M. Even in the shadow, the air was dry and fiercely, deadeningly hot. Gail glanced around. She had a Tswana staff of seven working under her. None of them was in sight.

She stripped off her T-shirt, dropped it on the bank and slid into the water. Then she unbuckled her jeans and worked them down over her knees. She was wearing nothing underneath.

"Have you got a cigarette?" she asked.

I lit one and gave it to her. She lay half-floating in the shallows with the smoke drifting up into the branches. Her body was firm and supple and tanned the same light bronze as her face. Her nipples cut the surface. The tiny fish that had nuzzled her toes clustered in sequined fans around them too.

The stillness, the heat, the naked girl twisting slowly in the golden, shadowed water—it should have been overpoweringly erotic. Strangely, it was not. She was utterly unself-conscious, utterly unprovocative. Her body was hot. Like an animal, she was cooling it in the river. That was all.

I asked her about animals. She thought for a moment. Then she laughed.

"It's funny," she said. "I came all this way, and you know what? I've been so goddamn busy I've never once made it up into the delta or out into the bush. I've just been stuck here in Maun."

"Does that matter?"

"I want to go, sure. I'll go just as soon as there's time. There's any number of guys who'll take me. . . ."

She paused and frowned. Then she glanced up at me.

"I bet they told you that across the other side."

"They said you had a friendly, outgoing nature," I answered tactfully.

"Crap!" Gail chuckled. "What they really said was if it hunts and wears pants she'll screw it. Well, they're right. Those boys, they're lovely. They come in from safari and they've been away for weeks and we have a really good time."

"You came here to be with animals," I said. "Instead you seem to have ended up with people who kill animals."

She spun the cigarette away and sat up. Water cascaded down her neck, flowed over her breasts and pattered back into the river. Her skin was clean and shining, and her wet hair clung to her back. Briefly her eyes were troubled.

"Look," she said. "Sure they kill, and sure I fuck them. I fuck them good and happy, because it is good, it is happy. Only there's more than that. When I'm with them I'm close to where they've been. They talk and tell me stories and almost it's like I'm there. One day I will be there. You see I've got this crazy idea . . ."

She reached out, took my wrist and pulled me down toward her.

"I'm standing in the bush and it's night and this elephant appears. He walks up to me and his trunk comes out and he touches me all over. Gentle as wind. I'm in his path and he's just feeling, exploring . . ."

She guided my hand down to her thighs. I felt the tuft of hair at her groin. Then she drew my fingers up across her belly, the nipples where the fish had pressed, her neck, her cheeks, over her closed eyelids, then her head.

"He feels everything. I just stand there still. When he's finished he knows I'm safe. I'm part of the bush too. So he steps round me and moves on. Afterwards I'm alone with just the plain and the stars and maybe . . ."

She stopped. Her eyes were still closed, and she was breathing quickly. Then a shout rang out from the bar. One of the staff was calling for her. She looked around, and suddenly she laughed. The laughter was warm and joyous and unrestrained.

"Cut the dreams and get on with the work," she finished.

"I might almost take up hunting," I said.

I handed her the T-shirt. She put it on, pulled up her jeans and buckled them round her waist. Then we walked back to the lodge. I left a message for Luke Carver and went down to the *makoro*.

"Come back soon," Gail called as I pushed away.

She was standing at the entrance to the bar. She shook out her hair and waved.

I headed upriver.

There were other wilderness groupies in Maun. They were all young, and they were all pretty, and some were remarkably intelligent—articulate, funny and well educated. There were no "dogs," in the vocabulary of pop music, among the camp followers of the wild.

By day they worked in the lodges. By night they wore bright dresses and decorated the bars. And most of them, like Gail, if not with the same generous gusto, slept with the hunters. It was virtually an obligation. After all, a groupie's first duty is sex. Sex with the wild isn't easy. Instead they lay down on their backs and parted their legs for the professional killers of the wilderness.

None of them saw any contradiction in what they were doing. None of them seemed to remember that the delta was a battleground between man and the wild, and in war giving comfort to the enemy by way of sexual favors is traditionally punished by shaven heads and shaven pubic hair. They simply scrambled out of their briefs and merrily coupled with the foe.

Perhaps they believed, as Gail put it, "When I'm with them I'm close to where they've been." It was difficult to tell. No one else was as candid and uninhibited, and even Gail couldn't explain it more precisely. Yet like debutantes dressed and awaiting a summons to the ball, they remained in Maun—sweet and fresh and yearning. One day their prince would come. He'd arrive in a carriage and they'd rattle out into the bush and there before an audience of antelope, lions and buffalo they'd waltz the night away to serenading owls.

# 9

HARRY SELBY is a short, compact man in his late fifties. His dark hair, thinning but without a trace of gray, is brushed sleekly against his head. Under it, his eyes bulge slightly beneath chameleonlike lids. The eyes are pale, watchful and shrewd.

He is courteous, quiet-voiced and articulate. He laughs easily. He is evidently a man of culture. Mrs. Selby, his wife, wears English floral dresses. She keeps her skin from the sun and walks her two little Pekingese dogs in the afternoon shade beneath the trees. She is devoted to her dogs. Harry and Daisy Selby live in a bungalow. The front lawn is neat and green. The house is decorated with taste. It is substantial but unostentatious—the sort of house a successful stockbroker would build on the edge of a country-club golf course.

Harry Selby could easily be taken for a successful stockbroker. He has the right air of authority, confidence and expertise. In his hands, your portfolio would be safe. There would be no reckless tips, no tainted insider dealings, no high-risk plunges. The pale, hooded eyes are indeed very shrewd.

Harry Selby is a professional killer. A white hunter. And more than that—by general agreement the finest white hunter of his generation. Very possibly one of the finest ever.

"Well, of course not a white hunter"—the correction is made quietly. "We no longer officially have any of those. Today we're all professional hunters."

The winds of change have swept away a term almost as synonymous with Africa as the Dark Continent. Now other winds are sweeping away more than a name. The hunter, call him white or professional, has become an endangered species. The last true examples of the breed work the Kalahari.

Harry Selby and I sat in his Maun office and discussed that arcane and mystique-laden subject—African big-game hunting. The first essential in understanding big-game hunting is that to the hunter, on one level at least, it is neither arcane nor charged with mystique. It is simply a trade. A man earns his livelihood from his trade. The wages pay the school bills, the mortgage and the wife's visits to the hairdresser. And because almost every trade can be made more productive through rationalization and the economies of scale, big-game hunting became a business many years ago. Selby is in business. To talk to him is to talk to an executive concerned with such issues as product development, marketing, inventory control, cash flow and tax depreciation.

Of course, his approach is inevitably rather different from that of a wholesale grocer. If your warehouse is a vast tract of desert wilderness and your most valuable stock line is Kalahari lions, you need a flexible business philosophy. Selby speaks and understands the jargon of finance and management as easily as the investment analyst he might have been.

"What attracted you to Botswana?" I asked.

"Political uncertainties in the traditional markets," he answered. "This country looked like a sound opportunity for diversification."

Until the late '60s, as a partner in the old-established safari company of Ker, Downey & Selby, he'd operated in the "traditional" markets of East Africa. Successive grants of independence there left the future of hunting, in his view, doubtful. To the south, Botswana, in his calculations, was quite another proposition.

The country was immense and largely uninhabited. The desert supported a wide variety of game in huge numbers. Politically, under the moderate but firm leadership of Seretse Khama and his British wife, Ruth, Botswana was stable. It was also poor—so poor that even by African standards the revenue from organized hunting could make an important contribution to its economy. Above all, it had the glamour of the Kalahari. Few but the boldest had ever hunted the great stone citadel. Now, with brushed strips, planes and good pilots, the desert could be made accessible.

"I set up a subsidiary company of the original KDS operation," Selby explained. "I managed to get concession areas. The first few years went well. So I took a view. I bought out my partners, who were still working East Africa, and carried on alone."

The key to Selby's success was his warehouses and inventory—the concession areas and the animals that roamed them.

On independence, for the purposes of hunting, Botswana was zoned. The process of zoning was an enormously complicated and delicate exercise in land allocation. Even colonial Whitehall, with its unrivaled experience of tarot-card interpretation and chicken-entrail reading, would have found the task hideously daunting. Whitehall, to the profound relief of the mandarins, was no longer responsible.

The problem belonged to the new country's government. On balance, it was handled with skill and wisdom—at least in the circumstances of the time. Large areas were declared reserves where no hunting at all was permitted. Others were formally given to tribes who'd long since established an exclusive right to take game there. Others still were brought under the direct control of the newly created game department.

But a number, including some of the most richly stocked with animals, were leased to the safari companies. Selby wasn't the only entrepreneur who saw the possibilities of the stone plateau. Four other groups bid for and were granted concession areas.

"I got leases on two," Selby said. "In Mbabwe and the delta. Not everyone was as lucky. One group, for example, was just given a plains concession. With plains and swamp I'm much more flexible. I can also offer almost double the range of trophy."

In an average year there are about twenty-seven species of big-game animal available to the Kalahari trophy hunter. Some—such as lion and elephant—can be found both in the grass plains of the desert and on the islands and in the water lanes of the Okavango basin. Others are restricted to one of the two habitats.

The combined area of Selby's two concessions is about the size of a small country such as Wales. Within them he operates much like a medieval baron. By way of annual tribute to his king, the central government, he pays rent. Then each year he agrees with the king's chamberlains, the staff of the country's game department, how many animals of each species may be killed.

Numbers and even species change from year to year. If the population of a particular animal drops, the trophy allocation will be reduced proportionately. If the fall is severe enough to threaten the survival of the species within the concession, the animal will be removed from the list altogether until such time as the stock has reestablished itself and a surplus is available once more. The reckoning, the inventory control, is of necessity rough and ready. It is easier to count breakfast cereal packets than wandering Kalahari lions. But given cooperation between the game department and the safari companies, the annual stocktaking can prove remarkably accurate. Once it is done, the baron is on his own. He can hire and fire. He can build and raze villages. He can call men to arms, march them against the foe and disband his companies when battle is ended. Above all, he can entertain his guests at the chase. Selby's guests are prepared to pay lavishly for the entertainment he provides.

"The cost? Well, let's take an average client on a full safari. He'll want twenty different trophies. Ten from the plains and ten from the delta. To have a fair chance of getting them all, he's got to allow a month. . . ."

Selby leaned back in his chair as he calculated.

"License fees, transportation, taxidermy, export permits, plus of course our own modest charges . . ." He chuckled. "You can reckon on a total of about a hundred thousand dollars."

From its start African trophy hunting has been the preserve of the very rich. Selby offers the rich a service. The cost is high, but nothing if not value for money. Throughout the client's stay he will be housed in luxury tented camps, each with its own staff of cooks, waiters, personal servants, trackers, skinners, guards and drivers. He will be flown by private charter from one concession to the next. He will be advised, entertained and treated like visiting royalty. Every smallest whim and fancy will be catered to. But in the end, the entire success or failure of the safari will depend on one man—the professional hunter assigned to the client as escort, bodyguard, guide, companion and mentor.

With few exceptions, mainly old clients who've become friends, Selby seldom fulfills the hunter's role now. His time is taken up with administration and forward planning. In his place, like the medieval baron, he employs mercenaries.

The transceiver crackled in the office next door. Selby went out to deal with some supply problem in one of the outlying camps. I left. It was midday. If there were any hunters in town they'd be gathering now at Riley's Bar. I walked down the road, passed Riley's and headed for the post office.

The post office was in the middle of the village. It was a single-story building. Bare, windowless and functional. From the outside it looked like a temporary public lavatory undergoing field tests in a sea of dust. Inside there was a narrow counter and a metal grill.

Two Herero ladies watched me as I walked to the counter. One had a turquoise turban, the other indigo and saffron. Their dresses reached to the floor in layers of rose and violet and crimson. They were tall and so stately I felt I should ask them to waltz. There was no music. Only the humming of clouds of flies and the smell of urine.

"May I have stamps for three letters to Spain?" I said.

I pushed the letters through the grill. The clerk was a young Tswana woman. She was dressed in a crisp white blouse and neatly cut skirt. She studied the letters carefully in silence. Then she asked, "Where is Spain?"

Her expression was severe but patient and thoughtful. I deliberated for a while.

"Spain is in Europe," I said.

She picked up the letters. She weighed them on a scale with little brass weights. She ran her fingers delicately across the envelopes over my handwriting. Then she put them down.

There was another long silence. An almost palpable tension had come into the room. The two Herero ladies stood utterly still, glowing in the shadows. The door creaked open and an old Tswana entered. He had a white stick and a dew-softened hide hat. He sensed the drama instantly and he stopped.

Finally the clerk said, "Is Europe close to England?"

"Not very," I answered. "But close enough."

Everything changed then. The girl's face lit up and she gave me a brilliant, heartwarming smile.

"If Europe is close to England," she said, "I can give you the stamps."

The Herero ladies nodded. The old man tapped his stick on the floor in approval. I thanked them all and went out.

I remembered the famous newspaper headline of the Edwardian era. "Fog over Channel—Continent isolated."

Carruthers was right. The sun hadn't set on empire yet. God's in His heaven. And here in the great Kalahari He's still English.

I headed back for Riley's.

On Saturday nights, Riley's Bar is like an old-time frontier saloon. Packed, raucous, throbbing with laughter, song and invective. But alas—still no clandestine exchange of money or a whispered allusion to leopards. Now, at midday on a Tuesday, the room was dusty and almost deserted. A couple of sullen-faced Tswana youths lounged indecisively at the jukebox. More of the interminable flies circled the air, and the lowered blinds bumped quietly against the windows.

I had left EBL at the lodge combing through the day's yield of images, feathers and grasses. The foot soldiers, anxious to make the best of Maun's assets, were with me. Big David led the way to the bar. Reminiscences of evenings at the Yak and Yeti, a legendary watering hole in the foothills of the Himalayas, floated to me across the room.

I ordered a Castle and carried it to the door. When I walked in, I had thought there was no one on the veranda outside. But glancing to my right, I noticed a sandy-haired figure perched in the sunlight on the wooden rail. He gave me a broad, open grin and jumped down.

"Good to see you again, man," he said.

"You too, Joe," I answered. "So how's it going?"

We'd met on my last visit to Maun. I called for the barman to bring out another Castle, and we sat down.

Joe Regan is twenty-seven, white and American. He has the thickly muscled wrists, scarred hands and strong, supple build of a steeplechase jockey. Under his tan, the skin on his face is pallid. In a jock the pallor would have come from sweating off excess pounds in sauna baths. Joe's problems are different. The whiteness and the strain carved in deep lines across his forehead are the consequences of his work.

Joe Regan was one of the men I'd been looking for—a professional hunter. That week he was having difficulty with elephants.

"Shit, man," he said. "I've never known jumbo so spooky. Pussy was just the same, except we got lucky on a buff kill up near Chief's

Island. But with jumbo I can't find spoor less than forty-eight hours old. Five days—would you believe it? I've got some goddamn pair of spics as clients and they're going out of their skulls."

Joe shook his head wearily. In hunter's jargon, "spooky" describes any game that's proving particularly elusive. Joe had driven into town from camp to hitch a ride on a plane flying north over the concession he was working, in the hope he'd spot an elephant herd from the air.

As we waited for the pilot to collect him, we sat in the veranda's shadow discussing hunting again. This time not from the point of view of the entrepreneur like Selby—Joe worked for a different company—but as the individual hunter in the bush saw it.

Commercial big-game hunting is less than a century old. Until twenty-five years ago it was carried on throughout virtually the entire continent. But when Kenya banned hunting in 1978 (proving Selby as shrewd as the watchful heavy-lidded eyes suggested), the Kalahari became the last major area of Africa where trophies could still be shot.

As the territory available for hunting shrank, so the number of professional hunters dwindled. That day, as I sat talking to Joe, there were probably fewer than forty left south of the Equator. With one exception, a witty, educated and outstandingly talented Cape Colored, they are all white.

"A black hunter?"

I'd raised the possibility with the head of another safari company when I'd been there before. He had paused, considering his answer.

"Sure," he had said. "Under the Africanization program that's what I'm meant to be training up. In fact, technically I can put the whole concession at risk if I don't. Only what the hell am I meant to do? You think a German industrialist's going to pay a hundred thousand bucks to put his life in the hands of some illiterate black by day, and then spend the evening discussing high finance with him over the fire?"

He had paused and shaken his head glumly.

"Listen, if I ever found a black who had the ability to be a hunter, he wouldn't be up here in the goddamn bush. He'd be running the country and lining his pockets as a cabinet minister down in Gab's. Jesus, the last thing on earth he'd want would be a hunter's license!"

To a professional hunter his license is everything. Granted by the game department on the recommendation of a safari company with separate endorsements from two of his already-licensed colleagues, it means he's served his apprenticeship. He knows the wild. He can spoor and stalk and kill. He can be trusted with people's lives. He can handle every hazard from a charging wounded lion to an encircling bush fire.

It is also, of course, his work permit. But even more than that, his license is the coveted membership badge which signifies he belongs to an elite. Joe Regan was a member of that small, proud and secretive elite.

"How did it happen, Joe?" I asked.

"My pa's an engineer," he said. "When I was a kid he was sent out from Kansas to work on an irrigation project in Tanzania. The family went with him. Back home he'd always hunted. One day he took me with him into the bush. We spoored a big sable ram for five, maybe six hours. Then he dropped it stone-dead at over two hundred yards with a single shot."

Joe shrugged. "Hell, it's difficult to explain. I just knew then that's all I wanted to do. To spoor, to get it all right, to kill clean. I wanted to hunt."

No professional hunter's license is easy to come by. Even in the days when the whole continent was open, few except the descendants of the old colonial powers—the British, the French, the Belgians, the occasional German—won the rare and treasured prize.

For Joe Regan, a young American lacking any links with or roots in Africa, the challenge was daunting. Yet Joe was stubborn and determined. He worked and grafted. He hung around the hunting camps taking any job that was going, the jobs beneath the dignity of the whites and above the ability of the uneducated blacks. If an axle needed fixing, an ammunition inventory checking, a mislaid and stinking trophy consignment delivering, Joe was there to do it.

"Shit!" Joe hammered his glass on the table. "If you knew how many magnum shells I've counted until the stars grow fucking pale, how many reeking maggot-ridden hides and heads I've trucked through the bush—and all for nothing, man, for nothing—you'd think I was nuts. Well, you'd be right. I was. Nuts! But I got that goddamn license."

Joe, like Harry Selby although more than a generation later, won his hunter's license in East Africa. And then, like Selby again, he trekked south to the Kalahari. That was in 1975. Since then he'd hunted the great stone plateau.

"I figure I'm good," Joe said. "Really good. But I know I'm not ideal. Sometimes I try to reckon the guy who'd make the perfect hunter. . . ."

Joe swung his legs up on the table and speculated, chuckling. "He'd start with a master's in Freudian psychology. Then he'd speak seven languages and tell dirty jokes in them all. He'd have political views somewhere out to the right of Genghis Khan, a hot line to the Dow Jones index, and when he wasn't in the bush he'd be shooting off par at Augusta."

Joe was talking about a modern hunter's clients. I laughed.

"Anything else?" I asked.

Joe thought for a moment.

"Well," he added, "if he can hunt a little too, that might come in useful."

He chuckled again.

A few minutes later the pilot arrived. Joe was going to overfly the concession with him and return to Maun in the late afternoon. Then he'd head back for his camp.

"Do you want to ride out and see it?" he asked. "Gordon's coming too to collect another truck. He can bring you back."

Gordon Masters was another hunter who worked for the same company. I agreed to meet Joe at the airfield at 5 P.M. Then he and the pilot left. Before they reached the end of the veranda I could hear Joe's voice drilling out a series of questions.

He'd already forgotten our conversation. All that concerned Joe now was his spooky jumbo again.

I glanced across at the foot soldiers. They were not likely to miss me for a few hours.

Joe's plane, a scarlet Piper Cub, came in to land five minutes after I reached the airfield. He jumped down from the cockpit and ran over to where I was waiting by the truck.

"Got the buggers!" he shouted. "Fifteen of them up by Shona bend—and they aren't carrying toothpicks! Shit, man, are we going to hit jumbo tomorrow!"

He gave a whoop of delight, swung himself up behind the wheel, hammered on the horn, and we set off.

Our first stop was at the safari company's headquarters—a sprawling complex of huts, tents and small warehouses—to collect Gordon Masters. Since my first visit to the Kalahari, the original five concession groups had merged through amalgamation or takeover into two. The dynamic of a free-market economy had proved irresistible. Even the calculating Selby was no longer independent.

One consequence for the hunters was that they now had their private bar. As we walked into the tent where they were gathered, I found the atmosphere instantly and puzzlingly familiar. The rifles stacked by the entrance. The frank masculine faces clustered round the drinks table. The casual military uniforms—khaki shirts and shorts, knee-length socks, leather boots. The slang, the schoolboy humor, the Indian jokes told in Bombay accents minted by Peter Sellers.

" 'My goodness gracious me,' the old man says when he sees the lady's drawers, 'what a terrible mistake!' "

A roar of happy, healthy laughter greeted the punch line—and I suddenly realized where I was. I'd wandered onto the set of a British officers' mess tent in some old World War II movie. The cast, the dialog, the dress and the simple, unquestioned values were identical to those I'd seen and heard in so many black-and-white childhood films.

Gordon Masters detached himself from the crowd and came forward. Masters is a stocky, cheerful man in his mid-forties. He has a balding head, an ancient briar pipe and an air of massive competence. In the movie he'd play the role of the veteran major who keeps the battalion transport running whatever Jerry's handing out.

"Good to have you back," he said.

As with Joe, I knew Masters from before. We left for the camp, this time with Masters at the wheel and Joe stretched out on a tarpaulin in the back. Before we'd driven a mile, Joe was asleep.

Masters glanced back and chuckled.

"Shortest commodity in hunting," he said.

"Sleep?"

He nodded. "Clients don't just buy trophies. They buy a whole damn package, and that includes company. If they want to stay up after supper talking, you stay with them. You may not understand a word they're saying, but you've got to be there and smile and act polite until maybe two A.M. Then you get to bed. They can sleep until daylight. You can't. Two hours later you're up again. You've got the truck and the guns to check, the tracker to consult, the day to figure out . . ."

The catalog went on from breakfast through the morning until the return at dusk.

"And it doesn't stop then," Masters said. "The clients can take it easy. Not the hunter. He's got the trophy to deal with, the skinning to supervise, the records to be written up, the stores for next day to prepare, Christ knows what. If you're lucky you'll get five minutes to wash up before supper. Then you start again."

We turned off the Savuti road into the bush. There was no track now, only the spoor of tires on the flattened grass. Occasionally a loop of yellow toilet paper knotted to a thornbush gleamed in the lowering sun. Each time, Masters slowed and made a detour. The knots of paper marked hidden ardvaark burrows.

Masters, another East African hand, has held a hunter's license for over twenty years. We discuss clients. Behind us, Joe murmurs in his sleep.

"You learn to read them fast," Masters said. "They come all sorts and flavors, but basically I divide them into two groups. Those who can shoot—and, Jesus, they can be good. And those who can't hit a barn at ten paces with a sawn-off scattergun. With the second lot I ask if they'd like me to put in a safety after they've fired. . . ."

A "safety" is a backup shot from the hunter. It's designed to avoid unnecessary pain for the animal and ensure that the client gets his trophy. Above all, it avoids the time and expense of tracking a wounded creature through the bush, as the hunter is bound to do—both by convention and by the terms of his license.

"Mostly they've got enough sense to agree. I mean, who's going to know back in some Belgian drawing room six months later who fired the shot that actually dropped the animal?"

"And if they don't?"

"The *macho* ones?" Masters shrugged. "I reckon, fine. You're the client, you're paying, you choose. But I say, Look, let's fire a few target shots before we go out. Just to check the sights and condition you to the light. . . ."

He paused. "You ever had a woman and watched her face when she comes?"

"Maybe once or twice," I ventured. "But that was years ago when I could still hear the chimes at midnight."

"Justice Shallow, *Henry the Fourth,* Part Two." Masters shook with laughter. "Well, I tell you it's the same. Something always happens a split second before. With a client I just need to watch him fire three shots and I know the very instant he's going to squeeze the trigger. When we get out in the bush and I've lined the trophy up, I keep one eye on the animal and the other on his face. Soon as I see the signal I fire."

"They don't notice?"

Masters shook his head contemptuously. "They've just 'killed' an animal. They wouldn't notice if someone loosed off a neutron bomb right then."

It was dark, and lights were flickering through the scrub ahead of us. I leaned over and shook Joe awake. He sat up yawning.

"Okay, man," he said. "Time for your party trick. Tell them I've found fifteen big gray bastards. Tell them this time tomorrow we'll have that cut to thirteen."

I frowned. The numbers had triggered something. Then I remembered.

There's an old Spanish children's song—I've heard it sung in French too—about elephants and a spider's web. The first elephant climbs on the web, finds it supports his weight and calls for another to join him. With each successive chorus the number of elephants grows. Finally, at the absolute discretion of the singer, the elephants decide the web can't take any more, and the song ends abruptly.

*Quince elefantes se balanceaban*
*Sobre una tela de una araña . . .*

"What's that?" Joe asked.

Unconsciously I'd been humming the song aloud.

"Fifteen elephants balanced on a spider's web," I explained.

"A spider's web?" Joe looked at me puzzled. "What the shit has that got to do with it?"

"Never mind, fellow," I said. "I'll just tell them you've found jumbo."

The truck came to a halt. We all climbed out. I stood for a moment outside the wall of cut thorn that encircled the camp.

For some reason of their own, my children invariably decided to end the song when they had fifteen elephants perched on the web.

From now on they could save their breath. They could stop at thirteen.

I walked forward to join Joe and Gordon Masters, who were already inside the thorn barricade.

Walking through a safari camp at night is like moving through the entrails of a vast opera house. Backstage, anonymous and unseen, known only to each other, is the army of mechanics which operates the production's intricate machinery. We passed the trophy-processing site where the day's kill was being skinned and butchered. Sweating figures hewed lumps of flesh from the carcass and heaved them up onto the meat larder, a wooden raft anchored high against a tree trunk above the raiding hyenas. The sand below was spongy with blood. It glistened scarlet in the firelight. Hides and drying strips of biltong hung like badly washed clothes from the branches.

We moved on and came to the armory tent. The stage props, the high-velocity hunting rifles, were being stripped and cleaned for the following day's performance. A gun bearer sat cross-legged polishing a mahogany stock. The air was thick with the scent of linseed oil and cordite fumes from the spent brass cartridges. Afterward there were the stores depot, the mechanics' yard, the gasoline tanks, the living quarters, the kitchen area—rows of heaped coals set in holes cut in the ground and shaped smooth like crimson butter pats.

Everywhere reflections and moving shadows and the quiet murmur of Tswana voices. And then suddenly a harsh white square of gaslight. We had reached the star's dressing room.

"*Buenas noches, señor.*"

The man was a tall Venezuelan with graying hair, a strong curved nose and a patrician face. He was wearing a black tie and velvet smoking jacket. He introduced me to his son—the same features but softer and slacker—and offered me a drink.

"*¿Qué prefiere usted?*" he asked. "*Tengo Johnnie Walker y Haig y Haig Black Label. También un malt magnífico, Laphrohaig. El único que no hay es J y B Rare. Pero eso es para mujeres, ¿no? ¡Mujeres norteamericanas!*"

He smiled.

"What's that?" Joe asked.

Joe had picked up the word "*norteamericanas.*" He knew about Mexican wetbacks. He knew it had to do somehow with his country.

"He's saying J and B Rare is a whisky for women, American women," I told him. "Your spic isn't so stupid, Joe. At least he's got that right."

"*¿Perdón?*"

The Venezuelan was frowning at me uncertainly. He had the bottle of Laphrohaig in his hands. I thanked him and asked for the malt. He poured a large measure into a crystal glass. Then we sat down and talked.

Brand names of the finest Scotch whiskies. A table laid with a white linen cloth. A conversation in Castilian Spanish—he and his son, questioning me eagerly about Joe's elephant find, spoke with elegant *madrileño* accents. In a glittering dome above us, the cold, wild Kalahari stars wheeled and tumbled.

They were prima donnas, those two. Two great divas, or ballerinas assolutas. They had flown in like a Callas or a Nureyev to La Scala or Covent Garden. It did not matter where. They neither knew nor cared any more, I guessed, than any musical superstar on a major world tour. They did not speak the local language—that was irrelevant. They lived, as they were used to living, in luxury hotel suites. We were sitting in Claridge's beneath the desert sky.

For the month they were there they would perform. Each evening they'd be presented with a bouquet. I had seen that night's on the rack beside the meat larder—a magnificent roan antelope's head dangling from the branches. All they lacked was a live audience to rise and applaud in ovation. Even that was unimportant.

After the tour there would be mounted trophies, photographs and stories to record what they'd achieved. Yet strangely, they weren't vain. They had come to the Kalahari to kill. To kill, in part, as a measure of their skill in marksmanship. But most of all to kill for the bare sake of killing. Killing involved the shedding of blood. As I listened to them, I heard Gordon Masters again as we drove to the camp from Maun.

"They scoop it up and spread it over themselves," Masters said. "Then they make me photograph them with the trophy as if they'd just gone ten rounds hand to hand. Bankers, they're the weirdest. You'd be amazed what they can want. . . ." He shook his head.

"I had one once," Masters went on. "A fat little American. He wanted lion and didn't give a goddamn how he got it. So I found a nice pussy, set him up and let him loose off. He might have hit the sky if he was lucky. I don't know. I just dropped pussy. . . ."

Masters chewed on the pipe stem as he talked.

"We walk up and I'm standing looking at it when I hear this tearing sound behind me. The guy's got out a knife and he's slashing away at his clothes like a maniac. He cuts them to ribbons, but he doesn't stop there. He actually makes a damn great cut down his own arm. Then he smears himself with blood, and I photograph him including the arm in close-up. . . ."

Masters shook his head in disbelief. "Well, I rush him back to camp and stitch him up. I tell him he's mad, he could have got Christ knows what infection. But the guy's as happy as a sand boy. He's got a scar he can show off for the rest of his life. He didn't even want the trophy. He'd already bought one in New York before he left. . . ."

Masters took the pipe out of his mouth and pointed it at me.

"Now, you figure that out. A man of maybe sixty, a pillar of society, flies to Africa and pays a hundred thousand dollars to mutilate himself over an animal he hasn't even shot for the sake of a photograph and a scar."

Looking at the sky, I thought of New York. Midnight among the soaring blocks of Manhattan. A penthouse high above Fifth Avenue. A little old man with a pot belly and a beautiful young girl. They have dined at "21"—all heads in the restaurant turned as the girl walked in. Now they are drinking champagne. The old man shows her the photograph and the scar. Then he tells her the story. An epic tale of danger, skill and valor in the darkest heart of Africa.

I studied the two Venezuelans again. The elder had told me he was also a banker. His son was following him in the profession. They had both killed pussy. Now they wanted jumbo. Joe, as a good hunter, was going to see that they got it. I wondered what fantasies jumbo would satisfy.

*"Señor, explícame una cosa. . . ."*

As I leaned forward and started to question him, a white-jacketed waiter announced that dinner was served. They pressed me to stay for the meal. Joe too, in an undertone, implored me not to go. But Gordon Masters was anxious to be back in Maun before midnight.

"My thanks indeed," I excused myself in Spanish. "Unfortunately, we must be away. *¡Suerte* for tomorrow, *caballeros!*"

They laughed happily and shook my hand with gratitude. I had used two good, strong words. I had wished them fortune, and I had addressed them as gentlemen.

"*¡Gracias!*" They waved me goodbye.

Joe walked with us to the truck. As we reached it, I gave him a friendly punch on the shoulder.

"Good luck to you too, fellow," I said. "I've a shrewd guess you've got the virtues of the Chilean colonels tonight over supper."

"*¡Gracias!*" He answered sourly, echoing the distant calls. "Where the hell's Chile?"

On the drive back, Masters spoke of the changes in hunting since he'd started a generation ago.

There were the obvious ones, of course—the contraction of territory and the dwindling stocks of game everywhere. Those, in turn, had had other and subtler consequences. As late as the early sixties, hunting had retained its prewar flavor. However highly charged the moments of the chase, the very nature of a safari was leisurely and open-ended for client and professional alike.

A week lost at the beginning because of a missed flight connection. A month added after the planned conclusion to secure an elusive trophy. Neither made any significant difference. The client had all the world's time and more on his hands. He was by definition rich. He paid—in money and days—for what he wanted. The additional cost was negligible. It wasn't even reckoned.

But when the winds began to blow, when independence came, when rising expectations, recession and soaring inflation followed, all of that changed. The hunter's overhead spiraled upward uncontrollably. The tight-knit feudal structure of the safari companies, the baronies such as Selby had lorded over, began to crack and crumble. Survival was possible first only by the application of modern business techniques, and then inexorably by amalgamation.

The sequence followed the iron laws of commerce in the industrial West. The individual, the lone operator, was absorbed in a corporate structure and the corporation in a conglomerate. And all the while, the pressures on the hunter intensified.

No longer could a client announce casually he was going to extend the safari. Labor, supplies, services and skills have been costed and sold to him on a computer-reckoned basis by the day, almost by the hour. If he's bought a month, a month is exactly what he gets. At midnight the sands run out. As his plane lifts from the desert strip to carry him home, another drops down from the sky bearing his successor.

The key to the constant through-put, the necessary cash flow, is marketing. Writers make coast-to-coast promotional tours to hype their wares. They wisecrack on television chat shows, they sparkle on breakfast radio, they attend picture-taking sessions and give sincere in-depth profiles of themselves to the local press. So now do professional hunters. They're selling jumbo, pussy and buff on the hoof. Showbiz razzle and boost has become the same for pen and sword. The African sword in the eighties is a high-velocity magnum rifle.

"Think they're bloody pop stars, some of them," Masters said scornfully. "Take young Charlie Randall. . . ."

Randall was another hunter I knew.

"Went on a tour of the States two summers ago. Came back with a trunkful of press cuttings and a fully booked season, boasting he'd had three different girls every night. Signing up clients or screwing girls, that's one thing. Getting the trophies once you're back here, hell, that's something else. Remember what happened to him."

Randall had fallen victim to the strain of trying to secure his clients' full trophy lists inside their allotted thirty days. Increasingly, as the season went on, the clients went back without all the animals they'd bought. The next year his bookings dropped dramatically. Randall took to the bottle.

A dependence on show-biz hype isn't all that contemporary writers and hunters have in common. They share the occupational hazard of drinking. Randall still hunted, but intermittently, and with a different company. Like a once-best-selling author whose last few books have died on the stalls, he'd changed publishers and headed downmarket.

"But what's happening now is nothing compared to what it'll be like in a few years," Masters went on. "This season a client's paying three thousand dollars a day. For that, of course, he wants his full list. What's he going to want when it's ten thousand a day? I tell you, by then I'll be taking people out to blast off at animals that might just as well be penned or tethered."

I frowned. "Penned or tethered?"

"It'll work like this," Masters explained. "Preseason, we'll dart our quotas from choppers. Every animal gets tagged with a micro-transmitter set at frequencies according to species. A client arrives with his list. Say he's got jumbo, pussy, kudu and sable. I switch on my receiver and tune it to pussy first. Then I do a directional scan. I get a signal that tells me we've got a lion in the concession due north of the camp. The signal strength says it's thirty miles out. Next day I can walk the client right up and watch him pump it full of lead. . . ."

Masters wasn't fantasizing. The technology had been available for several years. In the form he'd described, it was already being used to monitor the movements of several species, such as polar bears inside the Arctic Circle.

"But that's not all," he added. "Soon the client won't even need to come out here. He'll be able to rent visual and audio space on satellite. Say we get allocated thirty jumbo in Mababe. We auction them off. Some guy in New York buys one in and picks me as his hunter. I go out into the bush. I'm linked to him audiovisually. On my scope there's a video camera lens showing him what I'm seeing. I find jumbo and line it up in the sights. Then he fires—bang!"

"You reckon a client will buy that?"

"Buy it? He'll jump at it! Hell, just think of the possibilities." Masters hammered on the wheel. "He can throw a damn great party. He can have the sounds of the bush beamed to the room quadraphonic. He can spin the whole hunt out long as he wants. And then as a climax, while his girl and all his friends watch, he can kill jumbo or pussy in front of their eyes."

I gazed out at the darkness.

"See Joe's face?" Masters shouted over the engine's roar. "I tell you. Shit, is he going to hit jumbo tomorrow!"

The truck bucketed on. Masters was laughing uproariously. The metal bar was cold and hard. Over the hood, the winter-dry grains of stig grass broke in shining, phosphorescent waves.

It was dawn when we drove into Maun. The camp was in the grounds of the lodge under a twisted trunk of a huge old tree, plaited and twined by a strangler vine. Two louries, their blue-gray plumage soft in the morning mist, were drinking from the river's edge. I walked over to the line of camp beds where eight figures lay immobile in their sleeping bags. Only Syd opened one eye to check me in.

I kicked off my boots and crawled between the covers.

On a side table by my chair in Joe's camp had been a pile of booklets. As Masters and I left, I had picked one up. When I woke I examined it.

The paper was thick and expensive, the color illustrations crisp and glossy, the text that linked them bold and incisive. As a piece of production it would have done credit to a Swiss fine-arts publisher.

In fact it was a promotional brochure for one of America's leading taxidermists. The photographs showed examples of the establishment's art—room after room in mansions across the States crammed with trophies. Rearing polar bears, snarling wolves, bounding lions, fleeing antelope. All intricately mounted and suspended there for eternity. And in the center of each display, clothed and smiling but otherwise as lifeless as the animals, were the hunters, the men, women and children who'd killed them.

The booklet ended with a series of charts. I studied them. Each chart listed the trophy animals of the world's five continents. Every animal was given a rating from 1 to 10 in such categories as rarity, difficulty of approach, distance of shot, danger value and so on. Ideally, a hunter would have killed every animal on the list with maximum points in all categories.

For North America the danger value of a sheep was 1. I frowned. Then I turned back. On page 14, surrounded by his trophies in his private museum, was a certain Mr. Delton E. McCann, banker, of Detroit, Michigan.

"Delton McCann," the caption read, "has achieved the hunter's dream. He has a 100% record in every continent where he has shot! For skill, dedication and courage we salute Mr. McCann as one of the outstanding sportsmen of our generation!"

I searched the serried heads behind Mr. McCann. There was no black leopard. Finally I found the sheep. He or she—it was difficult to tell the sex—looked polite but gloomy. Its face reminded me of an elderly canon in the Church of England counting the take after Matins and finding more shirt buttons than coins in the collection plate.

Delton E. McCann. Banker. "They're the weirdest," Masters had said. I looked at the animal again.

"Cheer up, sheep," I said. "You nor lived nor died in vain."

"I beg your pardon?"

Bobby was gazing at me, puzzled.

"Sheep," I explained. "Bankers and danger value. Luckily, with men of Mr. McCann's courage—"

"Colonel," Bobby interrupted me. "No disrespect intended from the ranks, but you may have had a rather rough night. What about a little breakfast and a short lie-down?"

Twenty-five years ago the possibility that African big-game hunting might ever need defending would have been regarded by those who practiced it as inconceivable. The game was there in inexhaustible quantities. Man was a natural hunter. The bush was a destined testing ground for his skill and valor. It was as simple as that. Anyone who thought otherwise was an eccentric fool, a coward or a homosexual—the last two being, by definition in the bush, synonymous.

Today trophy hunting is increasingly under attack. In response, the professional hunter has become much more sophisticated. There are arguments to be put forward in defense of his craft, and he rehearses them fluently and convincingly.

"We have to," Masters remarked ruefully. "Every couple of seasons I get a client with a college-age kid who's come along for the ride. They've got 'ecology' dripping out of their ears. But I've got the answer. I can usually send them packing with their tails between their legs—politely, of course!"

He laughed. Of course. A hunter is never anything but polite.

And the arguments? They were first and most lucidly spelled out for me by Harry Selby.

"Game's a crop," he said. "It's just like wheat or barley. With good management, you can harvest it by rotation farming. The wild isn't depleted, and the local community benefits. . . ."

In the year after he set up his Kalahari operation, the district's budget balanced for the first time in fifty years from the concession rental he paid. Selby also created a hundred new jobs and generated substantial foreign earnings. The game population remained constant.

---

"More important," he went on, "controlled hunting actively supports and protects wildlife. What's the greatest threat to Kalahari game? Certainly not the tiny quotas we take out. No, poaching's the menace now. And I don't mean some old boy with a Tower musket. . . ."

The nineteenth-century Tower musket, plundered from some long-ago imperial battlefield to the south, was for long the Kalahari poacher's favorite weapon. A fine and fearsome-looking antique, it is not by modern standards a hyperefficient killing machine.

Selby was thinking of something quite different. The automatic repeaters that have filtered onto the plateau since the "liberation" wars around the desert's borders. They are not so much guns as instruments of mass extermination.

"You think I'm going to let a bunch of black cowboys strip my concessions bare? Roar through in their stolen trucks and slaughter every animal that moves? Believe me, my hunters are the best damn rangers/policemen in the country—and they don't cost the game department a *thebe*."

To the pragmatic Selby, conservation and self-interest were identical. The poacher who killed a single zebra was thieving redhanded from his warehouse. His private vigilantes, the hunters, were a powerful and unpaid deterrent to shoplifting in the wilderness.

"Finally, of course," he said, "what we do is no more than culling. People have this topsy-turvy idea that hunters invaded Africa and the settlers followed. Bollocks! It was exactly the other way round. The settlers came first and the hunters behind. If you like, we're just parasites, but useful parasites. We tidy up and keep the natural balance."

On the surface, sound and reasonable views. There was, of course, the occasional flaw in the argument. The concept of culling, for example. In the wild, culling means eliminating the old, the weak and the degraded by natural selection. The professional hunter, in contrast, has diametrically opposed priorities. Confronted by a pride of lions, he will select for his client not the poorest member but the finest—the dominant black-maned male or the proud and fecund reigning queen.

Bankers do not visit the Kalahari to vacuum the fleabag offal of the desert's species. They want the bold, the brave, the best.

Yet in the main, his opinions are those of an honorable, thinking man, and that—like Syd, like every Kalahari hunter I've met—he undoubtedly is. A courteous, concerned and learned man. One of the paradoxes of hunting is that the professional killer has as deep and vested an interest in the preservation of the wild as the most dedicated conservationist. Without game the hunter has no livelihood. And because game, like freedom, is indivisible—indivisible from the complex life-support systems of land, climate, vegetation, insect, bird and fruiting flower—the good hunter is axiomatically a good naturalist.

You seek to know where the African eagles fly? Where the morning wind-swift cheetah sleeps out the desert sun? Why the eland gallops straight, the greater kudu in curves and the long-horned gemsbok through elaborate figures of eight? How the elephant picks its path to water, and the reason the gold-backed jackal travels at evening a steady five paces to the west behind?

In the Kalahari you have a ready and expert source of answers at hand. Ask the man who kills and wishes to preserve them all.

So what, as the sun goes down—and all else aside, for them the sun is surely lowering—what of these men and their craft? What of the saturnine Selby, the jock-built Joe Regan with his rumpled hair and ready open grin; what of the stocky, pipe-smoking Gordon Masters, who keeps the battalion transport running under fire, and places unhesitatingly with chuckling delight a line from Shakespeare?

What of their few remaining companions in that elite and doomed fraternity—the last white hunters of Africa?

I thought of them all the next evening as I stood on the shores of Lake Ngami. We had finished with Maun and were on the move again. Ngami, our first camp on the trek south, was where the killing had started.

# 10

We rose even earlier than usual. There were the camp to be struck, stores to be taken on, farewells to be said. Carruthers, who'd heard we were leaving, passed by in his Land-Rover soon after dawn.

"See Boycott hammers those duskies, won't you, old lad?" he called out jovially. "Good hunting!"

He waved and drove on. Cameron Lyle was up early too. He came round and stood for a while cursing the chicken-obsessed Koszinski with savage Scottish oaths. Then he shook hands and wandered gloomily away. Lyle was followed by Gordon Masters—as spruce and wide-awake as if he'd been up for hours. Pipe clenched in his hand, Masters discussed the truck's engines with Syd, wished us well and strode off.

By 9 A.M. we were on our way. Looking back at the village as we drove out I felt a quick tug of regret. Even after a few days, the unprepossessing huddle of store and lodge and shantytown bungalow had become familiar and secure. On the stone plateau Maun had proved a true safehouse.

We headed south. The track was soft and sand-covered, but well marked. Pressing in from either side, the acacia thorn was thick and gray and hostile. The long, needle-pointed barbs speared out over the twin ruts that marked the route. To leave an arm carelessly hanging outside the truck was to risk having it stripped bare of flesh from shoulder to wrist. We had borrowed a canoe from the lodge to use on the lake. It was strapped precariously to the roof over the viewing hatch. I sat in its shadow as we jolted through the morning.

We were following the course of the Nxhabe River, and the track ran through cattle country. There were dust and swarming flies and occasionally, at the roadside, groups of Herero women in their brilliant turbans and long rainbow-colored gowns. The Herero had fled to Botswana from the west after fighting with their German colonial masters at the start of the century. Their dress was a legacy of the grimly modest Teutonic missionaries who'd been sent out to convert them.

Standing impassively in the heat they looked like guests summoned to some magnificent Kalahari ball the night before, but whom, unaccountably, the carriages had forgotten to collect when the orchestra stopped and the dancing ended. I expected them to raise their hands and ask for a ride home, but they made no move at all as we passed by. They might have been waiting for dusk and the violins to start up again.

We came to the lake in the early afternoon. When Livingstone arrived there, he saw a vast sheet of water stretching out to the horizon. During the night the water retreated, leaving the lake floor exposed. When it flooded back again next day, Livingstone became convinced he'd found an inland tidal sea, the first known to geography. For once, he was wrong. Ngami's shallow waters had been moved not by the moon but by the Kalahari wind.

There was no wind as we drove down to the shore, and the great expanse of water had long since vanished. Even in Livingstone's day it had been contracting swiftly. All that was left now was a series of inlets and lagoons separated by banks of reeds. Around the perimeter was a trampled belt of dry mud and broken grass stippled with endless hoofprints. Closer to the water, the mud became moist and dark. It was still corrugated everywhere by cattle.

We climbed out of the truck. An old man was beating a mule in front of us on the shore. The mule was pulling an iron drum filled with water. The animal lurched and stumbled forward as the man lashed its haunches. Behind them both a woman lifted her skirts and plowed wearily through the churned sand. They came abreast of the truck, looked at us sadly and trudged on. Afterward, lank cows, their eyes clotted with flies, congregated around us and then ambled away to drink.

For the next two hours we followed the lake's perimeter to the west. All along the shore the destruction wrought by the cattle was the same. The ground had been pulped and the plant roots smashed. Where once rich grass plain ran down to the water's edge, now there was only bare wasted earth, gray and sour-smelling. Every year the degradation bit deeper into the surrounding bush like an uncontrollably spreading sore.

As evening approached, the mosquitoes drove us back. They rose from the lakeside reeds and hung in black rustling curtains thirty feet high. In places the concentrations were so dense that they darkened the air. We recrossed the track and headed away from the water. A few minutes later, Syd stopped and swore. I looked out. George was standing disconsolately by the supply truck, which had broken down in the bush half a mile from where we were due to camp.

Leaving the others with Syd as he heaved out the toolkit, I walked back and climbed a ridge. Ngami was spread out below me in the sunset. By now, after more than a thousand miles, I had an overall image in my mind of the plateau's central and northern reaches. Everywhere we had traveled, the key to the life of the Kalahari was water. The fall of the unpredictable rains was critical, but so too were the arteries that run deep into the desert from Zimbabwe, down from the Chobe River, southward from the delta.

Of all the life-supporting reservoirs they'd created, the most significant was Ngami. It was here that the siege of the citadel and the wild had started. But for the lake's presence, the invasion might have been delayed a hundred years. Yet Ngami's water saved Livingstone's life, and unwittingly in return he became the agent not merely of the lake's destruction but of the assault on the entire plateau that followed. The game went first, those massive congregations which had covered the ground from horizon to horizon where I was standing. The heirs of the men who carried out that carnage were the professional hunters I'd left behind in Maun and at the camps scattered throughout the bush.

To dislike people like Selby, Masters, Regan and the others I knew was impossible. Unlike the mass slaughterers of the past, they were intelligent and responsible men. They cared deeply for the wild, and I had learned much from them. I counted them my friends. Their arguments, too, in defense of their craft were plausible and seductive. They acted as unpaid guardians of the wilderness, and what they and their clients killed, in comparison with what was lost through the ravaging of the land, was infinitesimal.

Yet in the end I found myself ranged against them. Harmless, even beneficial to the wild in themselves, they were in the service of an attitude—an attitude that accepted not merely the killing of animals for sport, but the destruction of the habitats they live in. As a naturalist, the hunter appreciates the difference. His clients do not. For them the two are inseparable. The hunter's clients as often as not are the remote instigators of the very programs that are clearing the wilderness.

After the first wave of hunters came the herders. To blame Livingstone for what they had done to Ngami was unjust. The cattle were there before his arrival, and the degradation of the lakeside pastures had already started. Yet the journey and its consequences undoubtedly accelerated the process. Now, with the pastures shattered and the game gone, the lake had lost its purpose. As if acknowledging the ruin, the waters had begun to shrink of their own accord.

As I watched, flights of white egrets began to wing back against the evening sky to their roosts. A flock of sacred ibis, their white wings scallop-edged with black, mingled with them. Behind, whirling like dust devils over the reeds, I could see clouds of tiny quelea finches. Then, farther away still, pelicans began to plane onto the water. As they touched the surface, their beating wings sounded like the distant trumpeting of elephants.

At least Ngami's birds hadn't deserted the lake. Behind me I heard Syd calling. The truck was repaired. I walked back, and we made camp in the darkness.

Uncharacteristically, both Big David and Bobby were silent and torpid next morning. David refused breakfast, and Bobby, after a single cup of coffee, slumped down in the truck's shadow with one of his books. His face was pale, and within half an hour he was sweating, although it was still too early for the day's heat to have reached us.

They were both clearly sick, but it was impossible to tell with what. Malaria, the obvious explanation two generations ago, was ruled out because, like all of us, they'd been taking a prophylactic. Carruthers had dealt with tsetse, and it was too soon for the symptoms of bilharziasis to have shown. The most likely answer was some viral infection from the water. EBL dosed them with a general-purpose antibiotic; we left them in camp and set out for the lake again.

On the shore we unloaded the canoe and paddled out through the reeds. The evening before, Ngami had seemed spent and broken, a dirty, fly-haloed cistern in place of the great shining waters thronged with hippos and crocodiles that had been there only a century earlier. But suddenly, away from land, everything changed. The clustering flies, the cattle stench, the sourness of the pitted and crusted earth all vanished. Instead there were long, brilliant lagoons, dragonflies and butterflies hovering over the surface, clean Kalahari air and sun. Above all, there were birds.

In spite of its contraction, the lake still covers an area of several hundred square miles. Depending on the water depth, in most years it supports one of the largest communities of birds in Africa. That year, for some species like the flamingos the water was too deep—the flamingos had deserted Ngami for the pans. But the rest, the hundred or so species which habitually use the lake, were there in numbers that defied counting.

There were those which feed in the waters below the surface—the cormorants, diving ducks, moorhens, gallinules and kingfishers. Those which crop the surface—the storks, herons, pelicans, skimmers and spoonbills. Those which hunt the shallows—the innumerable little waders—and those like the harriers which take their prey from the reed banks. And then all those from eagles to marsh owls to ibis to swallows which exploit the lake for drinking, for its insect life, for nest sites and nesting materials, for the prey creatures it sustains.

For two days, as we traveled the creeks, inlets and lagoons, I forgot about everything else—the animals that had vanished, the domestic cattle that had replaced them, the shoreside's destruction, the rank smells of the mud. Instead, I lost myself on the open water among Ngami's birds. They mantled us from dawn to dusk. Their calls and splashings and wingbeats filled every waking hour. At sunrise and evening I saw their skeins and colors and shapes against the desert clouds. Even in the darkest moments of the night there would be owls hooting; in the fiercest midday heat, an eagle or a falcon soaring.

At the start, I had reconciled myself to taking away from Ngami nothing but shadowy images of what had once been there, of the lost and half-forgotten. I was wrong. When the time came to leave, my mind was dazed and saturated with the lake's flocks. I was glad it was so. At least on the road I could hold to the memory of a bending wing, a drifting flight feather, a dazzle of plunging green and gold above a pool.

The journey south was worse than even Syd's grim prophecies had forecast.

The distance from Lake Ngami to Gaborone is almost eight hundred miles. The track runs in a great, curving sweep across thick sand layered over Kalahari rock. On either side there is nothing but scrub. Along the way, the scrub changes from low, sparse thorn to brush mopane and then back to thorn again.

The journey is long, monotonous and exhausting. Limestone outcrops and deep, soft sand beds punctuate the route. The uneven stone hammers a truck's chassis and lacerates its tires. The clinging sand slows speed to a walking pace. A good day may see two hundred miles covered. A bad one, less than half that. Throughout, there is heat and constant choking dust and, except at the irregular bore wells, no water.

Big David and Bobby were sick. They sat limp and morose and white-lipped on the jolting metal seats, their wrists shaking and their mouths intermittently flecked with froth. When we stopped, they stumbled out and lay down in the shade or at night fell without speaking into their sleeping bags. Their illness was baffling. Neither the antibiotics nor anything else we tried had any effect. It was only later, seeing David stripped one morning, that I realized what had happened. Close to the base of his spine was an infected puncture mark surrounded by an angry circle of bruised and swollen flesh.

On the inside of his thigh Bobby had the same. Both had contracted tick fever—a racking, dizzying infection transmitted by the bite of a tiny sand insect. The effect, the circulating flow of the poison in each, must have been agonizing. Neither complained; neither even mentioned it. They simply sat pale and shivering as we rocked and churned onward.

The rest of us, for different reasons, were exhausted too. From the start Syd had been bitterly opposed to the southern desert crossing. He sat hunched behind the Toyota's wheel, nursing his fatigue and anger like grievous wounds inflicted spitefully by the desert. EBL, her eyes reddening in the increasing dust, bounced and swayed numbly beside him. Even Little David, fresh from London and unmarked by the miles we'd traveled, began to drowse, wake suddenly and then drift back into apathy again.

Sand, stone, heat, dehydration and lacerating thorn. For mile after wearisome mile the pattern never changed. The sand lifted and clogged our nostrils. The stone beneath the track assaulted the Toyota and, rippling in shock waves up through its frame, kicked viciously at our bodies. The heat and its accompanying dehydration made us pant and shudder. The thorn was a constant threatening presence on either side.

Stubbornly, because we had no choice, we pushed on.

The village of Ghanzi, which lies one-third of the way along the route south, is the center of a dour and remote white cattle-ranching community, and another legacy of Livingstone's expedition.

In 1874, fired by reports of those who had followed the doctor across the plateau, a South African adventurer, Hendryk van Zyl, led a small column of pioneering settlers to the area. They arrived to find cattle country and a number of abandoned wells—left by Hottentot herders who had been there before them. Van Zyl built himself a two-storied mansion in the desert staffed by a hundred servants and furnished with French antiques. But his ranching enterprise was brief and ill-fated. A few years later he was murdered by San, and the venture collapsed.

At the end of the nineteenth century, Cecil Rhodes revived the project as a check to German colonial expansion from the west. The land was divided up into farms, and white families installed. By independence in 1960, there were almost two hundred working ranches around the village, watering their cattle from boreholes sunk into the desert rock. The boreholes have always been Ghanzi's lifeline, but even now no one knows whether the water drawn up is replenished yearly by some subterranean system leading down from the delta or whether it is ancient fossil water—and so finite.

If it is fossil water one day the wells will dry up, the ranches collapse and the land be returned to the plateau. Meanwhile, Ghanzi lies like a lonely little fortified outpost on crossroads that lead to nowhere. The village is dusty, grim-featured and silent. Throughout the desert it is famed for the local ranchers and for The Kalahari Arms, the saloon whose approach had almost moved David to tears. The Ghanzi ranchers are part of Kalahari folklore. They stand seven feet tall, sever barbed wire with their teeth, and can carry a seed bull under either arm through the midday heat.

We drove into the village in the afternoon. The ranchers were evidently out in the bush fencing their pastures or moving their stock. There was no sign of them, but the saloon was open. Before we adjourned there, everyone had letters to mail. We left Syd to organize the taking on of water and found the post office. It was smaller than the one at Maun, but there were three clerks behind the grille. I pushed the letters across the counter and asked for stamps. As I did so, the clock struck four.

"Closed," the senior clerk said.

He pointed at the dial and then at a notice. The notice informed customers that the Ghanzi post office was open for business between the hours of 9:00 A.M. and 4:00 P.M. By morning, we would be miles away.

I argued; EBL cajoled; Little David cursed; Big David, with increasing desperation in his voice, pleaded that the international monetary system would be put at risk if his mail didn't go off. To no avail. The post office shut at 4:00. We were ten seconds too late. The clerks looked at us stone-faced and silent.

Then Bobby intervened. He hadn't spoken before. Now he leaned over and addressed the senior clerk.

"Listen, Squire," Bobby said. "You're closed. Okay; no hard feelings. But how about this? You and I take a stroll outside. I give you the money for the postage—not officially, but as my mate. Tomorrow you come in here, buy the stamps, stick them on and tuck the letters in the cleft stick. Then you nip round to your side of the counter and it's business as usual."

The clerk thought for a long time. Then he nodded. Calculations were made, he and Bobby disappeared, the money was handed over and we set off for The Kalahari Arms.

"You, my fat friend, are deeply and seriously mad," Big David said.

"What do you mean?" Bobby looked aggrieved. "I've just arranged for your letters to be posted."

"You have just arranged for the purchase of three large whiskies." David glanced at his watch. "I give them no more than ten minutes. Let us see."

We went into the bar and sat down at a table in the corner. Exactly ten minutes later the door opened. Three figures marched in. They strode up to the counter and settled themselves in a row on stools.

"Three large whiskies, man," the senior clerk said.

For an instant Bobby froze. Then he leaped to his feet and crossed the floor.

"Please." The clerk was reaching into his pocket, but Bobby stopped him. "This round is on my friend in the corner. Gentlemen, let us drink to the glorious Kalahari mails."

The three turned to thank a startled David. Then they lifted their glasses, beaming, and drank. All our letters would arrive safely.

Soon afterward, Syd joined us scowling. The borehole pump was operating at a quarter strength. Instead of thirty minutes, it was going to take at least two hours to fill the water tanks. On any other stage of the journey, we'd have made camp outside the village as soon as George had finished. But Ghanzi's flies were as notorious as its ranchers, and even when the trucks were ready we'd still have to drive beyond the limit of the farms to avoid them.

We stayed in the bar until well after dark. Big David, to complete for him an evening of pure, boundless delight, found that the saloon stocked the ingredients for a drink called a Moscow Mule.

"A Moscow Mule," he explained, "is a delicate blending of raw vodka and old English ginger beer. In other words, old bean, a cocktail of pure nectar."

It turned out to be a favorite of the other foot soldiers too. The three of them sat there as the orders were repeated and the hours passed with the smiling, dreaming contentment of men who'd returned to safety after months of bitter trench warfare. Finally, with the water tanks at last full and George on his way ahead, we left.

Outside, it was bitterly cold, the coldest night of the journey. We drove shivering south through the darkness under the icy Kalahari stars with our breath pluming the air.

Two grinding, bone-chilling hours later, we spotted the supply truck's spoor angling away into the bush. We followed, and ten minutes afterward we pulled up before a blazing fire. Everyone that night slept long and deeply.

Only George, moving quietly among his kettles and pans, was up when I woke next morning. I climbed out of my sleeping bag and dressed. It was still icily cold, and as on the evening before, my breath lifted in clouds, but the sky above the trees was clear, and the day would be as hot as ever. George had chosen the site well—an acacia copse with open sand beneath the branches and a good supply of fallen wood for the fire.

For a few minutes I warmed myself by the flames. Then I walked away, following last night's tire spoor. It took me the same time to cover the distance to the track as it had taken the Toyota in the opposite direction. I reached it and stopped. The roadside clumps of grass were ungrazed—the signal to George that he'd passed beyond the boundaries of the ranches and could halt without being overrun by flies.

To north and south the twin ruts, walled as always by thorn, stretched out toward the horizon. The sun rose, the chill was drawn out of the air, and instantly the morning was crisp and fragrant; I smelled the scents of leaves and bark and resin. In the bushes' shadow, the sand covering the track was the soft blue-gray of autumn woodsmoke. A lilac-breasted roller dived, plucked an early-hatching insect from a wind's eddy and soared again. Somewhere close, francolins, the desert grouse, clucked and called among the thorn roots.

The quietness, the freshness and cleanness of a dawning Kalahari day held me for a moment unmoving. Then I glanced down. I was standing on the track. Around me there were crumbling tire marks and a scatter of black-and-white porcupine quills and the delicate splayed prints of a nightjar. I was standing on the Road of Death.

# 11

NOW SUDDENLY, my quest grew more intense. It was here if at all I would find the answers to the question posed by the poet and the politician. Here if at all I'd find the black leopard. We traveled the track all that day and the next. Big David and Bobby, after being briefly restored by Ghanzi's Moscow Mules, relapsed into the silent apathy of their tick fever. Syd clung grimly to the wheel as it jerked and spun beneath his hands. EBL and Little David dozed restlessly. I sat watching the dust spiral up behind us.

The Road of Death had been created to bring Ghanzi's cattle to market—to the abattoirs six hundred miles to the south from which the carcasses could be transported by rail for sale farther south still. It had earned its name from what characterized the journey. The trek could take three months. On the way cattle died by the score from thirst, starvation and heat. They perished too as prey of the great lion prides that lined the route—the prides Piet Maritz had been hired as a young boy to shoot.

As a business, desert cattle ranching was risky, hope-sapping, brutal in its physical demands, and often lethal. It was an enterprise for the solitary, the self-sufficient and the gambler. Often even the hardiest among those failed to survive the desert crossing. Wagon axles would crack, horses would break their legs on outcrops of stone, the rare wells would prove dry. Entire herds would die then—and so would the men who rode with them.

Gazing down on the sand in the morning heat, I remembered the last letter of the dehydrated and dying M. I had read it first almost thirty years before on the freezing landing of a Sussex farmhouse. What he'd written was still as vivid as it had been on that now-remote December day. I might never know his true name, the names of the friends he mentioned, the value and nature of the stamps he willed his children, the perplexing role of his wife in his career—none of the answers to the questions that had puzzled and obsessed me then.

Yet I had at least kept the childhood promise. I too had traveled the Road of Death. I had passed by his grave—it lay unmarked somewhere in the stone and thorn beside the track. And I had learned the answer to the most bewildering question of all: why had M come to the Kalahari? Like Livingstone, like the early traders and hunters, like the modern entrepreneurs, engineers, prospectors, pilots and storekeepers, he came in search of desert gold. Livingstone's gold was the charge of faith. For the rest it was, and remained, sturdy, ringing coin. M was no more than a digit added to the casualty figures in the ranks of the besieging army.

The Toyota swayed and rumbled on. By nightfall, as the temperature dropped again, we had completed half the journey. We made camp in a copse south of Lone Tree Pan. As I stood by the fire, Bobby wandered up. He was holding the inevitable book. Since the onset of tick fever his morale, like Big David's, had picked up each day with the arrival of dusk and the unloading of the expedition's liquor supplies.

He drained his glass and held the book out to me.

"The author's other major works," Bobby said, "are a paper on parachute design and a horticultural volume on growing begonias. This seems rather more relevant to our immediate circumstances."

I took the book from him. Stamped on the battered leather cover was the title: THROUGH THE KALAHARI WILDERNESS. Inside were printed LONDON and the date: 1886.

"As far as I can work out," Bobby added, "we're camping at the identical place where he pitched his tents. The problem with Svengali, of course, is that you can never be absolutely sure."

I opened the book and began to read. Bobby was right. There by the fire in the desert winter, we were standing where Svengali had stood gazing north up the Road of Death.

Of all the Kalahari invaders, he—the model for Du Maurier's creation—was the boldest and strangest.

He was not named Svengali. His name was Gilarmi A. Farini. That wasn't his name either. He was in fact William Leonard Hunt, an American born in New York in 1839, and even in the pantheon of the Kalahari's heroes—a company not noted for its modesty or lack of color—he stands out as a brilliant, gaudy and improbable star.

By profession, Farini—his adopted name fits him more comfortably than the prosaic Hunt—was an impresario. By instinct and experience, a street-wise hustler, a buccaneer, charlatan and rogue. But at heart he was also a dreamer, a dreamer of glorious, impossible dreams. A pursuer of rainbows and the crocks of gold at their end. A cavalier who launched himself on wild adventures, never found the fortunes they promised but always returned to weave marvelous tales out of the failure.

In promoting his extravaganzas Farini was fond of quoting Homer. He had much more in common with the old blind rhymer than he ever appreciated. How did this nineteenth-century fairground barker come to find himself in the southern Kalahari?

Farini's own story begins in 1864 when, imitating Charles Blondin, he crossed Niagara Falls on a tightrope. The feat earned him considerable notoriety. When his claims to have crossed the even more dangerous Chaudière Falls in Canada were accepted by his admiring public, he felt entitled to style himself "Farini the Great." Competition was snapping hard at Blondin's heels.

Fortunately for the great high-wire artist, Farini soon decided management was more lucrative and less hazardous than performance. He plunged into the entrepreneurial business, staged a variety of spectacles at Coney Island, and then in 1884 shifted his operations to London, where he'd bought an interest in an amusement center known as the Royal Westminster Aquarium. By this time Farini had also acquired a son and heir. His name was Lulu.

Lulu started his career as a ballistic statistic. Fired from a cannon into a net, he set the world distance record for a human missile. Delighted by his son's achievement and determined to put the record beyond reach forever, the enthusiastic Farini promptly doubled the gunpowder charge in the cannon's breech. Lulu soared over the net, made a pancake landing on a nearby sidewalk and broke his legs.

Somewhat disgruntled, Lulu decided on a change of occupation. He settled on portrait painting and photography. As a photographer he proved to be outstandingly successful—so successful that when in 1885 Farini decided to visit the Kalahari he took Lulu with him to record the journey. The reasons for the expedition, as with every venture Farini embarked on, were devious and obscure. Several years earlier, on one of his trips to Coney Island, with which Farini retained business connections, he had seen a fellow entrepreneur exhibiting a group of San. The tableaux enacted by the tiny Africans were attracting large and absorbed crowds.

Guessing that a similar exhibit would be just as successful in Europe, Farini dispatched his assistant Healey to South Africa with instructions to acquire another group. In due course Healey returned. He was accompanied by a tough old half-breed hunter named Gert Louw and six puzzled and seasick San—including a twelve-year-old girl named N'icy, "the daughter of two fine specimens that ran away."

The San didn't let Farini down. Exhibited as "Farini's African Pygmies or Dwarf Earthmen from the Interior of South Africa," they turned out to be even more popular than he'd anticipated. In particular, their "Exciting Torture Dances over War Captives"—with a little additional choreography by Farini himself—enthralled the London audiences that flocked to the Aquarium.

And there, with another of his strange and curious novelties doing a roaring trade at the box office, Farini's tenuous relationship with the Kalahari might have ended. It did not. Searching the San's belongings, by his own account, for poison, Farini claimed to have found several diamonds. Grizzled old Gert Louw had also spoken of diamonds in the great desert. Furthermore, the hunter had described the cattle-ranching possibilities of the Kalahari—and Farini was already involved in ranching in Ontario.

Diamonds, cattle or simply another and secret crock of gold at the end of a Kalahari rainbow? It does not matter. Whatever the true motive, in early 1885 Farini, Lulu and Gert boarded the *Roslin Castle* for Cape Town. Secrecy was paramount; but unfortunately, it had been breached. Word of the expedition had leaked out. To disguise their tracks and throw off pursuit, Farini decided the three would travel under assumed names. The one he chose for himself was Hunt. The only certain way he could think of to preserve his anonymity was to use his own name.

At Cape Town, Gert made himself responsible for securing wagons, bearers and provisions. Then the party headed for the interior. Early in the journey they came across a German trader, Fritz Landwer—or "I'll-Vatch-It," as Farini christened him after his favorite expression. Landwer was on the point of dying from thirst. With the help of their water he recovered, and he accompanied them for the rest of the trip.

In all, they were away some six months. They failed to find any diamonds, and the desert's potential for cattle ranching seemed small, but Farini turned the journey to good account with a book, *Through the Kalahari Desert,* which he published the following year. A suitably racy account of their adventures, it shows that even in the wastes of the stone citadel Farini's nimble showman's presence of mind never deserted him. Treed by a wounded lion, he spotted one of his San porters standing transfixed below. "Up here, man," Farini shouted, "or you're a gone coon!" Whereupon he leaned down, gripped the man by the hair and heaved him up into the branches.

Almost incidentally, midway through the book Farini recounts his discovery of the Lost City of the Kalahari. The story is illustrated by a drawing of a ruined building with "fluted pillars."

The book sold well, and Farini was invited to address the august Royal Geographical Society. He was received there with acclaim, but later a number of travelers challenged his version of his experiences—notably in relation to the Lost City. Unperturbed, Farini rapidly mounted another San exhibit and happily banked the take as well as his continuing royalties.

Not long afterward, Farini disappears from the spotlight. World War I found him interned in Germany. On his release he retired to Ontario, where he transferred his energies to cultivating begonias and died at ninety in 1929. Well before then, the lease of the Aquarium had been sold. The new tenant was Lily Langtry.

After the Jersey Lily made her final bow and left the stage, the building was demolished. Today on the site where once Farini's mermaids sang and dwarf earthmen performed their exciting torture dances, there stands the somber and disapproving Wesleyan Hall.

Yet the legend of the Kalahari's Lost City survives. And not merely survives—like a well-planted vine, it has grown and flourished. Since Farini, at least thirty-seven major expeditions have set out into the desert in search of what he claimed to have discovered.

What exactly was it that he, Lulu, old Gert and I'll-Vatch-It found? What was their precise route? What is to be made of Lulu's superb photographs?—and the photographs are indeed superb. Do the Kalahari sands truly roll and move as Farini insisted and many since him believe?

The questions accumulate. Fifteen years ago they were examined and answered with clinical detachment by the experienced South African anthropologist John Clement. In essence, he demonstrated that Farini was a fraud. A brave, enterprising and attractive fraud—but a fraud nonetheless. The route recorded in the book was impossible. Dates, distances and places were irreconcilable.

What Farini found, and what Lulu on his instructions photographed, was a strange geological formation. Vivid imagination and a showman's calculating eye converted the random stones into a marketable myth. There were no conveniently moving sands to bury the ruins after Farini passed by. The Lost City was a fable. One above all of the arguments marshaled to bury Farini's claims is irrefutable. A city needs permanently available water. Where Farini located his ruins there was not and never had been any water. The case was closed.

And then, fifteen years after the ghost of Farini's Lost City had been finally laid, a scientific paper was published. The paper's authors had no interest in the swashbuckling and now discredited Victorian huckster, even less in the detritus of some ancient Phoenician civilization or the ruined workings of King Solomon's mines. They were climatologists. Their field of study was the southern Kalahari. They had analyzed the sediment on the floor of the pans, and they had reached a conclusion.

Ten thousand years before, and quite possibly much more recently, the area was lake-filled, verdant, rich and fertile. It was ideally suited to human habitation.

When Farini first came under sustained attack, the *South African Star* commented wistfully: "The least the country can do for the lost city of the Kalahari is to proclaim it a national monument, 'whereabouts at present unknown.' "

The old rogue no doubt would have chuckled, consulted his Homer, and started composing copy for handbills to announce another astonishing novelty spectacular from the heart of Africa—admission, as advertised, one shilling.

---

We left the site of Farini's camp, and ours, soon after dawn. We were traveling fast and light now, and there were none of the elaborate dismantling procedures to be gone through. We merely rolled up the sleeping bags, heaved them into the truck, stamped out the fire and brushed away the embers, and set off again.

Our purpose was solely to leave no trace—the tire spoor apart, which the desert wind would brush away—that we'd traveled the southern Kalahari trail. We obliterated the camp and drove on.

We drove all morning. The day was hazy, arid and airless, and the track as bad as it had been all week. In five hours we covered less than twenty miles.

Sometimes we were in cattle country. At others, in the belts of ungrazed grass plain that intersected it. Unless one stopped and studied the ground, the only noticeable difference between the two was the presence of flies. The parched scrub was a uniform chalky-gray and the sky a sultry white. Close to the truck, the thornbushes were thirty yards apart; farther away, they merged into what appeared to be an unbroken spiny wall. It was only a trick of the eye: in reality they were the same even distance apart.

The Toyota lurched on. We sat inside cramped and sweating and irritable with fatigue and heat. Then at midday we reached a stockaded kraal under the shadow of an acacia. A Tswana woman came out and pointed toward the south. We saw the supply truck's spoor and followed it into the bush. Half an hour later we came to another stockade. Syd stopped by the arched entrance, and we climbed down.

There was no shade here, and the bone-dry stakes shimmered in the heat. The air was rank with the smells of man and cattle—smoke and dung and drying meat. A middle-aged Tswana appeared and greeted Syd. He spoke no English, but he was evidently a man of some substance and authority. As he and Syd talked, I suddenly noticed a face watching us from behind the stakes. It was a child's face, a girl of maybe nine or ten. Her eyes were bright, curious and unblinking. The face itself was flattened, but the features were sharper and more delicate than the ordinary Tswana's. Most striking of all was the color of her skin. It wasn't black but a deep, warm apricot.

She saw me looking at her and she smiled. Then she vanished so swiftly that it wasn't until I saw her again a few minutes later inside the stockade that I was sure she'd been there at all. She was a San.

There were seven of them at the kraal. Three women, three men and the child. They worked for the Tswana, a local headman, tending his cattle in what is known as "client status." To be a client means to receive a little food in return for labor. The term is, of course, a European one. It was minted by a commission set up to determine whether the relationship between the San and the Tswana amounted to slavery. The commission decided slavery wasn't involved and produced the concept of client instead.

We walked among them. Two of the men were cleaning a gemsbok hide. They worked apathetically, stripping the tattered flesh from the leathery skin with old kitchen knives. Periodically they would break off and hone the blades against pads of hardened skin on the soles of their feet. On the far side of the kraal a woman was squatting over a cooking pot. She was wrapped in a blanket, and she had the face of an angry bird. As I approached she scowled, chattered furiously and shook her hand at me.

I turned away. The third man wandered up. He was wearing a leather hat and a plaid shirt. Nothing else. The shirt was vaguely familiar. I stared and realized why. The plaid was Dress Stuart, the ceremonial tartan of the royal house of Scotland. It had been bleached almost to the color of dust by the sun.

The man was much the oldest of the group. It was impossible to guess how old. He moved stiffly; his skin was creased and gnarled like thorn bark, his tiny limbs wasted to brittle sticks. In Europe he'd have been at least eighty and probably more. In the Kalahari the San age rapidly, and he could have been twenty years younger. He stopped and gazed up at me. I gazed back.

His eyes were dark and clouded. They were the most unfathomable eyes I had ever seen. They were neither interested nor uninterested. I might have been a stake in the kraal wall, but they were utterly remote from me. He simply looked at me and then through me and then beyond the most distant point on the desert horizon.

He wasn't seeing the stockade or the bush or even the sky. He was watching something else.

Then he moved away and sat down. He hitched up his shirt and started to scratch his groin. In spite of his age, he still had the firm, erect penis that is one of the San people's proudest characteristics. A sudden gust of wind swept through the stockade. The wind covered his groin with sand. He gripped his penis with one hand and the shirttail with the other. Then, using the royal tartan like a duster, he carefully flicked around it and brushed the sand away.

The other two women were arguing. Or they seemed to be arguing. When you listen to any other language it's normally possible to guess the general tenor of a conversation even without understanding a word of what's being said. The sounds are at least recognizable as human speech; they belong to a familiar world. Not when the San talk. The clicks and snaps are birdlike, alien and impenetrable. They are the communication of a different planet.

The Tswana headman joined me. He remonstrated with the women. They ignored him so completely he might not have existed. The headman shrugged and stalked off. The two men scraping the gemsbok hide sliced away a strand of rancid fat, divided it and sucked out the juices. The woman by the cooking pot glowered malevolently. In a band of shadow at the back of the kraal the child danced. She reached down, scooped up a handful of sand and hurled it into the air. The sand sprayed out in a glittering phosphorescent arc above her. She leaped to catch the highest grain. Her hand closed around the Roman candle of flying sparks, and she dropped back to the ground like a tumbling salmon.

She skipped and smiled at me again. Her skin was gold, and her body was furred with sweat. The old man polished his penis with the faded Stuart plaid.

"What a whanger!" Little David said reverently.

Syd looked acutely unhappy.

"I had a Bedouin once. . . ." Big David wrinkled his face, remembering. "Came to a sticky end in the Negev. But he had a truly wondrous knob. We used to measure its shadow on the dunes in the evening."

"In the Amazon basin," Bobby volunteered, "I've seen ones you could fly flags from."

They stood together reminiscing. There were more untreated

hides in a grass-roofed rondavel. The stench was overpowering, and clouds of bloated flies buzzed round our heads. The headman watched us disconsolately. He'd hoped we would shoot another buck, but his son came into the kraal and reported that the gemsbok had deserted the pan where they'd been feeding. Syd looked more and more distressed about everything.

Later as we rocked back through the bush toward the Kokong track, Syd said, "Times change, Colonel."

He sounded both aggrieved and apologetic. He was like a man who's promised to show a visitor the glory of Niagara Falls and arrives there to find someone has turned off the water.

"Times indeed change," I agreed.

"I mean, I've got this Argentinan professor of anthropology," he went on. "He came out here a couple of years ago looking for Bushman. I heard of a group. I went on ahead to set up camp. When I got there, I found the little buggers were all wearing T-shirts saying, 'Coca-Cola adds life.' I only just managed to strip them off and dress the sods in hides before he arrived. . . ."

Syd shook his head glumly.

"He's been promising to come back ever since. I tell you, if he doesn't make it soon he'll have nothing left to study—T-shirts or not."

I stared at the thorn. I was thinking of my last visit to the desert.

Late one afternoon we came upon another group of San. We were driving through tall grass and we stopped, and suddenly they materialized in front of us, peering at the truck through the bending stems. They were also in client status, but unlike the ones we'd just left, they weren't penned in a kraal. They were tending Tswana maize fields, and they had their own camp in the bush beyond.

I got out and walked with them to the camp. They'd encountered Europeans before, and they knew what they were expected to do: plait rope from fibrous leaves, carve beads from ostrich eggshells, make fire from sticks. I sat down. Scrupulously and with great dignity they went through their repertoire. I watched. There was no thought of payment. It was simply a ritual obligation on both sides —the San to demonstrate their skills, I, the foreigner, to observe, which was what they'd learned foreigners wished to do.

They finished. I expressed my thanks and handed them some cigarettes. The San have a passion for tobacco and they gave me a volley of quick handclaps in appreciation. I stood up to leave. Then I paused. The whole performance had been as decorous and genteel as a church bazaar—and just as bland. I glanced around.

The last trick they'd performed from the deck of San arts was to weave a snare for a small animal. The snare's loop was pegged above the ground in a split sapling. I caught the arm of the man who'd woven the loop and propelled him toward it. For an instant he looked at me appalled, as if even touching him had been the grossest, most offensive assault. Then he saw I was smiling, and he understood. The San's passion for tobacco is as nothing compared with their passion for jokes.

The man broke away from me and trotted forward like a jackal. He put his foot through the loop, and the snare tightened round his ankle. He stopped; jerked his ankle back; studied it, puzzled, and shook his leg. Then he started to circle around the pegged sapling. He howled and jumped and worried at the noose and howled again.

The others laughed. Not the tentative gathering laughter of people uncertain at first whether something is really funny or not. But the laughter that breaks as thunderclap and rolls on as tidal wave. They were witnessing the funniest event in the entire history of the universe. It was a joke without precedent, beyond measure and beyond compare, and they knew it instantly.

They laughed until they fell. They rolled head over heels in the grass, beat the ground, staggered to their feet and collapsed again. Tears welled from their eyes. They clutched each other, tried to communicate the sheer extravagant unbelievable hilarity of what was happening, and reeled away gasping for breath.

For the man mimicking the jackal it was too much. No one on earth could have resisted the infectiousness of those pealing, bubbling waves of sound. He danced and barked and plunged. Then the barks spilled over into laughter too. He toppled onto his back and lay there with his legs in the air and his chest heaving with helpless delight.

"Whangers, mind you, are only whangers," I heard Little David saying reflectively.

"True, old bean," Big David answered. "But south of Baghdad they know a tradesmanlike knob when they see one. It's all a matter of proper respect and the use it's put to. I remember once . . ."

We hit a springhare burrow and I lost David's story. I thought of the dancing jackal in the winter grass and the child with the apricot skin who'd tumbled like a river-running salmon. And the San people.

As little as three hundred years ago, the San occupied most of southern Africa from the Cape northward. The land had always been their territory, and it supported a population of perhaps half a million of them.

Then, almost simultaneously, in the mid-seventeenth century white settlers landed at the Cape and migrating Bantu tribes started to press down from central Africa. They weren't the first arrivals—long before them the Hottentots and early groups of Tswana had trekked south across the continent—but the demands of the newcomers were different not merely in degree but in kind. They were both, black and white, true invaders. They wanted land—all the land.

As the two waves rolled toward each other, the baffled San found themselves caught in the middle. Land, to them, couldn't be owned any more than stars, water or sunlight could be owned. Land was a life-providing resource available to all under a delicate system of sharing agreements. Yet the invaders were enclosing it, stripping it and populating it with cattle. And if the San tried to appropriate as much as a single cow, they were shot down without mercy. The San were unused to fighting, but they turned and fought for survival.

They fought with the terrible unflinching valor of despair. The struggle was senseless. Often the enemy would find they'd come forward after an engagement to inspect a disputed valley or pasture. The San weren't interested in finding out what casualties they'd inflicted. They simply wanted to see again the richness of the grass or the play of light on a river pool—and somehow reassure themselves that what was being destroyed in madness was real. When they did that, they could be killed without risk or difficulty.

They had arrows dipped in lethal poison, they were superb marksmen and the bush was their home. Against white guns and the disciplined Bantu masses, it was not enough. It was hopelessly, pitifully inadequate. They were hounded, hunted down, rounded up and slaughtered.

They were even slaughtered for sport. As late as the early twentieth century, a Kalahari rancher describes setting out one Sunday morning in search of game.

He follows first gemsbok, then a solitary sable antelope, then a herd of impala. He loses them all. On the way back he spots a pair of San, a young man and a young woman. They have been cut off from the family group they belong to, and they are running. He spurs his horse, rides them down and shoots them from the saddle—the woman first and then, after a chase, the man.

He was back at his ranch in time for breakfast with the bodies draped across the horse's withers. He ate, and afterward, it being Sunday, he went to church for Matins.

The San resistance collapsed. Not that it had ever been resistance in any normal sense. The very word implies organization, common values and a joint will to resist a foe. The San had no organization beyond a few overlapping family units. No common values apart from those so blindingly obvious as the primacy of air and food and life. No joint will except a bewildered and futile desire to prevent the newcomers from committing murder at the same time as they committed suicide.

The San fought and died, and then those who were left fell back. They retreated to their last sanctuary, to the center of the Kalahari. There, in the inner keep of the upland fortress, they gathered to make a final stand against the lethal insanity of the invaders.

The invaders declined to pursue them. The citadel's heart was too brutal and remote to be worth the cost of conquest. The little people were welcome to its rock and thorn and heat. There weren't, of course, many little people left by then. The population of half a million had been reduced to some twenty thousand. Out of every twenty-five at the start of the twin assault, twenty-four had died.

For the San, the "war"—an alien and meaningless term—was over. The blacks and whites carved up the land from the desert's ramparts to the sea. The San hid themselves in the wastes at the center, in the arid, bitter places the newcomers scorned and feared. Occasionally, as the years passed, they ventured out toward the plateau's borders. When they did, more often than not they were trapped. Their young girls were taken as brides by the Tswana; the family group was coerced into client labor; the men were persuaded to abandon the desert and work in the vaults of the South African mines.

The San wasted away. Interbreeding blurred their identity. The tide of cattle spread out across the Kalahari plains and eroded their living space. Their way of life broke down. And then, toward nightfall in their history, something astonishing happened.

European man found the first convincing explanation of his beginnings. He found it in the archeological leavings of the African gorges and lakeshores. He pieced the fragments together and discovered that his ancestors might have been small apricot-skinned hunter-gatherers living on the desert plains. If he was right, Eden had another name. It was the Kalahari. He looked at the desert and realized, appalled, that the children of Adam and Eve were on the point of leaving the Garden.

The shadows of the last San were already lengthening on the plateau as they walked away.

The presence of the San had been with us throughout the entire journey. From the Boteti River onward, their tracks were inescapable. Two arched and long-abandoned sticks to mark a resting place on the grass plains. A set of the eyes, a high cheekbone, a golden cast in the face of an otherwise purebred Tswana girl. The trick of plaiting grass fibers and weaving them to rope strength demonstrated by an old man—whose skill was not his own but borrowed.

They were all the spoor of the little people, and their prints were everywhere on the plateau. The spoor remained, but the San were moving on. They came, they believed, from the Kalahari stars. Now they were climbing back up the ladders down which they'd been lowered from the desert night's constellations. With them as they went they were taking perceptions and understandings acquired across a hundred thousand uninterrupted generations—and that we, divided from them, separated from our brothers, had forfeited.

They were carrying away their stories. They had packed on their backs the experience necessary to live with the wild—the interpretation of gazelle and lion spoor, the reading of sun-slant, wind drift and the sail of rain cloud, the calligraphy of plant and night dew and pooled water. They were taking it all, and they were leaving. They were walking off with so much—in their eyes the precise color of a ripening berry, the scrawl of a tuber root, the strange junction of hive, badger and honey guide—that we could not even begin to believe what they were removing.

Anthropologists tried to unravel what was being shouldered away on the small, bright apricot limbs. They found the design of the world's first truly affluent society—a hunting-gathering society where two hours' work a day was enough to provide the group with a strong, rich, living and laughing existence. They discovered plenty and peace and culture interwoven by song, fable and legend. They discovered that the San communities functioned better, by all the criteria they could apply, than the most advanced civilizations of the West.

They learned the lessons—and as they began to digest them, the fugitive groups of their studies, the nomadic San, retreated into the central desert.

It was there that we camped on the seventh night of our journey south. We found no San. Instead, we found another searcher for Kalahari gold.

George heard the sound first. I saw him get to his feet on the other side of the fire and stand with his head cocked to one side, listening.

"Truck coming, *Morena*," he said to Syd.

We all stood up. After a moment I caught the distant hum of an engine. Then a pair of headlights appeared, bouncing and wavering through the darkness. The lights came closer and the truck stopped. The driver must have spotted our fire. He turned off the track and drove toward the camp.

"Shit," Syd said. "Who the hell's out here in the bush at this hour?"

It was 10 P.M. Like the rest of us, Syd was exhausted. All he wanted to do was sleep. But the conventions of the desert required us to greet the traveler, give him whatever help he needed and if necessary share the fire with him for the night.

The vehicle drew up. It wasn't a truck. It was a huge silver Chevrolet limousine, one of the special models made for the African bush. The waxed paintwork gleamed through layers of dust, and the firelight sparkled over the great chrome bumper. In the Kalahari night it looked as elegant and incongruous as a slumbering barracuda.

At the wheel I could see the silhouette of a Tswana driver. There was another figure behind. The rear door opened and a man got out.

"Is good evening," he said. "Excuse me, is lost."

He stood by the car ramrod-straight, with his arms rigid by his sides and his chin up, as if he were on parade. He was about thirty. He had unblinking ice-blue eyes and cropped fair hair, and he was wearing a spotless safari suit that might have belonged to a staff officer in Rommel's Afrika Korps.

For several moments, we all gazed at him astounded.

"I think we've just found Reinhard Heydrich," Big David murmured finally.

Then Syd gulped and asked, "Where are you heading, my friend?"

"Kokong," the man answered.

He wasn't German. He was Swedish, and his name, as far as we could gather, was Eriksson. By tradition, all Scandinavians speak fluent, perfectly accented English. Eriksson, if that was right, was the exception. The range of his vocabulary would have made the average talking parrot smug, and his accent was almost impenetrable.

What he did have was an expression of grim, fanatical determination such as I've never seen before or since. Eriksson had come out to Botswana on a Swedish aid program for livestock improvement. He was carrying frozen semen from a champion Charolais bull to impregnate the Kokong cattle herds. Eriksson was going to see that the seed reached its destination—or die in the attempt.

Syd carefully explained the route. Eriksson gave us all in turn a curt formal bow of thanks. Then he climbed stiffly back into the Chevrolet, and the silver limousine crunched away through the bush.

All of us except for Big David settled wearily into our sleeping bags. David stood for ten minutes watching the retreating car. When he came to bed at last, he was frowning.

"What's the matter, foot soldier?" I asked.

"I fear we have what we in the motor trade call an ongoing track-overshoot situation," he said.

David was right. The Swede had missed the track and plowed on into the scrub. A quarter of an hour later, I sat up. A pair of headlights was tracking the night sky above a churning engine. The sound grew louder; the car hurtled through the thorn a hundred yards to the west; then the roar died away. Five minutes afterward, the glow reappeared.

Big David was sitting up too. The others were all so numb with fatigue they were unaware of what was happening. Not David. He'd sensed an impending disaster, and he was sniffing the air as alert as a hunting caracal.

"Jesus wept!" he said happily as the Chevrolet thundered by again.

Over the next two hours the car circled us like some manic moth unable to tear itself away from the flames of our fire. At intervals there would be silence for minutes on end. Then, just as I thought it had finally broken free, the hum on the horizon would return and the lamps would scorch the darkness once more.

At 1 A.M. the car made a final scything sweep through the bush and came to a halt.

"Suitable moment to investigate, I think," David said.

We heaved ourselves out of our sleeping bags and walked over to where the car had stopped. Eriksson was standing by the hood peering at a map. He'd evidently made periodic searches on foot. His hair was matted with grass. His elegant suit was in shreds. His arms and legs were streaked with blood from thorn lacerations.

Yet his face was still set with implacable determination. Like the captain of some desert *Flying Dutchman,* he might be doomed to roam the bush forever—but he'd never give up.

"Is not wishing disturb you," he said apologetically. "Is still a little lost."

"Don't worry, old bean," David answered. "We'll see you right. . . ."

Then he added in a whisper to me, "I'll handle this one, Colonel. Just keep him occupied for a minute."

He picked up the map. I took the Swede aside. As I talked to him, I could see David bending in through the driver's window and hear the murmur of voices.

David rejoined us. "All sorted out. There's an alternative route to Kokong. Bit longer, but you can't miss it. You just leave it to the driver. He knows the form. You'll be there by morning."

Eriksson drew himself to attention again and started to stammer out his thanks.

"A pleasure, Reinhard," the beaming David cut him off. "Greetings to the Third Reich. Now off you go."

We guided the car back to the track. The driver turned east. The lights vanished, and after a while there was silence.

"What did you do, Dave?" I asked as we headed for camp.

"Reasoned with our tinted friend behind the wheel," David answered. "There's a village called Tubane. Same distance from here as Kokong, but on the Kanye road. That's where RH is going to find himself at breakfast."

"He doesn't want Tubane—"

"Listen, Colonel," David explained patiently. "Comrade Heydrich doesn't know one toto dorp from another. Breakfast, he'll see a circle of huts and some jolly old ruminants. Driver says it's Kokong. Kokong it is. Out with the semen. Arm up the uterus. Mission accomplished. Everyone, including local toto farmers, happy as clams."

"What makes you think the driver's going to cooperate?"

"Insurance."

We'd reached the fire. David held something up. I looked at his hand. I saw one half of a twenty-pula bill.

"Driver's got the other," David added. "Collects this if he reports success in Gab's next week."

I was silent for a moment. To the driver, twenty pula was two weeks' wages. The wretched Swede barely spoke English, let alone Botswana. The local cattle ranchers, well aware by now of the benefits of aid programs, would greet him like a gift from heaven.

"Dave, you're a thoroughgoing scoundrel," I said finally.

"Think so? Pity. Always considered myself a man of vision. I mean, imagine visiting Tubane in a couple of years and seeing the landscape littered with sodding great Charolais." David chuckled. "Sleep well, Colonel."

He got back into his sleeping bag.

He was still chuckling when he rose next morning. His tick fever had clearly gone. Whatever else, the wandering Swede had proved a more effective cure than any of EBL's antibiotics.

We pushed on. That night's camp would be our last before we reached Gaborone.

We stopped late in the afternoon. We had moved out of cattle areas and into what Syd called the clean country—the belt of grass plain studded with little pans that rims the southern desert.

Before supper I walked out into the bush. Half a mile from camp I came to a pan and sat down on the bank that ringed it. With the disappearance of cattle, the game had returned. Three gemsbok were grazing on the far side of the bowl, and against the horizon I could see the horns of a herd of hartebeests. The sun was on the point of setting. As it vanished, a sudden last flare of light poured over the landscape.

The southern Kalahari was Syd's favorite part of the desert. As the light washed round the bowl, I understood why to him it was the clean country. The air glittered. It had a clarity and radiance I had not seen even on the plains of the Boteti. Every distant detail—the velvet on the gemsbok's muzzle, a bending grass blade across the pan, a tiny moth in flight—was crisp and brilliant. There was no dust or haze or smell: only a chill and flawless purity.

Then the light drained away, stars appeared in the darkening sky and the shadow of a hunting owl drifted across the ground. I walked back to the fire. That night, for the first time in a week, I heard lions roaring close to the camp.

Next day we drove into Gaborone. We had come to the end of the Road of Death. With almost bewildering suddenness, the desert crossing was over. The following morning the expedition broke up.

EBL was the first to leave. I put her on the flight to Johannesburg, from where she'd catch a connection to London. She left brown and smiling and happy. With the plunder she'd garnered from the desert —the leaves, grasses, berries and feathers, her now-filled sketch pads and notebooks—she'd live with the Kalahari in her work for months to come.

The foot soldiers departed later in the day, heading for Little David's ranch in Zimbabwe. I accompanied them to the airport.

"Goodbye, Colonel," Big David said.

"Goodbye, Colonel," Bobby said.

"Goodbye, Colonel," Little David said.

I shook hands with them one by one. Then they climbed into the plane. As it took off, I glimpsed them through the window. Their arms were raised in farewell. I waved and turned away.

They had traveled with me almost two thousand miles across some of the harshest terrain in Africa. They had spent interminable hours trudging through sand and bush, or jolting wearily on metal seats in the backs of trucks. They had endured heat, thirst, boredom, cold, charges by elephants and buffalo, the assault of mosquitoes and the debilitating ravages of tick fever. Not once had I had a single complaint. Throughout, they'd been loyal, resourceful, funny and fearless. Livingstone had established a sound method of choosing companions for a journey into the wilds.

There were people I wanted to see in Gaborone, and I'd arranged to stay on there for another forty-eight hours. When they were over, I went to say goodbye to Syd. It was the second time we'd ventured into the Kalahari together. We'd had our differences, resolved them and completed the expedition. Once again, as a guide he'd proved peerless; but he was more than a guide now—he was a friend. I owed him much, and said so.

He waved me aside, chuckling. "Save your breath for this, Colonel."

He bought me a beer, and we stood talking—not about the past, but about the expeditions to come.

I took the evening flight out for Johannesburg. The flag of Botswana, the black and white and blue, lifted from the control tower in the desert winter wind as I walked toward the plane. Looking up at it, I said my farewell to the stone plateau. As the plane rose from the runway, I thought I had left the Kalahari. I was wrong.

# 12

At Johannesburg I booked myself on the morning's flight to London. Then I checked into the airport hotel. I dined alone, read for a while in my room and went to bed.

I could not sleep. It was like the night, two months ago now, before the expedition started. I felt restless and, for some reason I couldn't work out, troubled. In Gaborone I'd been preoccupied by the black leopard. Since then I'd crossed the desert in search of the animal and failed to find it. My plan had been to tread quietly, ask no questions and let the leopard come to me. It had chosen not to come.

Somehow, that didn't matter. Perhaps I had never truly expected to find it. Perhaps I had known from the start that it was a creature of myth and fable—a hunter's fantasy created and embroidered over a Kalahari fire in the winter dusk. I wasn't sure. I did know that what was troubling me was something different.

I climbed out of bed. There was no balcony to walk out onto and stand in the night wind gazing north across the plateau. Only a barred window and the sterile air-conditioned atmosphere of the little room, with the traffic fumes and the sodium lamps below. I picked up my book again.

It was the saga of the Viking chieftain Harald Hardraada. The Norse chronicler wrote in sentences as terse and vivid as cables from a trench-warfare command post. I read of the northern sea and the seabirds crying and the cold breakers and the flung spume, and suddenly I had an overwhelming desire to be where Hardraada had voyaged. He'd taken his longship down the gray Atlantic to the Hebrides.

I understood then why Livingstone to the last had clung to his vision of himself as an islander. The isles were clean and strong, austere and unperplexed. Their cliffs were hewn from granite. Their people wise and sure. Their garland of life modest—harebells in the lochside peat and red deer on the sunlit upland moors and a sentinel eagle against a Highland sky.

The isles were safe. Safe as the Glasgow doctor's faith if chance or choice or divine direction hadn't assigned him to the Kalahari. The desert destroyed him. Even in despair he reached for the island of Ulva. It was the only spell he could cast back against the terrible magic of the stone citadel. Like a frightened child in the dark, Livingstone clutched at the rocky ocean tower Hardraada left to starboard in a violent Hebridean storm.

Hardraada sailed on. He reached the Cumbrian coast and made a landfall. There were an estuary village and fat mountain sheep on the hill slopes above and Saxon-descended women with barley-colored hair and hips like rounded butts of mead. In the best tradition of good Vikings, Hardraada raped and pillaged. Then he set fire to the barns and sail to his longship.

As his boat circled out to sea, smoke drifted toward it across the waves. Hardraada left the coast with the stench of burning in his nostrils.

In the early hours of the morning, I canceled my London reservation. Instead, I booked back to Gaborone and from there on the Desert Airways flight to Maun. I was returning to the heart of the desert. I too had smelled fire on the plateau. The smell had been with me throughout the entire journey. That was what had left me troubled and sleepless.

Something in the Kalahari was burning, and I did not know what it was.

I landed at Maun the next afternoon. That night, in one of the trading post's bars, I found Luke Carver. Carver was on the point of setting out for his camp at Moremi, in the delta. He asked me to go with him.

The camp was one hundred miles to the west of Maun, on the edge of a lagoon. We left the following day and reached it in the evening. Apart from a few Tswana camp hands, there was no one else there. At night, hippos roamed between the tents and fish owls hunted the water. In the early mornings, herds of slender impala filled the surrounding glade, drifting so close as they grazed that they almost brushed our sleeping bags. Once an old black-maned Kalahari lion padded up to inspect us, grunted and ambled away.

We stayed a week. Carver was a good companion in the bush—quiet-voiced, slow-spoken, deeply knowledgeable about Africa and the wild. For most of his life he'd been a professional hunter. Now, like so many others, he'd put aside his rifle and turned to running photographic and game-viewing safaris. Each day he busied himself with jobs around the camp, preparing it for the expected visitors who'd arrive when Moremi's water started to dry up and the game congregated at the drinking holes that remained.

When he'd finished, we'd go out together. The African midwinter was approaching. By late afternoon the air was sharp with the first edge of the night's frost. In the last hour before sunset, the light was clearer and more brilliant than I had ever seen. It had the absolute purity of the delta streams, of water strained for mile after mile through sand and papyrus until every last grain of sediment had been filtered away and all that was left was a liquid diamond brightness.

The light held flawless and white until the sun lowered. Then suddenly the air was irradiated with gold. It cascaded down the sky, and instantly the grass, the lagoons, the animals were sheathed in golden armor. Golden elephants drank from golden pools encircled by golden pasture. Golden hyena and jackal followed the golden prints of their spoor. Golden birds and butterflies crowded the golden evening.

Afterward, just before dusk, it changed again briefly to rose. One evening I saw a lioness and her cubs watching me across a sheet of water lilies. The flowers, the water and the lions were all a deep sunset pink. I walked back to camp with the calls and night sounds of the bush ringing round me like small bells in the darkness.

For two months I had been traveling constantly. Now in place of the jarring movement there was stillness and silence. I woke at dawn to the quiet lapping of the lagoon. I sat for hours in a cone of shadow gazing across the grass meadows as the delta animals came and went in the sun. I took a *makoro* and paddled slowly through the waterways. Fish eagles mewed from the branches, and diving kingfishers rippled the stream's surface around the boat.

The days were so tranquil and unhurried I began to lose hold of the reason that had brought me back. The urgency faded from the unanswered question. Against the measured rhythms of the bush it became remote and insignificant. Sunrise, water and stars, the morning antelope and the nightly owl calls above the roar of lions—they were enough. They were the permanence of the Kalahari. The rest was as transient as the Toyota's spoor unreeling on the desert sand in the wake of that long journey.

On the final evening I smelled burning again.

Carver smelled it too. We were standing on the edge of the lagoon as the sun dropped and white egrets flocked in to roost. A small wind was blowing in our faces from the west. The smell came to us on the wind.

"The fires of June," Carver said. "Those poor bastards! When will they ever learn?"

He shook his head in anger and regret, and swore.

The fires of June. By June the Kalahari cattle have exhausted the grass raised by the summer rains. Sometimes then, in midwinter, another brief flurry of showers moistens the desert. In anticipation, the cattle herders set fire to what's left of the old dry stems. If the showers come and the deadness has been burned away, the roots below shoot green again.

The cattle are loosed on the new grass, but the roots cannot survive a second cropping. They have not had time to replace the resources lost in the first. The regeneration is artificial, a confidence trick. The plants die, and the pasture vanishes. Next year the cattle must be grazed somewhere else.

For the land, the fires of June are the fires of death.

That day a herder perhaps a hundred miles to the west of where we were standing had set the dry grass ablaze. At evening the desert wind had brought the smell to our nostrils. It was not an unpleasant smell. It blended the warm aroma of charcoal—hardwood must have lain in the pasture where the blaze was started—with the scent of hay and the fragrance of the flowers that had grown among the grass stems.

Then, mingled with it too, I smelled something else—the stench of charred hide. Smoldering wood and grass and leather. To the followers of Savonarola or Hitler the combination would have been instantly familiar.

It was the smell of burning books.

I knew then what had haunted me throughout the journey, and why I'd come back. Unidentified until that moment, the smell of fire had been with us since we started. It had pervaded the air by day and night. Sometimes, as in the flamingo clouds on the desolate Sua Pan, it had faded until it was almost undetectable. Always it returned, growing stronger and more acrid the closer we came to the grass plains.

I had known the pastures were being fired and destroyed. Now, at the end, I'd discovered what was being burned with them. Books.

On Kalahari sand there are stored the archives of man's beginnings—the reference library of our past. The library exists not in print but in manuscript, the manuscripts of birds and animals and plants. The manuscripts were written and illuminated to be studied together, and each is irreplaceable.

Every living organism—a hunting lion, a grazing antelope, a stooping falcon—carries within itself a quantity of unique information. The information was acquired at cost and hazard over millions of years in circumstances that can never be duplicated. Each set of data was scrutinized and tested against the most rigorous standards of proof. If the information finally proved sound, it was genetically incorporated in the animal's body, to be available for consultation across the succeeding millennia.

To destroy a species is to lose the meticulously researched and proved information it contains. It is like plundering a library shelf and tearing up every handwritten volume labeled A–D. The loss is irreplaceable.

Since the siege was mounted against the Kalahari, not merely shelves but stacks of shelves, whole vaults of recorded knowledge have been sacked and burned. The arson continues. It continues wherever the wild remains; but perhaps nowhere else are the consequences quite so incalculable as on the stone plateau.

If the avaricious and unlovely primatologists are right—and neither greed nor ugliness disproves their claims—the books being burned in the desert are our cradle books, the primers, grammars, diaries and nursery accounts of our emergence.

Toward sunset, we discovered the San. Hurrying beside them as they walked away—the garden gates were closing and the San were anxious to be off—we gleaned a little of what they knew. It was mere bazaar gossip compared with what we might have been told had we chanced on them earlier. Yet we learned of connections and relationships between man and the wild that staggered us by their intricacy, by the nets and pyramids of interdependence that linked them.

Most bewildering of all, we learned, scrambling across each other to overhear the little people's departing whispers, that there is in reality no wild at all. The wilderness as we conceived of it did not exist. There was only life, and life was indivisible. We were burning not merely the records of the past but the survival manuals of the future—our future.

Carver and I strolled back to the camp in the gathering dusk. The camp hands were building up the fire against the coming night. Watching the flames leap upward and the sparks cascade, I suddenly realized what report I'd take back to the poet and the politician, who on the now-remote London evening had unknowingly set me off on the journey across the plateau.

The fires of June were burning everywhere in the Kalahari. Poets, of their nature, have a passionate hatred for the destruction of any book. Politicians, of their nature too, are more equable. They are the expression of the common man—the poet, of the rare—and the common man by tradition tends to view books as a luxury. But if he and his politicians learned that the volumes being set ablaze on the desert sand contained instructions for their own survival, they might react with an equally violent sense of outrage.

Perhaps it was too late. Perhaps, as the doomsayers believed, all poets and all politicians had lost the ability to read. I did not know. I did know that all I could do was tell the two simply and clearly what was happening within the ramparts of the stone citadel. The rest I had to leave to song and the instinct of the gutter—the poet's song and the politician's gutter instinct for life. If the wilderness is a lost cause, life is a lost cause.

We left Moremi early next day and reached Maun in time for me to catch the afternoon flight south to Gaborone. I checked into the Holiday Inn. I made another booking for Johannesburg and the London flight the following morning. Then I went up to my room. It was a few minutes before 6 P.M. As I walked through the door, the telephone rang. The caller was Syd. Abruptly and without explanation, he asked me to come immediately to his house.

Syd lived less than a hundred yards from the hotel entrance. I arrived as the clock struck the hour. Syd was tuning his shortwave transceiver.

Radio communications in the Kalahari operate on a system of "skeds"—predetermined times at which an outlying camp will come on the air to report to base. Syd was acting as base for a geologist prospecting in the southwestern desert. He had skeds twice daily, at 8 A.M. and 6 P.M. He'd been out all day and missed the morning call, which had been taken for him by a neighbor.

At the same time as I was checking into the hotel, Syd had returned home to find a curious message on his desk. Normally, reports from the camp dealt with survey results or supply requirements. This one referred enigmatically to a leopard cub. I stood by Syd's shoulder. The static cleared and the geologist's voice came over the air. And then together we heard the story.

At dawn that morning a group of San had arrived at the geologist's camp. They had brought the cub with them. By gesture they had communicated that they wanted to exchange it for some sugar and tobacco. The geologist—I had met him briefly—was a forthright young South African. He was certainly no naturalist, but the animal puzzled and intrigued him. He knew that Kalahari leopards were rare in any event. This cub was particularly strange: its coat was almost entirely black. What, he wanted to know, should he do with it?

"Hold on," Syd said. He swung round and looked at me. "Do you want to go out there?"

I had listened to the crackling voice in disbelief. But I knew the geologist was speaking the truth, and for an instant my heart lifted in exultation. It was 6 P.M., and the camp was only three hundred miles away. All I had to do was take a truck and a Tswana tracker, drive for eighteen hours through the night and into the morning, and by midday I would be there. By midday I would have the cub—alive; a spitting, snarling physical presence—in my hands. I would be holding the black leopard.

The soaring, dizzying sense of triumph lasted a few seconds. Then I laughed and shook my head.

"Tell him what to do, Syd," I said.

Syd, the old hunter, chuckled back at me. He knew what had been going through my mind, what I had considered and rejected. He would have driven out with me again into the bush; but he knew just as well as I what the consequences would have been. By the time we arrived, the night would be over. With the night's passing, the one fragile chance of reuniting the cub with its mother would be lost. Even now it was probably too late. The cub had been contaminated by the alien print and feel and smell of another species. Almost certainly the leopardess would reject it.

Almost certainly—yet the chance remained. It was still conceivable she'd take the cub back. Take it back, wean it, teach it to hunt and then let the animal go its own way through the desert's winding corridors of thorn and stone. To grow and mature, to find another of its kind, to breed and raise other cubs in its turn. If that happened, the missing volume on the black leopard would have been returned to the library shelf.

"Listen. . . ." Syd was speaking into the microphone again. "Those Bushman probably drove the cub's mother from a kill to get at the meat. The place won't be far off. You make them take you back to where they found it. You leave right away. When you get there, let the cub go free. . . ."

I left Syd at the transceiver and walked out into the twilight.

Overhead, the brilliant wheeling constellations were filling the evening sky. Three hundred miles away, under the same stars, that night one of the desert's garrison, a tiny angry charge of life, would be returned to the still-unbreached keeps and towers of the citadel. I had no illusions about the odds against the cub's survival. By any reckoning they were vast. Yet the chance was there, and however slender, however remote, the wild would grasp it with a ferocious tenacity.

When I reached the Holiday Inn, there was darkness over the Kalahari. I headed for the bar. As always at that hour, it was crowded with both the old and the new pioneers of the desert. Hunters, traders, game wardens, pilots, prospectors, entrepreneurs. I shouldered my way among them, through the jostle and clamor, to the counter. I counted out the last of my *pula.* I had just enough to buy a glass of champagne.

I ordered my drink. Then I lifted my glass and drank to the black cub in the night.